The Democratic Revolution in the West Indies

Studies in Nationalism, Leadership, and the Belief in Progress

edited by Wendell Bell

Contributors: **Wendell Bell**
Yale University

James T. Duke
Brigham Young University

Raymond W. Mack
Northwestern University

James A. Mau
Yale University

Charles C. Moskos, Jr.
Northwestern University

Ivar Oxaal
University of Guyana

Andrew P. Phillips
California State College, San Francisco

with a Foreword *by* Vernon L. Arnett

SCHENKMAN PUBLISHING COMPANY, Inc.
CAMBRIDGE, MASSACHUSETTS

THE DEMOCRATIC REVOLUTION
IN THE WEST INDIES

INTERNATIONAL STUDIES IN
POLITICAL AND SOCIAL CHANGE

Series Editor: Wendell Bell, Yale University

The Democratic Revolution in the West Indies: Studies in Nationalism, Leadership, and the Belief in Progress
edited by Wendell Bell

Social Change and Images of the Future: A Study of the Pursuit of Progress in Jamaica
by James A. Mau

The Sociology of Political Independence: A Study of Nationalist Attitudes Among West Indian Leaders
by Charles C. Moskos, Jr.

Black Intellectuals Come to Power: The Rise of Creole Nationalism in Trinidad & Tobago
by Ivar Oxaal

Mau Mau — and After
by L. S. B. Leakey

To the people of the West Indies,
whose revolution it was and whose
democratic principles were the
inspiration for all that we did

Acknowledgements

We are indebted to many persons whose assistance and encouragement made possible the studies reported in this volume. Especially, we thank the Carnegie Corporation of New York for a grant that allowed us to initiate our West Indies Study Program and to plan our activities over a number of years with some financial certainty. The studies that are reported here, with the exception of Professor Mack's contribution, and the next three books in this series are the major results of that Program. Additionally, we thank the Social Science Research Council for a total of five man-years of Pre-doctoral Research Training Fellowships for three of the participants (Duke for 1960, and Mau and Moskos each for 1961–63); the U.C.L.A. Political Change Committee for support for Moskos and Bell during 1963–65; and the Center for Advanced Study in the Behavioral Sciences, Stanford, Calif. for a fellowship (Bell for 1963–64) during the tenure of which the major editing of the manuscript was completed.

Although we aimed our studies of elites and nationalism in the West Indies toward substantive research objectives, we also tried to conduct a modest experiment in graduate education. That we were able to do so is a result of the understanding, forbearance, and cooperation of our former colleagues — including members of the administration as well as of the faculty — at the University of California, Los Angeles, where the Program was based. We should mention by name James S. Coleman, Donald R. Cressey, Melville Dalton, Thomas P. Jenkin, Clement W. Meighan, Richard T. Morris, Raymond J. Murphy, Anthony Oberschall, Theodore Soloutos, Melvin Seeman, Eshref Shevky, M. G. Smith, Rita Sann, Fred Thalheimer, Ralph H. Turner, and David A. Wilson for the help they have given us. And we should mention those expediters extraordinary, Robert A. Rogers, Chief Accounting Officer, and Franklin D. Murphy, Chancellor.

v

Although our program was officially a U.C.L.A. affair, it also relied heavily on the facilities, services, and expertise available at the University of the West Indies, ranging from such mundane essentials as food and housing to active participation in the design of research and the collection of data. We wish to express our gratitude to West Indian leaders-administrators-scholars H. Dudley Huggins, Philip M. Sherlock, and Hugh W. Springer; to historian Douglas Hall, sociologist Lloyd Braithwaite, and economists George E. Cumper and David T. Edwards; and to former U.W.I. students Joan Lai Fook, Leonnard Hardyal, Donald Harris, Locksley Lindo, Premdath Gairaj Ramphal, LeRoy Taylor, Roy Thomas, Arthurine Tomlinson, Beverly Townsend, and Junior Wong.

There is insufficient space to give recognition to everyone in the West Indies who helped us with our research, but it should be evident that without sponsorship and cooperation from the West Indian community, especially from West Indian leaders, the studies reported here would have been next to impossible to carry out. Mr. Vernon L. Arnett, Member of the Jamaican Parliament, played an important role in advising and supporting our research efforts from the outset, and we have thus asked him to write the Foreword for this book. Additionally, we are obliged to both him and his family for making Jamaica a second home to us.

Also for help while in Jamaica we thank J. D. Barnes and his family, Morris Cargill, Elfreda Mitchell, Hartley S. Neita, Deryck E. Roberts, O. A. Roberts, Theodore Sealy, and the officers and staff of the Jamaica Social Welfare Commission.

In Trinidad and Tobago, we were fortunate in receiving the aid of Dr. Eric Williams and other P.N.M. leaders, especially Senators W. J. Alexander and Nicholas Simonette, and Mr. Andrew Carr. On the other side of the political fence, we are grateful to Dr. Rudranath Capildeo for his candor and assistance in helping us to understand the problems of the Opposition. Others who gave us assistance were Senator and Mrs. Ronald Williams, the Hon. Donald Granado, Leionel Seukeran, Bernard V. Primus, C. L. R. James, Edna Roxburgh, Eugene Borde, Stanley Roberts, Carlton Comma, Ulric Lee, Randolph Rawlins, Lennox Pierre, Esla Molineaux, and "Sputnik" and the Crossfire Steel Orchestra.

Both Mr. L. Forbes Burnham and Mrs. Janet Jagan of British Guiana were exceptionally helpful, as was Mr. Lloyd Searwar.

Clearly, we are indebted to persons of different political persuasions as well as members of different social classes. Thus, in a single breath we thank the workers and the Managing Director of the Antigua Sugar Factory, Mr. George Moody-Stuart; the Hon. V. C. Bird, Chief

Minister of Antigua; His Honor I. G. Turbot, Administrator of Antigua; the Hon. Dr. L. R. Wynter and Mr. Oscar Bird of the Antiguan Government; and also from Antigua Sir Alexander Moody-Stuart, Mr. and Mrs. E. Dalmer Dew, Frank Goodwin, Everard S. Richards, F. H. S. Warneford, and the Rev. George Weston.

Local historian F. A. Hoyos, Victor A. Archer, and the Hon. Wynter A. Crawford were particularly helpful to us in Barbados; in Dominica Dr. Edward Armour, Jenner Armour, Stanley Boyd, Charles Maynard, Dr. and Mrs. Bernard Sorhaindo, Joan Sorhaindo, and Bernard Yankey extended both hospitality and advice; and in Grenada we especially thank Walter St. John, Derek Knight, and Mrs. Eric Gairy.

We also appreciate the suggestions and support given us by American scholars Walter E. Freeman, Raymond W. Mack and Richard C. Snyder (both of whom served as consultants to the West Indies Study Program), and by those old Caribbean hands, Lambros Comitas and David Lowenthal.

Four West Indians returned with us to U.C.L.A. to work toward their Ph.D. degrees in Sociology. They became our friends and advisers, making numerous contributions to this book. We thank Dr. Andrew G. J. Comacho, former acting Principal of Queen's Royal College in Trinidad; Neville W. Layne, sociologist and historian from Guyana; Trinidadian Anthony Maingot, Ph.D., whose knowledge of the French, Spanish, and Dutch Caribbean in addition to the British was of great help; and Barbadian Dudley E. Parris.

We wish to express our appreciation to Professor Joseph LaPalombara who read with care and commented in detail on an earlier version of this book.

For typing and editorial assistance, we thank Irene Bickenbach of the Center for Advanced Study in the Behavioral Sciences and Lorraine Estra of Yale University. We are grateful to Janet G. Turk for indexing and proofreading.

Four of us in the U.C.L.A. West Indies Study Program had wives — or in one case acquired one — during the time we were doing this research, and they have helped in many ways — if at times mainly in being long-suffering — to bring this book to completion. We must here acknowledge our gratitude and appreciation to Lora-Lee Bell, who also served as Administrative Assistant for the Program; Ruth Duke, whose second child was born in Los Angeles while her husband was in Jamaica; Gail Mau, whose enthusiasm infected us all; and Cecile Oxaal, for whom her husband recommends highest honors, for, in his words, "putting up with the tedious daily spectacle of a mumbling, obese sphinx poised over the typewriter."

Of course, none of these organizations or persons necessarily approve by virtue of their assistance any of the statements of views expressed in this volume. We must accept full responsibility for these reports.

Finally, earlier versions of a few of the chapters presented here have been published before. We thank the following publishers and editors for their permission to revise and republish these materials in this book:

Moskos and Bell, "Attitudes towards Democracy Among Leaders in Four Emergent Nations," *British Journal of Sociology*, 15 (December, 1964), pp. 317–337.

Moskos and Bell, "Some Implications of Equality for Political, Economic, and Social Development," *International Review of Community Development*, 13–14, 1965, pp. 219–246.

Mack, "Race, Class, and Power in Barbados: A Study of Stratification as an Integrating Force in a Democratic Revolution," in H. R. Barringer, G. I. Blanksten, and R. W. Mack (editors), *Social Change in Developing Areas*, Cambridge, Mass.: Schenkman, 1965, pp. 131–154.

Moskos and Bell, "Emergent Caribbean Nations Face the Outside World," *Social Problems*, 12 (Summer, 1964), 24–41.

Additional acknowledgements of quoted materials are made elsewhere throughout the book.

THE AUTHORS

Bethany, Connecticut
July, 1966

Contents

ix

Foreword

I am a Citizen of Jamaica. This formula may be multiplied seventy times with a mere change of nation to mark the sealing of the constitutional instruments which has in the past few years removed the colonial patchwork from the map of the world. A few scattered protected territories are today the embarrassing residue of the pride of empire. The proconsuls have packed their bags and handed over the keys. Keys to a brave, new world?

The future of all the peoples of the world depends on the answer to this question. With the transfer from colonial rule to independence, national equality has been achieved in the United Nations Assembly for peoples in Africa, Asia and the West Indies who were formerly the subjects of one or other of the metropolitan powers. These were the have-nots who could clearly be identified as colonial. They have now joined the other have-nots who won their citizenship from the revolutionary 18th century on or whose subjugation has never been politically formalized. In the community of nations today, therefore, the haves and the have-nots face each other across the vast gap which marks the division between the many nations of the greater part of the world and the handful of nations who have achieved hegemony at their expense. Can this gap be bridged and, if so, what are the new relationships that will make this possible? And, if there can be no meeting, what happens to all the world?

There are those who see the answer to this question as one conveniently to be decided by the men in Washington and Moscow. But, mighty as these men are, one would be undervaluing what is motivating the stir and the commotion in the world today to conclude that even these men have an unlimited time span and range of power in which to ride the storm of change. This storm has not been spent by formal transfers, and political independence has merely provided a new setting for its motive power. Though thermonuclear weapons, the power to destroy, have become the authentic stamp of world leadership, there is the constructive force of aspirations which has been unleashed and is now free to use an abundance of human and natural resources for different ends. The political and economic domination of the have-not world by the great powers has run its course into the cul-de-sac in which the supreme achievements of science and technology have become agents of destruction, and world peace (or absence of world war) is enforced by sanctions too terrible to consider. If humanity is to get out of the dead end, then the lead must be taken by those for whom stalemate is not self-preservation and who now have the papers of release: the right to stay, the right to go and the right to change.

I may be challenged by those who regard the division of the world between East and West, free world and Communism, good and evil (from whichever side of the fence one is looking) as inevitable. Those who hold this view regard hundreds of millions of men and women as actively or passively awaiting their turn for apportionment between one camp or the other; that the struggle in Vietnam or in Santo Domingo, the Sino-Soviet differences and incipient realignments are all transitory phenomena to be resolved finally within the hard and fast lines laid down by two powers who alone have a sufficiency of the bombs which both keep them at arm's length and enable them to rule the rest of the world. But is it really true that the peoples of the greater part of the world, no matter how small and poor, are prepared to be parcelled out and done out of their own release from one imperialist power or the other? What then would be the spirit and substance of the nationalism of the new nations? Are the leaders putting on the paraphernalia of retired rulers and only grasping the symbols of political power? Or are they assuming the responsibility for creating the new society in which independence is the blood and bone and equality the framework? If they are not doing the latter, then they are not only betraying their own peoples but they are also betraying the ideal of the universal quest for liberty, to be engaged in for the first time not by separate groups in separate nations, but by new nation-states acting in concert.

Ideas about liberation are universal. They flow across boundaries of nation, race, colour and creed. These ideas have an internationalism of their own. Writing in Jamaica in the year 1965, I remember that one hundred years ago it was an English Committee, inspired by John Stuart Mill, which moved to bring Governor Eyre of Jamaica to justice and so make some contribution to the cause for which Jamaican Paul Bogle died. Though it has often seemed to be painfully so, the freedom fighters have never had really to fight alone. The French Revolution, the American Revolution, the Bolivars and the Martis have their links in time and space and these have been seen in *The Democratic Revolution in the West Indies* as joining with the social revolutions of the twentieth century and into a new Europe, Africa, Asia and the West Indies.

The climacteric of independence was seen by Nehru. Inaugurating the Asian Conference in New Delhi in 1947, he said, "standing on this watershed which divides two epochs of human history and endeavour, we can look back on our long past and look forward to the future that is taking shape before our eyes." Nehru saw more than a billion people living in new independence in a world of technological advance and shrinking distances, farming and exploring the wealth of soil, of sea and all the universe. If nuclear research and achievement have so far done no more than lead the world into a dead end, overshadowed by clouds of destruction, then those who are fresh on the march and with still a great distance to go must take the lead out of the dead end.

Are Jamaica and the other emergent nations of the West Indies too insignificant to have a part in this? The only solution for the small and weak lies in co-operation just as much as the powerful have chosen rivalry. In 1962, Jamaica and Trinidad joined with the Afro-Asian bloc to add their weight against two-power confrontation in the Caribbean. There is at least one world organisation, however tainted by international bullyism, in which each nation has the right of one voice only. However cheerless the prospects may be of the United Nations being always able to survive through the power plays, the present choice at least seems to be between destruction and the alliance of the greater part of the world, however powerless as individual units, in a compact of growing strength. We in the West Indies can at least join with others at the watershed and make our own decisions. What manner of men form these new nations and what manner of men are their leaders and their future leaders? The nature of the decisions to be made has been discussed in *Decisions of Nationhood* and now there are these studies in *Nationalism, Leadership, and the Belief in Progress;* true, of the West Indies alone, a tiny part of the cosmos of the new nations but nevertheless confronted with the generic problems created by the past.

The seven Americans who have taken part in this study have essayed a contribution to West Indian history. I am sure that no West Indian would be churlish enough to regard this as an intrusion or to view Professor Wendell Bell and his associates as agents of exploitation as they may view the United States as replacing European powers in the Caribbean. Professor Bell emphasizes that the democratic revolution is unfinished business everywhere and that he and his colleagues are part of the universal enterprise that is social science, dwellers in universities and intellectuals whose thinking goes beyond their own nation-state, and who are, as such, in a way themselves agents of the democratic and egalitarian revolution. "A concern for human dignity and common decency transcends national boundaries and is the responsibility of all men." No one will question the sincerity. Indeed, some may feel that the study has done too well by us in the West Indies in the presentation of an over-optimistic view of the future.

The new nations have taken with them into independence a great backlog of problems. They are economically under-developed and many labour under a sense of inferiority. But even with the will — where are the tools? Or how are they come by? How must the effort go? There is the double task of bringing everyday life closer to the standards of advanced societies which have given us their laws and culture but not their lathe and plough. Then there is the task of re-claiming and rehabilitating a mass of the population, already beyond school age and worn down by adversity, while trying to cope with the care and education of the newcomers. In Jamaica, for example, with 100,000 children for whom there are no school places, there are 50,000 children now annually reaching the age of five years. With un-employment at over 16% of the work force, the vast majority of the idle are in the 15–19 age group with only 15% in that age group pur-suing full time studies. The temptation is very great to choose a new father in different clothes and for the new image (if ever clearly seen) to be blurred by the shadows of the old.

It would be wrong to conclude, however, that the achievement of political independence has created a new situation, fraught with diffi-culty and risk, as well as promise, for the have-nots alone. Much public attention has been drawn to the obstacles which they face in achieving economic viability for their societies and higher standards of living for their peoples. Aid by way of finance and technical services is stressed and advertised as essential from the more advanced countries. It has become fashionable, now that colonialism is not in vogue, to revert to the motif of the "white man's burden" because of a protective and bene-ficial relationship to the advantage of the protected and at the expense of the protector. Foreign aid may therefore be represented as a con-tinuation of these idealistic policies but might equally be represented either as a form of recompense for past exploitation or as a means of preserving and extending economic control since aid is tied not only to goods but also to behaviour. The fact that former overlords are also at risk in the new situation should not be over-looked; and it is a risk which looms for their economies as a whole just as directly as it is a risk for those of their nationals who have come to own, in many in-stances, the greater part of the productive and trading enterprises of the former colonial and semi-colonial territories.

The maintenance of an uninterrupted flow of food and raw materials to keep the industrial complex humming is a matter of fundamental concern. The modern capitalist state is run at heavy cost not only to its own citizens but also to citizens of the have-not world who have far greater cause to complain of the burden. The latter are making it possible for the industrial nations to keep their people at work, well fed, clothed, housed and provided with social security all at standards incomparably higher than those enjoyed by themselves. In addition, they must help also to maintain the nuclear striking force of destruction.

Is this true? And how does it come about? An analogy may be taken from the total effort involved in the Second World War. England was then described as an island sinking under the weight of armaments resulting from her own mobilisation and her role as the arsenal and forward post of United States forces. It is not too fantastic to view in the same perspective a small portion of the world population inhabiting a small portion of the globe loaded down with science and technology and investment and creating their own problems of automation and cybernetic progress. Here technology is outpacing the useful activity of men and women, of young people whose simple skills (or lack of them) have thrust them into a corner from which they look out on an empty future. Surpluses are created: unwanted food and other goods along with an excess of productive capacity. But over the vast stretches of the rest of the world, there are teeming multitudes enduring starvation, poverty and illiteracy and having to do without the services and tools of the modern world. The supply of needs in the world, despite scientific and technological progress, has grown far beyond the range of our limited mechanisms for the exchange of goods and services, and resources cannot be shared. Yet to maintain this grotesque and absurdly limited mechanism in the interests of the few who control it, the many must do without.

The problem of the haves and the have-nots has been obscured by ideological schisms based on legendary concepts. The real problem is how to harness science, the energies of man and modern techniques for the exploitation of material resources and how to integrate all cultures into the universal culture of the equality of man, of all races and colours and of all tongues and customs, so that the struggle against nature becomes a social enterprise.

The under-developed world does not have to pay merely by doing without, however. There is the example of Latin America. I go first to the facts given in the February 1964 Economic Letter of the First National City Bank of New York. This Letter stated that income from private US investment abroad is one of the props of the US balance of payments position, though foreign aid constitutes *in theory* an outflow of capital beneficial to the have-nots and representing for the donor a sacrifice of scarce resources. In the year 1963, US investment income from overseas was over $4 billion, an increase of $1.6 billion from 1958, plus $500 million in royalties and fees (the toll for patents and know-how). On the other hand, the Inter-American Development Bank reported total credits in a three-year period for Latin America of $26 million, but US private operators increased sales by $235 million through supplies to the International Development Agency. To complete the picture, against the $4 billion investment income received, direct investment of only $1.6 billion went out.

In little Jamaica, in the year 1964, net outflow of investment income was £11.7 million while the provisional estimates of capital inflow were no more than £4.6 million. Since these are only figures, unintelligible for more than one reason too many, I will translate the £11.7 million into goods and we must bear in mind that Jamaica's wealth comes mainly from the export of agricultural products and raw ores. The total of investment income going out would equal Jamaica's receipts for bananas (the second largest agricultural export) at £6 million plus the £5 million received for all other products such as citrus, coffee, cocoa, pimento, ginger and their products. Net outflow of investment income was more than twice the value of manufactured exports, and more than half the value of Jamaica's main and prized industries of sugar, rum and molasses at £21.8 million. Local receipts from the mining of bauxite and conversion into alumina at about £15 million would have gone for the most part in meeting the foreign investment bill.

But these are the direct fruits, the sort that can be easily checked off by entries in a bank book. Indirectly, there is a far greater gain to the metropolitan country in the terms of trade. Simply stated, the yield from primary products in food and raw materials (including minerals) tends to depreciate in relation to the cost of imports of consumer and capital manufactures. The have-not primary producers are steadily losing more each year in relation to the goods they must buy from the industrial nations. In Jamaica in 1963 the Economic Survey says:

> The continued deterioration in the terms of trade, or the rate of exchange between Jamaica's exports and the commodities imported, is clearly illustrated. [The net terms of trade had dropped from 1954 (base year) 100 to 76.]

Looking at the position in regard to Latin America, the Economic Commission of Latin America in 1963 estimated that changes between 1955–1960 in average import and export prices resulted in a loss of $7,400,000,000 to Latin America.

The few great of the earth, therefore, appear to have a tremendous material stake in the maintenance of a system in which there are many poor. There is the compulsion of maintaining an economic relationship and of trying to contain the impact of new, lusty nationalism on the social and cultural pattern which made economic exploitation an accepted feature of society. Nationalism and independence clearly present a threat to this. Landownership is concentrated in a few hands, there is foreign ownership and exploitation of resources, the economy is based mainly on export agriculture and the import of consumer goods. Against this, there are poverty and unemployment at one end and conspicuous consumption at the other. Opportunities are severely limited and status is denied to the majority. This complex can be the base for revolutionary action. There may be confiscation because of the choice between paying (some say twice) for wealth that has been created and providing the means of development. There may be drastic changes in economic power and in the direction of the economy towards more food, houses and education and away from the maintenance of vested interests.

Nationalism can therefore be an explosive force primed by discontent and the desire for change. For those whose interests lie in the preservation of the status quo, there has been a weapon close to hand in the attachment of the tag of Communism to the nationalist movement with international consequences. The smear has become the war cry against the move for self-determination and the natural desire to use political power, backed by universal suffrage, to achieve economic independence. Intervention, aid or embargo, and the skills of diplomacy are the manoeuvres on the battlefield and strange bearers carry the banners of freedom.

In the result, capital and technical aid, Peace Corps and food for peace can become suspect as part of the plot to keep things as they are. Are science and technology, the establishment of international agencies, the efforts of the United Nations, the enlargement of trade and exchange facilities — all so urgently needed — to be under the aegis of economic domination and continued exploitation? Are these things to make the gap wider between haves and have-nots, fueling the anger? Is there no way out of parcelling the world willy-nilly between two camps?

Consequently, the new nations in seeking change for themselves cannot confine the effects to their own societies. The changes they must make and the new things they must do will have a profound effect on the greater nations. The struggle of the haves and the have-nots is more than the internal conflict within each nation — new or old. The conflict is now international. Accommodations between Washington and Moscow will not solve the issue as between those who now have political power and seek to use it to take economic control over their societies from those who will have to learn to live without it. Can a new relationship be established or will economic imperialism, divested of political power, intensify the threat to world peace in the effort to hold what they have?

There has been no period in world history in which there have not been wars for the control of territory, resources, trade routes, goods and people. These wars have always been fought in the name of freedom. Wars in the past could be localised according to spheres of influence and power. It was not until this century that two world wars came. Today the border conflicts or the conflicts between racial or cultural groups cannot be as easily confined. The world position has been sharpened to the edge by the right of the new nations, acting in political independence, to bring off internal coups or to hold peaceful elections as the case may be, and these may result in realignments. A war is escalated in Vietnam, a match sputters in the Dominican Republic, the Congo may flare or India and Pakistan or Malaysia and Indonesia may cause the explosion. The new nations have come to independence dependent on some great power or other economically and militarily. A new nation may occupy no more than a strategic position such as Cyprus. It is the new nations who are first in danger. When a nuclear conflict comes it will be over their dead bodies. If they seek to achieve equality within their own boundaries, it may set the match to the powder keg. The cynic holds that it is best to live with the parcelling of the world between the two powers who hold the nuclear aces. How far can the new nations go? At least, they must put the matter to the test and do so better collectively rather than as single spies. Can equality be achieved in an unequal world and can the new nations find sufficient strength among themselves to make their impact in the creation of a new world order? Each nation must try for itself and with others. Their effort will be the test of democracy and the validity of freedom. But no new nation can do the job of freeing itself until it first frees its own people.

The political independence of the new nations, therefore, can be seen as setting the stage for two revolts: the revolt of the new nations against the dominance of the powerful nations who have up to now had the power to arrange world affairs between themselves and, failing agreement, to come to blows and, secondly, the revolt of oppressed classes within these new nations themselves. The significance of the latter revolt lies in the fact that, like their counterparts in the industrial countries, they must now make their demands and press their struggle against their own national leaders instead of combining with those leaders, as in the nationalist movement in a colonial country, to wrest the right of political self-determination from an imperialist master.

In their introduction to *The Democratic Revolution in the West Indies,* Professors Bell and Oxaal say that the six studies in general deal with "the spread and development of the democratic revolution through time and space from the eighteenth-century Atlantic community to the twentieth-century global society." The word "revolution" is accepted in this study, they say, in the meaning attached to it by R. R. Palmer as a conflict between incompatible images of the future and opposing views of what the community ought to be, because it includes serious political protest and a series of rapid changes resulting in the reconstitution of government and society. Bell and Oxaal say,

> We take as our underlying hypothesis the proposition that much of the political, economic, and social change that is going on in the world today, and has gone on in the recent past, can be understood as a continuation of the democratic revolution — especially as an extension of the drive toward equality — to which the Europe and America of the latter part of the eighteenth century gave birth as a realizable human aspiration in this world.

Bell, who had come to Jamaica in 1956 on a somewhat different task, was immediately perceptive of (and sympathetic to) the fundamental changes in history-making that were proceeding in the West Indies, at first on the federal pattern but then decisively in 1961 on the basis of unitary independence for Jamaica and Trinidad and Tobago. So here are studies in nationalism, leadership and the belief in progress: the actuating motives of the men in charge and how their images of the future guide their decision-making, the decisions of nationhood. Bell and Oxaal treat the vital decisions in their Introduction. Shall we be independent or not? There is in our own region the example of Puerto Rico and outside that of Northern Ireland with umbrella-like arrangements. There is the question of federation which for a time was a confusing, contradictory element in the West Indian scene. There are questions of uniting in one nation those of different racial origins and cultures. There is the question, now being answered in Africa, as to the parliamentary system itself or variations of it. There is the role of government in the society: how positive shall this be? There are foreign relations — do we include all who will be friendly or do we cling to former attachments? There is the question of the creation of a social structure in which different traditions and cultural behaviour can be melded into a national character.

The fundamental question must be asked: Can or will the new nations, now having the right to change, follow the path of the old?

The development of the parliamentary system as a means of breaching the privilege of feudalist classes was accompanied by the industrial revolution, and new social and economic organisation partnered political democratisation. In the new nations, universal adult suffrage and elected governments have succeeded foreign bureaucratic rule but the use of political power for social and economic reorganisation does not necessarily flow as the natural consequence since to a great extent the means are in the hands of the former political masters and caught up in the external trading and financial mechanisms. The will to change, even if not for social and cultural reasons, is conditioned accordingly.

Bell, for example, quotes R. R. Palmer as seeing the democratic revolution aimed against feudalism, aristocracy and privilege and he includes colonialism. This power may be broken constitutionally within the country where the persons who hold this power, in whatever form, are an elite within the community. In the case where political and economic power are in foreign hands, the democratic revolution must be in two stages: the power of choice (political) and the use of this power for social and economic change. Without exception, the new nations of the 20th century must face not only vested class interest within the community but the vested interest also of those without the community who enjoy the backing of the greatest and richest countries of the world. The difficulties are that much greater, some say immeasurably greater, but the new nations still have their future to make for themselves. They must have an image of the future and they must have the will and the endurance and the capacity for sacrifice to work towards it. If they lack the will, then the keys they have been handed open only into a cave of dead sea fruit.

If this, broadly stated, is the core of the problem, the role of the social scientist and the studies of the sort encompassed herein must be of profound interest insofar as the motivations of leaders and people may be interpreted at a point in history when profound changes are inevitable. The past has left its mark and scored significant patterns for great and small and poor and rich. Existing modes of production and a social organisation which have developed out of the needs of the past cannot be rationalised and made the means in a future in which the new men of the new nations have in their grasp the effective power to decide what they wish to do and how they choose to do it. The industrial revolution of the 19th century and all its consequences, including the sowing of the seeds of equality, can evolve today into what Bell describes as the spread of the democratic revolution throughout the world. But whether democratic or not (or peaceful or not), revolution is inevitable since the wine of independence is heady and cannot be contained in old skins. It has come in the West Indies to a society which on the surface had adopted the culture of the former rulers: their religion, concept of rule of law, parliamentary system, social stratification and concept of property rights, and worship of the Western gods of creative activity. But there is a great mass of the population for whom these concepts have little more significance than the appurtenances of a privileged class to be enjoyed or not as the opportunity may arise. It is largely this section of the population for whom the existing society has brought no benefits, and since they see no real opportunity of improving their lot they can hardly be expected to have absorbed reverence for a culture in the same way as those for whom it has given status, security and hope of advancement. This is the natural consequence of colonialism which could not have achieved even the limited ends it set itself without dividing the population and creating its fifth column suitably inspired with a "well nurtured sense of inferiority."

Imperialist exploitation of the West Indies was not a tip-and-run affair necessitating at the most the control of a port as a trading centre. Jamaica and the other West Indian islands were ideally suited to the cultivation of sugar cane and Britain joined with France and Spain in this exploitation, embarking on the essential and profitable sideline of transporting captured or purchased Africans to be entered in the estate books as pieces of equipment, necessary capital to be written off as obsolescent or added to as the case might be. There was other machinery to be protected and gradually a large investment in sugar, later expanding into coffee, chocolate and cattle rearing. Stability was necessary for this investment (and still is) and stability could not indefinitely be assured by arms or even by expatriate owners and overseers. Progress towards a stable middle class, satisfactorily acculturated to the needs of the imperialist power, was hastened by formal and informal alliances between white and black producing a coloured middle class who understandably sought by all means at hand to advance themselves as rapidly as possible away from an African mother to a father from the master race. There was the plantocracy — the upper ruling class and at the other end a mass of enslaved Africans who were to be left to their own devices at emancipation while their owners received cash for the value lost. In between, there grew up a skilled, professional and trading middle class advancing into a local capitalism, subservient to the needs of imperialism, counting all their blessings of status, wealth, conspicuous consumption and opportunity as flowing from a foreign domination and culture.

The studies against this background are of great interest. Professor Ivar Oxaal makes a detailed study of the leaders, the circumstances and the occasions forming the historical process of the "decisions of nationhood" in Trinidad and Tobago. He documents the links between the ideologies of the West and the nationalism of Trinidad by looking at the motives of individuals, their backgrounds and careers and their subsequent roles in the nationalist movement. Oxaal also touches on the conflict that arises in working towards idealistic objectives where global contradictions of ideology reproduce themselves in the little theatre.

Professor Charles C. Moskos, Jr., surveys the field of West Indian nationalism. He asks how is it that certain members of a colonial society begin to question the old order and make the first steps towards independence while others look on with alarm at the course of events. He constructs a typology of nationalist attitudes and behaviour that runs from true nationalism at one extreme to "colonialist" at the other. He uses an "Index of Enlightenment" to reveal the meaning of West Indian nationalism and the extent and for whom it was considered to be the means for the achievement of social and economic equality. He constructs an overall image of the future which is an optimistic one but he notes the threats to it.

Moskos and Bell take up in detail the context of elite attitudes within which decisions regarding form of government and global alignments were being made. Furthermore, they show how attitudes toward equality were particularly significant in shaping attitudes toward these and other decisions of nationhood.

Professor Raymond W. Mack's study of Barbados reveals the effect of the transfer of political power on the stratification system, since status aggregates or groups cut across racial boundaries. The weakening of social distinctions associated with race is seen by Mack as the accommodation by whites to black political power as a means of protecting economic power.

Professor Andrew P. Phillips has studied the sugar factory in Antigua and his survey challenges the theory that the workers are lazy or do not care to work. Rather the workers (or some of them) saw little to work for; that it is not so much that indolence retards progress but that lack of progress stimulates indolence.

The studies of Professors James A. Mau and James T. Duke are set in Jamaica. Mau focuses his study on the belief in progress and concentrates on the problems of the working-class area in the West of Kingston. Since he also tests attitudes of a number of Jamaican leaders who are concerned with this area, he is able to compare not only the different images of the future held by elites and masses but also the image of each group as seen by the other. The results may be surprising to Jamaicans and I draw attention to one conclusion: that leaders who perceive hostility in the masses generally were less likely to be knowledgeable, powerful and egalitarian than leaders who did not perceive such hostility.

In his study of Jamaican youth, Duke concentrates on the analysis of questionnaire data for over 200 university and over 2,000 secondary school students from whose ranks many future leaders of Jamaica and the West Indies will come. The egalitarians here seem to be those in the higher levels of education, those who would choose a job of a social or creative nature in which their talents might be expressed, and those indicating dissatisfaction with the nature of the existing stratification system.

Jamaica and the West Indies, like every other new nation, are now free to decide. To what extent the decisions they make will be influenced by the legacy of the past will significantly determine the future of these peoples. An effort of will is needed to take hold of the future and, where necessary, make the clean break with the past. Leaders and people will have to combine in an effort to secure united identification as one people. If the present divisions are to be abolished, it can only be as a result of a policy for equality and full participation in the social and economic structure of the society. It is essential as a first step for the leaders to divest themselves of the "inferiority complex" of colonialism. In my new country, they must seek to hold up an image of Jamaica for the Jamaican people and not strain after an artificial image for the powerful financial centre of the world. They must be prepared to go a Jamaican way, hew it out if need be, rather than stick to a way merely because a more powerful nation might be willing to go that way with them. There is a limited time in which to make these decisions. The revolution is inevitable. If it can come about as the result of a national choice and be dynamised by a national effort then it can be the democratic revolution of this study.

The leaders of the new nations owe it to their own peoples and to all the peoples of the world not to try to contain the desire for change but to channel it into the national movement. While there is much to be done and while the tools for the job are often inadequate and, in some cases, lacking, the revolution of rising expectations will find the men, and the men will find the means. The new world of science and ideas which has accompanied the political liberation of the last decade has opened up for those who have had so little and have so much to gain. What is needed is the will and the endurance. I am confident that the new world has these qualities and it is because of this that the new nations have an essential role to play in creating a world in which man, and not the bomb, is master.

VERNON L. ARNETT
Member of Parliament, Jamaica

Kingston, Jamaica
June, 1965

The American Revolution coincided with the climax of the Age of Enlightenment. It was itself, in some degree, the product of this age. There were many in Europe, as there were in America, who saw in the American Revolution a lesson and an encouragement for mankind. It proved that the liberal ideas of the Enlightenment might be put into practice. It showed, or was assumed to show, that ideas of the rights of man and the social contract, of liberty and equality, of responsible citizenship and popular sovereignty, of religious freedom, freedom of thought and speech, separation of powers and deliberately contrived written constitutions, need not remain in the realm of speculation, among the writers of books, but could be made the actual fabric of public life among real people, in this world, now.

R. R. PALMER, *The Age of the Democratic Revolution*

CHAPTER 1 Introduction

WENDELL BELL AND IVAR OXAAL

THE DEMOCRATIC REVOLUTION

The studies reported in this book are about some islands in the Caribbean Sea and one fairly large piece of land on the South American continent, all of which constitutes the bulk of what has been known as the British West Indies. But the story we try to tell stretches far beyond this limited area. It touches on matters of concern to the new states of Asia and Africa, it includes materials relating to modern intellectual currents of Europe, and it moves into the past to eighteenth-century Europe and America. It is based on the belief that history can be read as the story of the growth of human freedom and it purports to reveal a small part of what Robert Redfield once called "the historic trend which has tended to make the totality of human conduct more decent and more humane."[1] In general, it is about the spread and development of the democratic revolution through time and space from the eighteenth-century Atlantic community to the twentieth-century global society.

In his excellent two-volume work on *The Age of the Democratic Revolution*, R. R. Palmer[2] attempts to summarize "what happened in the world of Western Civilization in the forty years from 1760 to 1800" and explores the meaning of these years for the subsequent history of mankind. His thesis is that the events of the eighteenth century should be seen:

> . . . as a single movement, revolutionary in character, for which the word 'democratic' is appropriate and enlightening; a movement which, however different in different countries, was everywhere aimed against closed elites, self-selecting power groups, hereditary castes, and forms of special advantage or discrimination that no longer served any useful

[1] *The Primitive World and Its Transformations*, Ithaca, N.Y.: Cornell University Press, Great Seal Books, 1957, p. 163.
[2] R. R. Palmer, *The Age of the Democratic Revolution: A Political History of Europe and America, 1760–1800*, Princeton, N.J.: Princeton University Press, "The Challenge," 1959 and "The Struggle," 1964. (Quoted here and elsewhere by permission of author and publisher.)

1

purpose. These were summed up in such terms as feudalism, aristocracy, and privilege, against which the idea of common citizenship in a more centralized state, or of common membership in a free political nation, was offered as a more satisfactory basis for the human community.[3]

Palmer uses the term "democratic" to refer to this movement because it was the last decade of the eighteenth century "that brought the word out of the study and into actual politics."[4] He points out that then the words "liberal," "radical," and "progressive" did not exist, and that when ". . . moderates or conservatives wished to indicate the dangerous drift of the times, or when the more advanced spirits spoke of themselves, they might very well use the words 'democrat' or 'democracy.' "[5]

Although the term included the political notion that "the possession of government, or any public power, by any established, privileged, closed, or self-recruiting groups of men" was wrong and that "the delegation of authority and the removability of officials" was right, it also "signified a new feeling for a kind of equality, or at least a discomfort with older forms of social stratification and formal rank. . ."[6] In fact, the democratic movement had as an overriding central theme "the assertion of 'equality' as a prime social desideratum."[7] And the ideal of equality came to take on a variety of related meanings and to apply in many different situations:

> It could mean an equality between colonials and residents of a mother country, as in America; between nobles and commoners, as in France; patricians and burghers, as at Geneva; ruling townsmen and subject country people, as at Zurich and elsewhere; between Catholic and Protestant, Anglican and Dissenter, Christian and Jew, religionist and unbeliever, or between Greek and Turk. . . It might refer to the equal right of guildsmen and outsiders to enter upon a particular kind of trade or manufacture. For some few it included greater equality between men and women. Equality for ex-slaves and between races was not overlooked. For popular democrats, like the Paris sans-culottes, it meant the hope for a more adequate livelihood, more schooling and education, the right to stroll on the boulevards with the upper classes, and for more recognition and more respect; and it passed on to the extreme claim for an exact equality of material circumstances, which was rarely in fact made during the Revolutionary era, but was feared as an ultimate consequence of it by conservatives, and expressed in Babeuf's blunt formula, 'stomachs are equal.'[8]

[3] *Ibid.*, "The Struggle," p. 572.
[4] Palmer, "The Challenge," *op. cit.*, p. 20.
[5] *Ibid.*, pp. 13–14.
[6] *Ibid.*, pp. 4–5.
[7] Palmer, "The Struggle," *op. cit.*, p. 572.
[8] *Ibid.*, p. 573.

The word "revolution" he uses because the movement posed a conflict between incompatible images of the future, opposing views of what the community ought to be and what it was, because it included serious political protest, and because it involved a series of rapid changes that resulted in the reconstitution of government and society. Violence and destruction need not necessarily accompany a movement or situation for it to be called a "revolution," although, of course, brute force, civil war, and terror sometimes dominate the scene.

> By a revolutionary situation is here meant one in which confidence in the justice or reasonableness of existing authority is undermined; where old loyalties fade, obligations are felt as impositions, law seems arbitrary, and respect for superiors is felt as a form of humiliation; where existing sources of prestige seem undeserved, hitherto accepted forms of wealth and income seem ill-gained, and government is sensed as distant, apart from the governed and not really 'representing' them. . . The crisis is a crisis of community itself, political, economic, socio-logical, personal, psychological, and moral at the same time. Actual revolution need not follow, but it is in such situations that actual revolution does arise. Something must happen, if continuing deterioration is to be avoided; some new kind of basis of community must be formed.[9]

With very few exceptions, Palmer restricts his discussion to what is now called the Atlantic community, Europe and America (mostly Anglo-America) of the last forty years of the eighteenth century. The last paragraph of the second volume, however, suggests a wider application:

> All revolutions since 1800, in Europe, Latin America, Asia, and Africa, have learned from the eighteenth-century Revolution of Western Civilization. They have been inspired by its successes, echoed its ideals, used its methods. It does not follow that one revolution need lead to another, or that revolution as such need be glorified as a social process. No revolution need be thought of as inevitable. In the eighteenth century there might have been no revolution, if only the old upper and ruling classes had made more sagacious concessions, if, indeed, the contrary tendencies toward a positive assertion of aristocratic values had not been so strong. What seems to be inevitable, in both human affairs and in social science, must be put in contingent form — if x, then y. If a sense of inequality or injustice persists too long untreated, it will produce social disorganization. In a general breakdown, if a constructive doctrine and program are at hand, such as were furnished in the eighteenth century by the European Enlightenment, if the capacities

---

[9] Palmer, "The Challenge," *op. cit.,* p. 21.

of leaders and followers are adequate to the purpose, and if they are strong enough to prevail over their adversaries, then a revolution may not only occur and survive, but open the way toward a better society. The conditions are hard to meet, but the stakes are high, for the alternative may be worse.[10]

The spread and elaboration of the democratic revolution into the twentieth century are the subjects of this book. We take as our underlying hypothesis the proposition that much of the political, economic, and social change that is going on in the world today, and has gone on in the recent past, can be understood as a continuation of the democratic revolution — especially as an extension of the drive toward equality — to which the Europe and America of the latter part of the eighteenth century gave birth as a realizable human aspiration in this world.

We have, of course, been limited in the amount and scope of data we have been able to bring to bear on this sweeping generalization, and as social scientists we have strongly felt the obligation to bring a new set of relevant data to light as part of our contribution. Thus, our thinking has concentrated mainly on the transformations that have characterized the breakdown of colonial domination and the rise of new nations since World War II, and our actual data collections and specific data analyses are limited to the emergent nations of the British West Indies: Jamaica, Trinidad and Tobago, British Guiana — or Guyana as it is known since independence, Barbados, and a sample of islands from the Leeward and Windward chains.

THE DECISIONS OF NATIONHOOD

In our attempt to understand the facts of modern political and social development in the West Indies, we used theories and concepts from many sources, but the conceptual framework we formulated as a result of our work directly derives from our research task — understanding the recruitment, socialization, and, above all, the performance of new national elites, and it results from a basic commitment which we shared: to define and to do socially significant research. We have called this approach, which we propose as a widely applicable scheme with considerable analytic utility for the study of all new nations, "the decisions of nationhood."[11]

10 Palmer, "The Struggle," *op. cit.,* pp. 574–575.
11 Wendell Bell and Ivar Oxaal, *Decisions of Nationhood: Political and Social Development in the British Caribbean,* Denver, Colo.: Social Science Foundation, University of Denver, 1964; and Wendell Bell, *Jamaican Leaders: Political Attitudes in a New Nation,* Berkeley and Los Angeles: University of California Press, 1964. We have drawn liberally from these sources in this section, and in the following one on the West Indian setting.

The transition from colony to nation-state, of course, involves the formal transfer of political power from an old elite representing the established interests, especially from officials representing the imperial "mother country," to a new elite composed prominently of elected nationalist politicians representing new national citizenries and of local persons who man the posts of an emergent governmental bureaucracy. With the transfer of this power, the responsibility for the future is placed into the hands of an emergent indigenous elite while the problematics, possibilities, opportunities and hazards are underscored by the very realization that the character of the new nation will be to a considerable extent determined by the conscious, volitional acts of the new leaders. The political, economic, and social facts of the new states since World War II combined with the ideologies of the modern world have resulted in the leaders' adoption of what can be described as a rational decision-making model. This is not to evaluate objectively the degree of rationality with respect to some extrinsic criterion, but simply to say that the new national leaders' *definitions of the situation* are such that they view themselves as conscious actors within a set of conditions, means, ends, and motives — as actors who are to some extent manipulators of the present and creators of the future. Thus, we arrived at the decisions of nationhood in part from our knowledge of the maps of social reality, only more or less accurate to varying and unknown degrees, carried in the minds of the new elites. Such perceptions of reality, of course, are consequential both for the terms of emphasis in which political, economic, and social problems will be specified and for the nature of the solutions which will be implemented. Real consequences follow from the leaders' perceptions of the tasks before them. Thus, our formulation of the decisions of nationhood results in part from our effort to see the new nations through the eyes of the persons who are establishing them (or in some cases trying to prevent their establishment), and we have asked: What do men *think* they must do and *think* they must become in order to establish and maintain what they *think* is the type of organization called a nation-state? The answer, of course, may not be a single subjective reality, but may be multiple subjective realities if different actors have different perceptions of the situation.

Additionally, our specification of decisions of nationhood follows from a consideration of the requisites of nation-states, both as examples of the general conditions of organizations and as examples of the specific conditions of nation-states as a special kind of organization. For example, nation-states have some features they share with all social organizations, such as the problem of the maintenance of boundaries and the regulation of the relations with other organizations; they have others which are distinctive, such as those that result from their claim to be that social unit that legitimately demands the highest priority and overriding loyalty from its individual members.

From the notion of organizational requisites, we may ask: What must men really do and really become in order to establish and maintain the type of organization called a nation-state? The answer defines some of the specific problems that require solutions if men are to build a nation successfully. What men *think* they must do and what they really must do from an independent observer's point of view, of course, are not necessarily the same thing, and here and there in the course of our studies in the West Indies we have been able to show where organizational constraints, causes, and effects existed in contradistinction to the subjective meanings of social reality held by some of the West Indian leaders.

Furthermore, we arrived at the decisions of nationhood from our analysis of the underlying values of the people of the emerging nations of the British Caribbean. "Values," writes Neil J. Smelser, "are the major premises of the social order; they set the bearings of society toward general kinds of ends and legitimize these ends by a particular view of man, nature and society."[12] Values at this high level of generality and societal importance are not the same thing as organizational requisites of a national society. The difference lies in the distinction between how men must behave in order to create and maintain a nation-state and the various purposes which they may give for doing so. The relationship between the two is an empirical problem. Often it appears that new societal values emerge when major changes in the overall institutional order are being undertaken. On the other hand, there is likewise a tendency to legitimize innovations in the name of the old verities.

Nonetheless, it may be observed that when men do things which importantly change, or attempt to change, the boundaries, membership, autonomy, coalitions, organizational structure, internal relationships, history, and personal character of an organization (and all these things are involved in building a new nation), they generally advance what they believe to be important reasons for doing so. Societal values, therefore, can be regarded as including the more generalized qualities of an image of the future toward which historical action is directed. As such, they are what the big decisions of nationhood are often about.[13]

Finally, the decisions-of-nationhood approach grew out of our

[12] *Theory of Collective Behavior*, New York: The Free Press of Glencoe, 1963, p. 35.
[13] Bell and Oxaal, *op. cit.*, pp. 5–6.

consideration of a variety of works including prominently the decision-making approach as formulated by Richard C. Snyder and others,[14] developmental analysis as delineated by H. D. Lasswell,[15] and the concept of the image of the future as elaborated by Frederik L. Polak.[16]

We phrase the decisions of nationhood as a series of questions that require some answer, if a nation-state is to be created and maintained. Often national debate representing basic cleavages and differences within the society surrounds a decision, thus pushing it into the forefront of public consciousness. At other times, a particular outcome or an answer is so taken for granted that it does not even appear as if anything so high-sounding as a "decision" has been made. No alternative possibilities may be considered, there may be no controversy, and any issues that may be contained in the nature of the outcome may remain buried deep within the public unconscious. Among the different new states, of course, there are, because of varying historical circumstances, variations in the amount of public concern and disagreement over the outcomes of particular decisions. Needless to add, we are indebted to many writers for many of our formulations, particularly political scientists writing on the twentieth-century formation of nations throughout the world and historians who have detailed the rise of nationalism in Europe at an earlier time.

Our list of the decisions of nationhood, which we regard as preliminary, is as follows:

1. *Should we become a politically independent nation?*
This decision may have priority over all others in time, since the other decisions of nationhood may never arise if this one doesn't, and in importance, since the purposes and objectives behind the desire to create a politically independent state have implications for particular preferences with respect to the alternative outcomes to the other decisions. Of course, opinion within as well as without the territory of a potential nation-state has been far from unanimous regarding the desirability of independence. There have been active individuals who were dedicated to the idea of independence and who participated in the nationalist movements, but there have been equally active individuals in many

---

[14] "A Decision-Making Approach to the Study of Political Phenomena," in Roland Young (editor), *Approaches to the Study of Politics*, Evanston, Ill.: Northwestern University Press, 1958; Richard C. Snyder, H. W. Bruck, and Burton Sapin, *Decision-Making as an Approach to the Study of International Politics*, Foreign Policy Analysis Series No. 3, Organizational Behavior Section, Princeton University, June, 1954.

[15] For example, see Heinz Eulau, "H. D. Lasswell's Developmental Analysis," *Western Political Quarterly*, 11 (June, 1958), pp. 229–242.

[16] *The Image of the Future: Enlightening the Past, Orientating the Present, Forecasting the Future*, Volumes I and II, New York: Oceana Publications, 1961.

countries dedicated to preventing independence and expressing anti-nationalist sentiments. And, of course, there have been others — often large numbers of the general population in some countries — who have been relatively indifferent to political change. We ask: Who fought for nationhood and who opposed it? What reasons did they give for doing so? How did their images of the future conflict? How did the nature of the existing polity, economy, society and culture generate or suppress particular attitudes and actions? Thus, involved in deciding to be independent are ideas — potentially conflicting, sometimes subtly, sometimes wildly, different — about what an entire society should aspire to be, ideas that are carried by individuals and groups that have been shaped by the past, sustained by the present, and influenced by the images of the future toward which their action is directed.

2. *How much national sovereignty should the new nation have?* This question is explicitly stated among the big decisions of nationhood in recognition of the fact that potentially there are various degrees of independence, although most of the new nations since World War II, just as the older nations at an earlier time, decided on full autonomy as far as their national *political* status is concerned. Few were very inventive on this question and ironically they followed the path of the older European nations whose shackles they were trying to throw off in the search for their own distinctive identity. And they did this at a time when the older European nations were experimenting with the workability of supranational organizations, such as the Common Market and Euratom, which could result eventually in the erosion of the national sovereignty of European countries. There have been a few countries, however, that have stopped short of full political independence. The notable case in point is Puerto Rico which is a free state in association with the United States and which has achieved with remarkable success many of the goals that the modern nationalist movements set for themselves. Unless independence is viewed as an end in itself rather than as a means to an end, an independent observer may wonder why more thought was not given by the new nationalist leaders throughout the world to alternatives to complete political autonomy.

Militarily and economically, of course, the new nations are less independent than they are in formal political status. Not having adequate military power to protect their own lands from actual or potential threats from more powerful enemies, some — Malaysia comes to mind as a prominent example — call upon the military strength of the former imperial power or upon that of some powerful friend for assistance. In some cases, this call for aid has been the result of an inability to control internal disorder among their own peoples, such as in the cases of Kenya and British Guiana. Furthermore, economic autonomy has been striven for by some of the new nations through expropriation, nationalization, or otherwise increasing control over foreign-owned land and enterprise within their borders, but many have devised policies designed more to lure the former imperial rascals in than to throw them out.

3. *What should the geographical boundaries of the new nation be?*

Given notions about what constitutes a nation-state and the fact that human life is concentrated on the surface of a sphere, the problem of drawing lines on the sphere to create the boundaries between one nation-state and another arises. When a collectivity of people seek to establish a nation-state, they must decide, if they are going to succeed in their task, on the geographical boundaries that are to delimit the new state. This decision, like the others, is made only more or less by the new national leaders themselves. The heritage of colonialism enters in as well, to some extent in the form of advice, more or less insistent as a condition for permitting early independence, voiced by the European colonial officials during the transition to independence, and to some extent by the historical facts of European domination that have over the years set certain patterns of language, communication, transportation, association and orientation in the former colonies. The facts of existing territorial divisions which demarcated European empires and which resulted from wars between European powers, for example, were of great importance in explaining where many of the geographical boundaries of the new nations were to be established. They help explain why Gambia, a former British colony nearly surrounded by Senegal, a former French colony, in West Africa, is even in existence as a separate state and why in many ways it is nearer to London than to Senegal, while Senegal is nearer to Paris than to Gambia; and they help explain why some islands that can be seen with the naked eye from others in the Caribbean are nearer in social space to their respective European metropoles thousands of miles away than they are to each other.

Forces both for consolidation and fragmentation have been at work among the imperial purposes as well as among the emergent national circumstances. Federations were formed, and some collapsed; sometimes cultural groups were cut asunder and divided between different nations, and other times many diverse groups were placed together within the same colonial administrative districts, the boundaries of which were carried over into nationhood. Many of the problems of selecting boundaries — or dealing with existing boundaries once they had been selected — are related to the next big decision of nationhood.

4. *Should the state and the nation be coterminous?*

This question pertains to the degree of cultural homogeneity that the new state should strive to attain. Here, we must use the term "state" strictly to refer to the legal and political definition in order to distinguish it in the discussion from the cultural, linguistic, religious, or communal connotations contained in the term "nation." Should the state have the exact same boundaries as the nation, and should the nation have the exact same boundaries as the state? That is, should the political boundaries defining the new state be coterminous with the boundaries of some culturally distinct and homogeneous group?

Such a decision is obviously related to the decision regarding geographical boundaries, since the correlation between culture and geography makes juggling the boundaries one way of making the state and nation coterminous, as was done, for example, in the split between India and Pakistan. Another way, of course, is the mass migration of people from one location to another.

The boundaries that have been set up have sometimes made the state smaller in scale than the nation at least for some of the groups within the state, but frequently have done the reverse, and have created a state larger in scale than the nation. For example, one writer summarizes the situation as follows:

> In South-Southeast Asia, the former colonial area with the longest history of political independence, not a single country has escaped the problem of dissident groups. Pakistan has her frontier peoples; Ceylon, the Tamil-Sinhalese conflict; Burma, her hill peoples; Thailand, her Chinese and southern Malays; Laos, the non-Mekong Lao; Cambodia, the Vietnamese; Vietnam, the Cambodians and other ethnic and religious groups; Malaysia, a delicate balance among Malays, Chinese, and Indians; while India, the Philippines, and Indonesia must cope with a multitude of different ethnic, language, and religious groups. In many Middle Eastern countries, tensions have arisen over alienated groups such as the Kurds, the Armenians, and various Muslim sects. In Africa, many of the new states are torn by tribal rivalries.[17]

Most of the leaders of the new states have answered *Yes* to the question of state and nation cotermineity, although they don't always agree on how to bring it about. Some have succeeded or still hope to succeed by fragmentation, taking some primordial group smaller in scale than the state and creating a state coterminous with it by secession from a larger state. Others, confronting a culturally plural state, hope to create a nation by breaking down communal ties within the state and building up the priority of loyalty to the state over sub-group

[17] F. R. von der Mehden, *Politics of the Developing Nations*, Englewood Cliffs, N.J.: Prentice-Hall, 1964, p. 2. (Quoted by permission of author and publisher.)

loyalties by bringing a statewide culture into dominance, a subject that will be discussed below under cultural traditions. And a few seem to have considered the possibility of rejecting the melting-pot concept in favor of a cultural mosaic, as Canada did at an earlier time, in which ethnic minorities are encouraged to maintain their cultural identities while the unity of the state is achieved through legal rules of the game and political cooperation.

5. What form of government should the new nation have?
For the new nations of the twentieth century, perhaps the most important aspect of this question has been whether or not to have a political democracy, by which we mean a representative system based upon wide participation in the political community *and* the maintenance of public liberties. In such a system, dissent is not only possible, but more probably institutionalized. But countries such as Indonesia and Ghana, to name just two examples among the new states, despite considerable democratic rhetoric have opted for authoritarian systems that fail in important respects to fulfill the definition of a democratic political system as understood in the West. Often, the explanation is given that the mobilization of effort that is needed to lift the relatively poor new states out of the economic doldrums into the main stream of self-sustained economic progress cannot be achieved under a democratic political system. Debate and division of opinion, according to this view, must give way to unity in order to maximize the success of achieving collective national goals. Yet other nations, such as those under consideration here, facing much the same conditions of poverty and underdevelopment, strive to maintain political democracy. In fact, the new and near nations of the British West Indies may be particularly instructive in this regard, since they have managed so far to establish and maintain political democracies based on universal adult suffrage and public liberties while at the same time, at least in the cases of Jamaica and Trinidad, succeeding in their attempts to grow economically at relatively rapid rates.

We do not view the organizational requisites of a nation-state as requiring any particular type of political system; they demand only that *some* form of government be established and maintained. Rather the particular type of system that is created will depend on the complex interaction of many factors including importantly the patterns of priorities given within a new nation to civil and political rights on the one hand versus economic, social and cultural rights on the other. To those people who place higher priority on the former, political democracy tends to become an end in itself, a feature of the Good Society toward which they should strive; to those who place higher priority on the latter, the political system may be viewed as a means to an end to such a degree that any political system is acceptable, even an authoritarian one, as long as it is effective in producing the desired level of economic progress and, as we shall see, economic, social and cultural equality.[18]

6. *What role should the government play in the affairs of the society and of the economy?*

Whether or not the government plays a large role in other institutional sectors, of course, is a question that can vary quite independently of the question regarding the *form* of government. An authoritarian regime can play either a large or small role in the lives of the people and so can a democratic regime. These two things are commonly confused by the tendency to equate an authoritarian regime with a government that has elaborated and extended its control and services throughout the society and economy and to identify a democratic regime with a government that offers a minimum of functions and services. In fact, such thinking is often promoted by those persons who oppose the extension of government services and control, since they frequently argue that such extension represents a trend toward authoritarianism. But there is no necessary connection empirically, since we have cases to the contrary, for example authoritarian and economically stagnant Haiti compared to democratic and economically advanced Sweden, and it is fallacious theoretically.

In most of the new states, the nationalist leaders are committed to the modernization of their countries, and, whether authoritarian or democratic in their present political policies, they are often deeply dedicated to the welfare of their people — *all* of their people — and tend to view their new control over the governmental machinery as well as an increase in the power of that machinery itself as being among the most important ways — some go so far as to say *the* most important way — of achieving it. It was after all the control of the *political* institutions that was placed into the hands of the new national leaders, and it has been through the utilization of the resulting new political power that such leaders' influence on other sectors of society, whether by persuasion, threat or force, has been most evident.

7. *What should the new nation's external affairs be?*

Another example of a decision every new nation must face . . .

. . . concerns the new nations' entry into international relations. Prior to political independence, these countries had little or no control over their foreign affairs. As colonies, their contacts with the outside

[18] Cf. Charles C. Moskos, Jr. and Wendell Bell, "Attitudes Towards Democracy Among Leaders in Four Emergent Nations," *The British Journal of Sociology*, 15 (December, 1964), pp. 317–337.

world, apart from those with the imperial power itself, were indirect and circuitous. But with the successful drive toward nationhood, the question of the most desirable and beneficial international relations could be raised from the point of view of the emergent nation's own welfare. Although there were limitations imposed by economic ties, as well as by bounds of sentiment and culture, to the European power that had dominated them during the years of colonial rule, the new national elites faced the outside world with considerable freedom of choice to formulate their new nations' foreign policies.[19]

External affairs are perhaps dominated by a nation's relationships with other nation-states, by international relations. But they also include relationships with supranational organizations at the global and regional level, and in some cases they include relationships with subnational units such as those with ethnic communities or local governmental bodies.

There are examples of new states that are more aligned with the Communist bloc — now either Chinese or Russian versions — than with the Western democracies, others that seem to be fence-straddling trying to play each side of the cold war off against the other, and still others more inclined toward the West than the East. As the new nations have grown in number and stepped onto the stage of world affairs, however, a distinctive result of their foreign policies has been the emergence of the so-called neutralist bloc of countries, generally committed neither to Communist nor Western viewpoints but to their own particular interests and world views. This attitude is ably expressed by the Jamaican political leader, Mr. Vernon L. Arnett, in his Foreword.

8. *What type of social structure should the new nation have?*

9. *What should the new nation's cultural traditions be?*

10. *What should the national character of the new nation's people be?*

These decisions can be properly thought of as containing problems that are primarily *sociological* in the case of the question on social structure, *anthropological* with respect to the question on cultural traditions, and *social-psychological* with regard to the question on national character. Of course, the facts of the past leave any society in the present with a particular social structure, set of cultural traditions, and a typical psychological type of person; and the new national leaders, no matter how divergent their aspirations for the future are from the actualities of the present, cannot create a new social order, a new culture, or a new basic personality structure among themselves and their people very quickly. Yet most of the new national leaders have set

[19] Charles C. Moskos, Jr. and Wendell Bell, "Emergent Caribbean Nations Face the Outside World," *Social Problems*, 12 (Summer, 1964) pp. 24–41.

about the tasks of just so transforming their new states. It may take decades, more probably generations, but the effects of their policies can already be observed in many countries. In fact, in large part the new nationalist movements promised just such transformations. They promised more egalitarian and socially inclusive social structures; more distinctive, unified, impressive, and purposive cultural traditions — more modern while also being linked with their *own* past; and new national men and women within whose characters would be embodied new hope for perfection within this earthly world. There were exceptions, of course: nationalist movements that represented splintering, exclusive movements; and even in the case of the nationalist movements that professed the highest humanitarian ideals, the threat of deflection toward limited and parochial goals remains.

As stated earlier, this book is about the democratic revolution, especially the spread of equality in the twentieth century, but it is also about the decisions that every new nation must face and how some of these decisions were being made in the new and emerging nations of the British Caribbean. We call them the "decisions of nationhood," because it was the transition to nationhood that raised the underlying questions, that molded the new elites who were to act as leaders in the decision-making process, and that altered the nature of the political community within which they were to be decided. The decisions are not such that once made they cannot be altered. In fact, the questions can be raised again and again in the life of a nation and different decisions from the original ones reached. Nonetheless, the way the questions are resolved in the early life of a nation often sets the course for subsequent developments and in some cases may close the issue for generations.

It is obvious to say that the different decisions are more or less interrelated and that a certain outcome with respect to one may have implications for the range of choices possible with respect to others. Also, we realize that the broad, holistic approach we have used in the specification of the decisions of nationhood of necessity leaves many details relevant to each of the decisions beyond our grasp. We have here, of course, given only a brief outline of the decisions-of-nationhood framework, and, although there is (mostly at the macrosociological level) an elaboration of the framework in the studies that follow in this book, hundreds of particular studies could be made on certain points contained under the general formulation of the questions. We hope that some of our colleagues will be inclined to carry out such studies not only in the British West Indies, but in the other new states — or for that matter in the old states during the time they were becoming nations — as well. Furthermore, we should reiterate that many other writers — too numerous to cite by name here — have informed us about the new states, nation-building, and nationalism and that many of the decisions of nationhood, as we have formulated them, have been phrased in one way or another and discussed by others. Nonetheless, to our knowledge they have not been stated in quite this way by anyone else, nor put together in a single schema, nor used as systematically as a framework for studying the historical facts and future aspirations that accompany the transition to nationhood for a few particular places, nor have they been employed as part of an effort to project an idealistic and scientific image of the future for entire peoples and whole societies.

THE WEST INDIAN SETTING

The emergent nations that we have studied are contained within what has been known as the "British West Indies"or the "British Caribbean,"[20] and the inhabitants, whatever their backgrounds, have been collectively called "West Indians," although this term may be giving way to the more particular territorial designations since different roads have been followed to independence. Most of the field work on which the reports contained in this book are based was done during the period from 1960 through most of 1962. It was a time of great excitement and expectancy in the British West Indies. It was to see the collapse of the West Indies Federation and the achievement of political independence by Jamaica (August 6, 1962) and Trinidad and Tobago (August 31, 1962). Since then, British Guiana has become independent Guyana (May 26, 1966) and little Barbados, after some discussion about forming a larger union with the Leeward and Windward islands, appears to be destined to "go it alone" as one of the tiniest independent nations of the world.* All but one of the remaining islands — Antigua, Dominica, Montserrat, St. Kitts-Nevis-Anguilla, St. Lucia, and St. Vincent — are at the time of writing still fragmented and working out some kind of half-way house between being politically dependent colonies and fully independent nation-states, where internal self-government would be combined with British responsibility for defense and foreign affairs. The exception is Grenada which may join with Trinidad and Tobago in a unitary state.

Jamaica, lying 90 miles south of Cuba, has a population of 1.7 million people; Trinidad and Tobago, located in the Eastern Caribbean just off

[20] British Honduras and the Bahamas are excluded from this discussion because of fundamental differences between their political development and that of the other territories of the British Caribbean.

* Since this book went to press, Barbados on November 30, 1966 became politically independent.

the coast of Venezuela; 800,000; Guyana, on the continent of South America with 83,000 square miles of land — by far the largest of the territories under consideration — has 600,000 persons settled chiefly along the Atlantic coast; and the remaining eight islands have a total population of about 700,000. Excluding Guyana, these new and emergent small nations of the Caribbean have an average population density in excess of 360, although in Barbados the density reaches a high of nearly 1,400.[21]

Almost all of the present-day inhabitants of these territories are descended from slaves and indentured laborers brought over in previous times to satisfy the labor demands of a plantation economy. While containing a cultural and racial mosaic — including descendants of English, Irish, Welsh, Scottish, French, Portuguese, German, East Indian, Chinese, and Lebanese immigrants — the total proportions of all these groups except for the East Indians are small compared to the number of descendants of Negro slaves. The East Indians, both Hindu and Muslim, were imported as indentured laborers after the end of slavery in the British Empire in the 1830's. From India they were brought chiefly to Guyana and Trinidad; in the former they today outnumber the Negroes while in the latter they constitute over one-third of the population.

The class structure of the area — in oversimplified terms — consists of a small white or near-white, upper class, a mostly brown-skinned middle class, and predominantly dark-brown or black lower class.[22] These traditional designations, however, no longer show the same high degree of correlation between color and status as has held in the past. Brown and black men are today found in large numbers as leading professionals, politicians, labor leaders, educators, clergymen, and civil servants. Aside from East Indians, however, they are heavily underrepresented in management of business firms where the lighter-skinned minorities still prevail. Thus, the classic West Indian color-status pattern is to be found most pronounced in the economic sphere, particularly in the commercial community, where family capitalism remains an important mode of organization. This tendency toward ethnically-based polarization of political and economic power has not, however, resulted in a chronic pattern of critical conflict between light and darker-skinned elites. Although many non-white politicians identify themselves as "socialists" and lead parties based on organized labor, they have generally adhered to a conception of economic development

[21] George W. Roberts, "Some Demographic Considerations of West Indian Federation," *Social and Economic Studies*, 6 (June, 1957), p. 270.
[22] M. G. Smith, *The Plural Society in the British West Indies*, Berkeley and Los Angeles: University of California Press, 1965.

which stresses the need for partnership and cooperation between government and business, and between the latter and organized labor.

Life styles of the West Indian middle and upper class – regardless of color or ethnicity – are distinct from that of the mass of lower-class West Indians but are typically similar to those of comparable social strata in more economically advanced countries. The English language, as most frequently heard throughout the British Caribbean, is peppered with Africanisms and echoes with the intonations and vocabularies of other languages. Trinidad, the most polyglot island, is the home of a dialect which has been described as "Spanish in origin, French by tradition, English by adoption, and not without traces of the languages of India, Pakistan, China, Syria, and Palestine."[23] Trinidad, however, was one of the last colonial acquisitions of the British in the Caribbean, having been wrested from the Spanish at the end of the eighteenth century. At the other extreme there is the relative cultural antiquity of an island like Barbados which has been under continuous British control since the 1620's, and which after the original slave settlement has not been host to a large influx of non-Negro immigrants from outside the West Indies. Thus the British Caribbean has occupied a unique position in relation to other areas in the Empire: it was peopled chiefly by dark-skinned immigrants originating in Africa and Asia. It was therefore unlike either Britain's major North American or Pacific possessions – both settled by European immigrants – and unlike its Asian or African colonies which, despite some instances of heavy European colonization, were peopled chiefly by indigenous populations. This aspect of West Indian history has in several instances served, as will be seen, to bolster a diffuse kind of immigrant mentality running counter to exhortations for unity issued by the leading nationalist politicians.

The West Indian economy, today as always, is largely dependent on agricultural production for the world market, with all the vulnerability to fluctuation and chronic uncertainty that this can entail. The major export crop remains sugar although such tropical specialities as bananas, coconuts, spices and citrus fruits are also marketed abroad. The major extractive industries, all foreign-owned, are bauxite in Jamaica and Guyana and petroleum in Trinidad. Some small-scale manufacturing is conducted locally – notably in Jamaica and Trinidad – and tourism has become an important source of income for some of the islands – notably Jamaica and Barbados. The last decade has seen some success in Jamaica and Trinidad toward economic development and the raising

[23] S. Moosai-Maharaj, "Problems of Race and Language in the British Caribbean," in P. A. Lockwood (editor), *Canada and the West Indies Federation*, Sackville, N.B., Canada: Mt. Allison University Publication, No. 2, 1957, p. 79.

of per capita income but, despite the general modernity of the area compared to some underdeveloped countries, the West Indies are poor, suffer from high rates of under- and unemployment, widespread poverty and exploding population, low per capita productivity, land that is often poorly utilized, illiteracy and inadequate educational facilities. The revolution of rising expectations is so much an accomplished fact in the West Indies that, between 1955 and 1960, Jamaica alone sent over a hundred thousand migrants to the United Kingdom — and exodus curtailed by the 1962 Commonwealth Immigration Act.[24]

The modern political history of the British West Indies began in the late 1930's when outbreaks of poverty-induced strikes and riots spread throughout most of the area. The economic discontent of the West Indian people was given voice by new labor leaders and nationalist politicians, and led to a series of constitutional advances which got underway in the mid-40's. The old Crown Colony system gave way to modified ministerial forms of government, and by the early 1950's all of the colonies had achieved universal adult suffrage and were being primed for self-government. These measures were aimed ultimately at bringing all of the British territories in the area into a federation, which would be the vehicle intended to take them collectively on to Dominion status. This, at any rate, was the expressed wish of both British colonial authorities and leading West Indian politicians at the Montego Bay conference of 1947. Over a decade later, however, when the provisional West Indies Federation was inaugurated in 1958 the federal ideal was still plagued by a number of serious ailments, any one of which could prove fatal to the transitional organization housed, symbolically, in a "temporary" headquarters in Port of Spain, Trinidad. Guyana had decided not to participate in the federation from the outset and the ten islands, unable to agree on a final federal formula, were chopped into three major sections after a 1961 referendum in Jamaica had decreed an end to that island's participation in the federal system. At the northern end of the islands, Jamaica went on to independence alone, closely followed by a similar development at the southern end of the chain when Trinidad and Tobago became independent. Led by Barbados the remaining eight islands — some of which are dependent on British subsidies to balance their budgets — began searching for some form of political consolidation, which gave rise to the nickname of the "Little Eight" as a potential addition to the family of nations. Further fragmentation has occurred: Barbados sought a separate independence and the remaining islands do not seem able to unite.

[24] R. B. Davison, *West Indian Migrants,* London: Institute of Race Relations, Oxford University Press, 1962.

Guyana, in the meantime, saw its progress toward independence thwarted in 1953 with the temporary suspension of the colony's constitution, an act followed by a splitting of party politics along ethnic lines of East Indian versus Negro, which led to two mass riots, internal political stalemate, and an impasse in negotiations for independence. Finally, Guyana moved on to independence in 1966.

Thus, the British Caribbean at the time of writing contains three newly-independent nations — Jamaica, Trinidad and Tobago, and Guyana; one near nation, little Barbados; and the remaining seven placid but poverty-stricken orphans of the federal experiment who remain as wards of the Colonial Office, uncertain as to what their future will be.

From even this brief introductory description of the area it can be seen that, despite its diminutive size and power in the world, its political and social development has been highly complex. For purposes of the analysis we are about to undertake it has the advantage of providing illustrations of various approaches to the big decisions of nationhood while at the same time placing convenient limits on the number of cultural variables which a full-scale global analysis would entail.

CHAPTER 2 The Intellectual Background
to the Democratic Revolution
in Trinidad

IVAR OXAAL

*The planters do too much or too little in this matter. If they will educate the
slave, then they do too little for their own safety in persisting to debar him from
those privileges to which he will soon feel that he has acquired an equitable
right . . . It will be impossible to march the Negroes on the road to knowledge
and compel them to stand at ease within the old entrenchments of ignorance.*

— H. Coleridge, *Six Months in the West Indies in 1825*[1]

*And as in material, so also in intellectual production. The intellectual creations
of individual nations become common property. National onesidedness and nar-
rowmindedness become more and more impossible, and from the numerous national and local literatures there arises a world-literature.*

— Marx and Engels, 1848[2]

BUT why march the Negroes, and much later, the East Indian estate
workers, on the "road to knowledge" at all? If Crown Colony Trinidad,
as Eric Williams would charge in his Independence *History*, was based
on sugar workers and needed only sugar workers, not citizens, what
purposes gave rise to limited but in some respects excellent institutions
of learning inaugurated in nineteenth-century Trinidad? Why was
the lid of the Pandora's box which contained European ideas on enlightenment and progress raised even slightly?

There were three fundamental reasons, none of which were incompatible with the major interests of the sugar industry; first, there
was the sheer necessity of colonial administration to bring some order
into the milling *anomie* of Trinidad society; second, there were the
proselytizing endeavours of the missionaries and priests; third, there
was the unavoidable seepage of British humanitarianism and the doctrine

[1] H. Coleridge, *Six Months in the West Indies in 1825*, London: John Murray,
1826, p. 321.
[2] Karl Marx and Friedrich Engels, *Manifesto of the Communist Party*, New York:
International Publishers, 1848, p. 13.

of trusteeship brought to the colony by some of those who administered it.[3] These purposes combined to establish and expand the system of formal education in Trinidad but they were not entirely complementary. Secular and religious educational authority clashed from the outset in the colony and resulted in a system of dual jurisdiction. That system was still in effect when the People's National Movement was formed in 1956 and the apparent intention of Dr. Williams and some of his closest associates to modify it heightened the crisis of political legitimacy which confronted them in the years immediately preceding nationhood.

NINETEENTH CENTURY BEGINNINGS

From its very inception to the time of independence, the educational system of Trinidad was divided between the overlapping, and at times conflicting, jurisdiction of Church and State. At stake were the competing interests and aspirations of those persons and groups who have seen in the education of the young a means whereby a unified earthly city might be forwarded and the descendants of Augustine who were equally ardent in advancing the claims of the heavenly city. In the early 1840's, Governor MacLeod, pressed by various religious groups for increased subsidies to the various small denominational schools which had been established since Emancipation a few years earlier, decided that the time had come to attempt to institute some unified, state-supervised system of education. In letters to the Secretary of State for the Colonies, MacLeod, as one historian has paraphrased the documents, pointed out:

... Trinidad's unique position among British colonies owing to its very mixed population. The immigration of peoples from so many scattered nations as well as the differences of religion made it imperative that there should be some system in the colony. Education, he stressed, should be under Government control and should be accessible to all

[3] Cf. Shirley C. Gordon's invaluable compendium of colonial documents, *A Century of West Indian Education*, London: Longmans, Green and Co., Ltd., 1963. More complete documentation of the process described here for Trinidad is available for the entire West Indies through these documents. In a circular dispatch from the Colonial Office dated January 26, 1847, for example, the following points are stressed: "a) Religious Education — to inculcate the principles and promote the influence of Christianity; b) The English Language — to diffuse a grammatical knowledge of the English Language as the most important agent of civilization for the colored population of the colonies; c) Requirements of Small Farmers — to communicate such a knowledge of writing and arithmetic . . . as may enable the peasant to economise his means, and give the small farmer the power to enter into calculations and agreements . . . ; d) Relationships With Authority — The lesson books of the colonial schools should also teach the mutual interests of the mother-country and her dependencies; the rational basis of their connection, and the domestic and social duties of the colored races." Gordon, p. 58.

nationalities and religious groups. This would ensure that in future generations the English language would be understood by all the inhabitants, *two-thirds of whom were still speaking French or Spanish.*[4]

These circumstances could hardly be tolerated, the Governor stated; it was only proper that " . . . peoples living under British rule and claiming the benefits of British citizenship should at least be able to read the laws by which they were governed."[5] Aside from this compelling administrative necessity he noted that the churches, each of which was using the schools to advance their own doctrinal points of view, would continue to claim government subsidies; the colonial government was already undertaking to pay half of their teachers' salaries.

Governor MacLeod's tentative inquiries addressed to the Secretary of State in the early 1840's did not result in any changes in the denominational school system as it was then constituted. In 1851, however, after East Indian indentured immigration to the sugar estates had begun, Governor Harris took steps to organize a system along strikingly secular lines — a move which met strenuous opposition not only from the Roman Catholic authorities, whose supremacy dated from the days of Spanish rule and French Creole social ascendancy — but from some of the other denominational leaders as well. The Harris educational reforms stipulated that primary school education was to be free, open to all children, conducted in English, maintained entirely from the rates of local districts, and devoid of any religious instruction whatsoever. The reforms further made the entire management and control of the schools, the hiring of teachers, the selection of textbooks and courses of instruction the responsibility of a Board of Education consisting of the Governor, members of the Legislative Council (appointed in its entirety by the Governor), and such other laymen as the Governor might select.[6]

The Harris system was the high-water mark of secular education in Trinidad, but it did not survive for long. As a result of denominational opposition the Secretary of State in 1869 sent one Patrick J. Keenan out to the colony to recommend changes. Keenan had been Inspector of Schools under the Commissioners of National Education in Ireland, and because of this Roman Catholic background a modern reformer suspected he " . . . was obviously not a liberal choice for the job . . ."[7] The Educational Ordinance of 1870, which embodied many of the

---

[4] Gertrude Carmichael, *The History of the West Indian Islands of Trinidad and Tobago, 1498–1900*, London: Alvin Redman, 1961, p. 33 (emphasis added).
[5] *Ibid.*, p. 224.
[6] *Ibid.*, pp. 252–253.
[7] *Education Report, 1959, of Committee on General Education* (The Maurice Report), Port of Spain: Government Printing Office, 1959.

recommendations of the Keenan Commission, saw the substantial beginning of the reassertion of denominational control of education. The beginnings of the Dual System, as it was called, involved the maintenance of both government and denominational schools, with the latter enjoying considerable autonomy, and with the passing of years, ever greater subsidization by the government. Power to appoint and dismiss teachers in the grant-aided church schools was given to the religious managers of the institutions. By 1890 the government was paying three-quarters of their salaries and operating expenses. In 1878 there had been 47 government primary schools in operation as against only 35 denominational schools; by 1898 the number of government schools had increased only by 10, to 57, while the number of denominational schools, assisted by increasingly generous subsidies, had leaped to 147. During the same twenty-year period at the end of the century, enrollment in primary schools of all types swelled from barely 7,000 in 1878 to almost 25,000 in 1898. More Trinidadians were receiving a rudimentary formal education, but it was increasingly being taken over by the humanitarian and missionizing programme of the Christian churches.[8]

One of the most remarkable of these missionizing endeavours was that conducted by the Presbyterians of the Canadian Mission led by Reverend John Morton. The programme of the Canadian Mission, which addressed itself to the neglected education of the rural East Indians, illustrated how the Government, in effect, abdicated responsibility for education to the priest and missionary. In 1869 Morton proposed to the Governor that his administration should undertake to fully underwrite the Mission's expenses. The Governor admitted to the Legislative Council the need for a greater effort at educating the East Indians, pointing out that " . . . hardly an Indian child has attended a ward school, whilst the small number of these immigrants who are receiving any education are almost exclusively to be found in private schools of the strictest denominational character and uninspected by the State."[9] Very little financial assistance for Morton's mission to the East Indians was provided by the Government, however. By 1874 Morton had opened twelve primary schools in southern Trinidad, only one of which was government supported, one supported from the funds of the Mission itself, while the remaining nine were paid for by the (presumably British Protestant) planters of the area who had been receptive to the Mission's appeals. Many later-prominent East Indians were educated in the Canadian Presbyterian primary schools and

[8] *Ibid.*, p. 12.
[9] Quoted in Carmichael, *op. cit.*, p. 265.

many, too, received their secondary education at the Mission's Naparima College in the town of San Fernando — one of the first three secondary-level institutions in the colony.

In an educational system geared chiefly to teaching the English language, spoken as well as written, and the verities of the British Empire and the Christian religion, secondary education was not extensively developed in Victorian Trinidad. In addition to Naparima College, secondary-school education in the last quarter of the century was available at only two other institutions. One was the government-operated Queen's Royal College which provided a secondary education, free of charge, to the sons of civil servants; the other was the Roman Catholic St. Mary's College. Both were located in Port of Spain. However, from its foundation in 1870, Queen's Royal College did offer a limited number of scholarships and exhibition prizes by which a few exceptionally promising primary-school graduates could continue their education. This inauguration of scholarships at the secondary level was of great importance since it opened up the possibility of higher education to at least a few of the most gifted sons of poor local parents. A secondary school certificate eventually became the ticket of admission to junior positions in the civil service, and it was likewise the necessary formal prerequisite for those few who sought a university education and a berth in the private professions. With the addition of the so-called Island Scholarships as another link in this embryo meritocracy a few of the most talented of the secondary school graduates could, on the basis of performance in gruelling, competitive, examinations, obtain a university education in Great Britain, and then possibly enter into studies in medicine or law. The "scholarship boys," as they came to be called in Trinidad, were exemplary figures in a society which otherwise provided very limited opportunities for the vast majority of its citizens; they were the exceptional ones who rose in the social scale by virtue of brains and hard work. The term "scholarship boy," however, would sometimes be used derisively, as connoting that "the scholarship boy" tends to be a snob, or a joyless grind. There would be three Island Scholarship winners in the first P.N.M. Cabinet: Dr. Williams himself; the P.N.M.'s Deputy Political Leader, Dr. Patrick Solomon (M.D.); and Dr. Winston Mahabir, an East Indian physician. Ellis Clark, a brilliant constitutional lawyer, pillar of the Roman Catholic Church, who was appointed as Trinidad and Tobago's first Ambassador to the United Nations, also began his career as an Island Scholarship winner from Queen's Royal College (or as it is nick-named, "Q.R.C.").

There thus appeared during the Victorian era an avenue of social mobility based very largely on the educational system which led to a high degree of correlation, within the Negro community, of social position and education. From this ladder of opportunity the East Indians – owing to their rural location, neglect, and an official bias against drawing them off the land through education – were relatively excluded until much later. Rewards for exemplary academic performance were the limited expression of official colonial policy which aimed at providing some avenues of advancement into the professions and civil service for talented local persons. An experienced British schoolmaster living in Trinidad in the nineteenth century eulogized that policy in these terms:

> In consequence of the liberal exhibitions and scholarships open every year to deserving pupils of elementary schools no matter what nationality or creed, 'the humblest peasant,' to quote . . . from a report of the Inspector of Schools, 'may aspire to a college course at Cambridge or elsewhere free of expense, and enter as a candidate for the Civil Service of India. The advantages offered to boys by our educational system are hardly surpassed in the world . . . It may indeed be said that the highest positions in the British Empire to which mental acquirements are a passport are opened to the poorest boy in Trinidad by the educational advantages at his command.'[10]

Not only the exceptional scholar, however, benefitted from the establishment of the education system: that system had to be staffed and, although a great many of the primary grade teaching positions, and virtually all the secondary level posts, were filled by expatriate teachers, the growing school system provided expanding opportunities for local citizens to achieve at least the status of a minor professional. Naturally, there were other criteria which became the basis of social ranking within the Negro community in Trinidad, color being perhaps the most important of these, but with the growth of the professions and the civil service in the twentieth century, education, and the opportunities which education provided, began to assume ever greater significance. At the top of this status hierarchy would be the university-educated professionals, below them the more educated of the civil servants, and, still lower, the primary school teachers who had been trained by the "student teacher" method, perhaps supplemented with a course in the local teachers' training college.

The exportation of education from the "advanced" nations of the Victorian era to Trinidad was not without difficulties aside from the government's periodic difficulties with the denominational authorities. The attempt to maintain the same standards "as at home" is unrealistic, the schoolmaster quoted above laments, because of the heterogeneous

---

[10] J. H. Collens, *Guide to Trinidad*, London: Elliot Stock, 1888, p. 246.

nature of the population. "Speaking from experience," he wrote, "I can truly say a teacher's life 'is not a happy one.' "[11]

EDUCATION FOR NATIONALISM

Just after the turn of the century, two members of the new stratum of Negro primary school teachers in Trinidad acquired sons who would make their mark on the world in a rather exotic profession. One of the boys was named Cyril Lionel Robinson James, the other, Malcolm Nurse. Both would achieve distinction as professional revolutionary organizers and intellectuals. The fathers of the pair were good friends. The James family was descended from the class of free colored artisans; James' grandfather had been a respected mechanic and first Negro engineer on the government railroad.[12] Later, James' young brother, Eric, would continue in the family occupational tradition and become an important railway official himself. The father of young Nurse was also an exceptionally successful colored man by the standards of the colonial society of the period, for he served as an Agricultural Advisor to the government Department of Education.[13]

The young James and Nurse seemed to have been casual friends in their boyhood days. Writing many years later, James recalled that they had together explored their rural and forested environment, tramping along the base of the Northern Range and bathing in the Arima River.[14] Both boys eventually attended secondary school. James was a precocious scholar and won an exhibition at nine years of age to Queen's Royal College; Nurse attended St. Mary's College. Not that opportunities for secondary education had increased very much by 1911, the year in which a Negro clerk in the Port of Spain post office acquired the distinction of becoming the father of the future Dr. Eric Williams, and which was approximately the year in which James and Nurse were embarking on their secondary school education. Secondary education was expensive, straining the limited resources of the colored middle class and virtually out of the question for the sons of parents living in regions so remote from the urban centers as to make necessary the boarding of their sons in town. The official scholarship bridge between primary and secondary school, and from the latter to a university education abroad, was in reality a razor's edge. The government itself provided only

[11] *Ibid.,* p. 245.
[12] C. L. R. James, "Nationalist Strain," *New Statesman,* January 18, 1958, pp. 67–68.
[13] C. L. R. James, "Notes on the Life of George Padmore," *The Nation,* October 2, 1959.
[14] *Ibid.*

four free places in the secondary schools, and the university scholarships for the United Kingdom numbered but three annually.[15]

The quality of the secondary school instruction was, however, in
comparison to the ordinary level in the primary schools, deemed to be
extraordinarily high. On this point there is the testimony of a leading
West Indian educator — Dr. Eric Williams himself. As an alumnus
of the system, he later wrote that both Q.R.C. and St. Mary's had a
staff and curriculum the equal of the British public schools after which
both were modelled. Classical literature, languages, geography, mathe-
matics, history — even including a course in West Indian history —
were all taught and taught well. Also of the greatest importance in
accounting for the high level of scholarship in Trinidad was the fact
that the colony's secondary schools were *the first colonial institutions
to participate in the external examinations of Oxford and Cambridge.*[16]
Thus identical criteria were established for the performance of the local
scholars in an inter-Empire educational system. The annual publication
of results produced great public interest. And the Trinidad scholars
did very well; as Eric Williams, old boy from Q.R.C. wrote later in an
article dealing with the social anatomy on the island in the year of his
birth:

> One of the island scholars of 1911 was placed first among 57 candi-
> dates in the British Empire in Agricultural Science . . . He gained
> distinction in five subjects; so did four other students in the Empire, one
> in Ceylon, three in England. Of 83 candidates who gained distinction
> in history, four were from Trinidad . . . At the 1910 examinations one
> island scholar from Queen's Royal College was placed first in the Senior
> Cambridge examinations throughout the Empire, whilst another from
> St. Mary's College topped the candidates in the entrance examination
> to St. Bartholomew's Hospital in London. W. J. Locke, island scholar
> for 1879, became a successful novelist; another scholar for 1884 became
> Sir Robert Falconer, President of the University of Toronto.[17]

An adventurous alternative for the secondary school graduate who
had been unable to obtain a university scholarship was to go to the
United States and attempt to work his way through a university.
Malcolm Nurse would take this route in the 1920's. However, the only
profession in Trinidad which could be entered on the basis of an
American degree was that of dentistry. In 1911, twenty of the twenty-
four dentists practicing in the island had been trained at American

[15] Eric Williams, "Education of a Young Colonial," *The P.N.M. Weekly*, August
30, 1956.
[16] *Ibid.*
[17] *Ibid.*

schools, indicating that this avenue of advancement, which thousands of West Indian students would later take, was already well-trodden.[18]

And then there was cricket. The stem of one palm tree branch provided a bat, three more, propped up against each other, supplied a wicket for the plebeians who had observed the British gentlemen engaged in their favorite sport. Inter-Colonial cricket had been inaugurated in Trinidad in 1893, the year in which the elite Queen's Park Oval Club was organized. In 1895 a team from England had been beaten by an all-Trinidad side; two years later, during the centennial celebrations of British rule, cricket was prominent on the agenda, and in 1900 the first West Indian team visited England. Cricket clubs, and the inevitable village cricket pitch, could be found all over Trinidad. Everyone knew the game; young C. L. R. James was a cricket fanatic, and so was Learie Constantine whose father had himself been an outstanding exponent of the game. In the 1920's Learie Constantine went to England to play in the county leagues for Nelson in Lancashire. He soon established a reputation as being one of the best "all-rounders" that the game had ever seen, a sportsman of legendary prowess and one of the early heralds of the phenomenal ability that West Indians were to bring to the game.

Someday, perhaps, a Trinidad writer will attempt a full-scale social history of the complex little island civilization that was Trinidad in the early years of the century. In his cricket memoirs, *Beyond a Boundary*, James provides glimpses into such facets of the period as the Puritanical code impressed on the Q.R.C. schoolboy, the metropolitan sophistication of a group of local intellectuals and literators, and the manner in which membership in the various local cricket clubs was determined by very fine class and color distinctions. The excellence of the cricket played was a product of the sublimated class conflict which found an outlet in the keen rivalries between the clubs; also of importance was the ready, informal, availability of top players for matches at every level. Under the veneer of class and caste there had taken shape a self-confident, robust, uninhibited national character for which cricket — like Carnival? — provided a disciplined, formalized, means of expression. West Indian social conditions of the period, particularly in Trinidad, James seems to be saying, were analogous to the vigorous, pre-Victorian ethos which had produced W. G. Grace and the modern game of cricket — an England still unconquered by the Industrial Revolution, not finicky in morals, committed to enjoying life with gusto.[19] The parallel, if tenuous, is nonetheless fascinating. In Trinidad the lively, innovative neighborhood organizations of the urban underworld *jamettes*

[18] *Ibid.*
[19] C. L. R. James, *Beyond a Boundary*, London: Hutchinson and Co., 1963, p. 157 and *passim*.

had counterparts in many areas of the countryside. Tunapuna, a district intimately known to James and Constantine has been described by Dom Basil Matthews as a frontier town, intensively clannish, and united as a semi-secret organization against outsiders. The cultural background to James' theory on the relationship of social conditions to the excellence of sport — as well as insight into the perhaps subconscious origins of the intense populist faith which he later developed into a unique method of revolutionary action — is suggested in this master portrayal of the Trinidad from which he emerged by Reverend Matthews:

> Beneath the geographic-economic conditions of the village neighborhood, a human factor was active and creative. The flight of runaway slaves and the forging or assimilation of novel kinship links (godparent relationships) in the social pattern, to say nothing of the development of folk literature are evidence of creative activity. Nevertheless, the neighborhood, that is, the village, frequently cast or drawn into the shadow of the plantation, largely conditioned and also determined the structure, form and expression of the traditional Trinidad family and society. Just as before Emancipation the slave plantation was the center of all life; and, as in recent times all life and activity, even in the remotest village, point, like the roads, to the commercial towns and industrial centres; so, in the intervening hundred years, the shut-in village neighborhood was the hub and matrix of society . . .
>
> Membership in a territorial group used to be a test of manhood. Initiation involved the spilling of blood of the petitioner in a war-like ceremony which has been witnessed by many people who are today [*circa* 1953] not above twenty-five years of age. The secret society aspect of the territorial group is nowhere as remarkable as in Tunapuna where . . the original Tunapunians hold their community secrets to this day against all comers, whether they be the law or private citizens.[20]

During this period the great French Creole nationalist, Cipriani, seems to have made a deep impression on many youths in Trinidad, an impression which was more than political; it was emotional as well. Although many members of the colored middle class, some directly dependent on the British authorities to maintain their standing within a tight little social structure, were leery of supporting Cipriani openly, many sympathized with his cause and covertly gave him support and encouragement. While speaking at Woodford Square, Cipriani would often point rhetorically toward St. Vincent Street (the "lawyers row" of Port of Spain) and, apparently without great success, exhort its timid denizens

---

[20] Dom Basil Matthews, *Crisis of the West Indian Family*, Port of Spain: Government Printery, 1953, p. 95.

to join in the struggle for local self-government. James has written a reminiscence on Cipriani in which he recounts how he and a friend were listening to Cipriani speak: "As Cipriani came to a pause at the end of his opening words, I felt thrills running up and down my back and I looked at John: his eyes were filled with tears." On another occasion, when in his capacity as English tutor to the French Consul in Trinidad, the latter official asked James, "If the Governor arrested Captain Cipriani, what do you think would happen?" James immediately answered, "The people will burn down the town."[21]

This, then, was the curious mixture of the rustic and urban, the provincial, yet cosmopolitan, environment to which schoolboys and young men born after the turn of the century would be exposed in the Trinidad of the twenties. During that decade Malcolm Nurse tried his hand in local journalism but then set off for Fisk University in Nashville, Tennessee, and then moved on to Howard University in Washington, D.C. James taught at Q.R.C., at the Government Teacher's College, and was also on the verge of leaving the colony by the end of the decade. Eric Williams had a series of successful scholarship competitions behind him and was about to climax his graduation from Q.R.C. by winning an Island Scholarship.

On a day in 1931 James ran into Eric Williams on a street near Q.R.C. They knew each other well — James had been a tutor to Williams while the latter was a pupil at the secondary institution. Both had made plans to leave the colony. James had been working on a biography of Captain Cipriani and was determined to go to England and become a writer. Williams, having just won his university scholarship, had decided that the conventional career pattern of the scholarship winner — law or medicine — was not for him; he was going to Oxford University and do History.[22] His father, who had favored a regular professional career for his son, protested, but to no avail — after all, as the Trinidad scholar-statesman dryly observed during a B.B.C. interview in 1962, "It was I who had won the scholarship — not he."

Thus the two Trinidad intellectuals set off — like many other bright, adventurous and ambitious young men from the provinces of the Empire — in search of an education, and possibly even a career, in the metropolitan country. Many had preceded them, and even more would follow. Not all, however, went to the Mother Country; some, like Kwame Nkrumah who left the Gold Coast about three years later, or the son of an East Indian estate overseer, Cheddi Jagan, who left British

---

[21] C. L. R. James, "Andrew Arthur Cipriani," *Trinidad Guardian* (Independence Supplement), August 26, 1962.
[22] C. L. R. James, "Dr. Eric Williams, P.N.M. Political Leader — A Convention Appraisal." *The Nation*, March 18, 1960.

Guiana a decade later, would go to the United States. All, however, were "foreign students" in an advanced country and by exposure to the intellectual milieux of these countries they found individuals and groups which instilled, and encouraged, nationalist aspirations which gave the impetus to the incipient colonial revolution.

"The colleges and universities," writes Edward Shils, "attended by the students of underdeveloped countries became academies of national revolution."[23] In London, the Fabian-founded London School of Economics which had Harold Laski as its leading political theorist upheld a universal democratic ideal for the young colonials; the *New Statesman*, under the editorial guidance of Kingsley Martin and with J. M. Keynes and the Guild Socialist G. D. H. Cole as the dominant influence in the paper's approach to economic affairs, made the cause of independence for India its own during the Thirties.

> . . . It was not only the universities of London and Paris but the cafes and cheap restaurants and dingy hotels and boarding houses where they spent most of their days and the offices of their nationalist organizations which educated the students in nationalism, gave them first some degree of national consciousness, made them see how retrograde their own countries were and what they could become if only they became their own masters and modernized themselves. Personalities like Mr. Krishna Menon, Dr. Nkrumah, Dr. Panda, *et al*, were themselves formed in these milieux and in turn formed many of those who were to play an active part in the movement in their own countries.[24]

The intellectual and political *Zeitgeist* which greeted James and Williams in the England of the Thirties was perhaps more strongly to the Left than it had ever been before, or was to become thereafter. The Western Democracies were entering a period of political ferment and crisis associated with the Great Depression and the ideological and military skirmishes between fascism, Communism, and capitalist democracy. In this highly charged political period the education of colonial students tended to acquire great ideological intensity, but not all of the young colonials were exposed to, or gravitated toward, identical Left milieux. Their status and experiences had much in common, but the nationalist image of the future which they acquired would sometimes reflect the divisions within the European Left of the day. Between Keynes and Lenin, between Laski and Trotsky and Stalin, there were important differences of theory and practice. These were distinctions which the seriously political colonial student would at least be aware

[23] Edward Shils, "The Intellectual in the Political Development of New States," Committee on Social Thought, University of Chicago (mimeographed), n.d., pp. 19–20.
[24] *Ibid.*

of, and toward which he would often acquire at least tentative ideological leanings and preferences. Political socialization in the metropolitan country, that is to say, was not uniform, although there was a broad common exposure to everyday British life. Cricket was everywhere cricket, but in those times the London School of Economics was not Oxford.

In the diverging careers of James and Williams in the England of the thirties these differences in milieux stand in sharp contrast, partially because James was not a university student, but perhaps of greater importance, his was a more radical and romantic temperament . . . and he lived chiefly in London. Another colonial intellectual who was a university student in London, Jomo Kenyatta (studying anthropology under Professor Malinowski), was a member of the same radical circle that attracted James.

James arrived in England in 1932, apparently a few months ahead of Eric Williams. He spent three months in London and then went to live for some months with Norma and Learie Constantine in Lancashire where he found employment for his literary skills in helping Learie to write his first cricket book. Returning to London he made his living by reporting county cricket for the *Manchester Guardian* while, as he later wrote, "I educated myself." There was to be, however, a curious similarity in the careers of these Trinidadians in the Mother Country, and that was that though they came to learn, *they stayed to teach.* Constantine was an acknowledged master at cricket, James would teach them politics, Williams would teach them history; and, some years later, Dr. Rudranath Capildeo — Q.R.C. graduate and head of the East Indian opposition party in Trinidad — would undertake to teach them physics.

As Williams began his career at Oxford, James, then just over thirty years of age, almost immediately embarked on the education of the British. He plunged into the radical milieux of London, not merely as a spectator but, fresh from completing his *Life of Cipriani*, he began to participate by lecturing on *The Case for West Indian Self-Government* which Leonard and Virginia Woolf's Hogarth Press published in 1933. At the same time, he later wrote, "I was reading hard and I was already a long way towards becoming a Trotskyist."[25] In the midst of this early, formative, period in London he was invited one day to attend a speech by "a great Negro Communist" named George Padmore in Gray's Inn Road. He was going to every meeting in those days and the Negro aspect of the invitation was an added attraction. He went and found about 50 people in a small auditorium, most of

[25] C. L. R. James, "Notes on the Life of George Padmore," *op. cit.*

them Negroes. They waited for some time and then ". . . in stepped Malcolm Nurse." His old chum, James learned during a reunion which ran far into the night, had pursued an exciting career since he had left Trinidad and gone to the United States. At Howard University he had shown signs of a militantly revolutionary temperament when he had (so the story went) thrown a sheaf of anti-imperialist pamphlets in the face of a visiting British Ambassador. He then entered into organizational work for the U.S. Communist Party in Harlem and took the "party name" of George Padmore.[26]

Intelligent, cultivated, young Negro radicals like Padmore and James were at a premium in these early days of the stirrings of Negro radicalism in the United States, West Indies and Africa. First Padmore, and later James, rose very rapidly in the leadership hierarchy of the various contending branches of the international Left. Compared to Negroes in the United States and Africa, the West Indian colored colonials had had educational and social advantages far superior to those attained by the Negroes suffering under the American caste system or under the cruder, less "enlightened" British trusteeship in Black Africa. Thus in 1928 the Sixth Conference of the Communist International established a new international trade union organization, the Profintern, and in charge of its Negro department, with offices in Moscow, was placed George Padmore. Despite his outward air of being a respectable, cultivated colored Englishman, Padmore appears to have been an ingenious and indefatigable organizer. One of his early achievements had been the organization of the first international conference of Negro workers, staged in Hamburg in 1930, which had involved him in considerable world travel, often of a dangerous, clandestine variety.[27]

Padmore invited James to assist him in his work for the Communist International, which had then brought him to England, but James was unable to take up the offer. "Between Communism and Trotskyism," he wrote almost thirty years later, "there was a line of antagonism and conflict, stained with blood, incredible cruelties, murders and death." Nonetheless, both were Trinidadians, "sons of the soil," and as old friends in an alien land they never quarrelled, ". . . the simple stream of home kept us together."[28] They would see each other intermittently during the next several years, and soon it would be Padmore who changed ideological ranks and became for many years a central figure in the early efforts to organize African students into nationalist move-

[26] *Ibid.* See also J. R. Hooker's, "Tacarigua to Moscow: Padmore's Early Life," *Trinidad & Tobago Index*, Winter, 1966, pp. 16–29.
[27] James, "Notes on the Life of George Padmore," *op. cit.*
[28] *Ibid.*

ments in London. During the 1940's when James was living in New
York as leader of a Trotskyist sect named the Johnsonites (James had
also, as was the fashion, taken a revolutionary alias — J. R. Johnson),
he as a matter of routine wrote a letter of introduction to George
Padmore for an African foreign student named Kwame Nkrumah
who was then en route to London.[29] In his autobiography Nkrumah
states that he learned the techniques of underground organization
from James,[30] and in London his association with the other revolutionary from Trinidad would result in Padmore becoming political
advisor — until his death in 1959 — to the founder of the newly-
independent state of Ghana.

In estimating the ideological exposure of the young colonials in
Britain, and in reconstructing the world orientation of nationalist
politicians in the West Indies it is important to remember that the
dominant British leftist orientation of the thirties on the question of
global alignment was, if not actively pro-Communist, at least pro-
Russian. The Bolshevik Revolution and its aftermath had been examined by the Fabian socialist leaders, Beatrice and Sidney Webb,
who reckoned that in Soviet Communism a new civilization was being
created. Aside from the general admiration of the Soviet Union in
the Labor Party and among the intelligentsia, there was a strong
clinching, *Realpolitik* argument — strenuously advanced, for example,
by the *New Statesman*[31] — that the only practical defense strategy
available to the Western democracies against the rising militarism of
fascism lay in alliance with the Soviet Union. As history is re-written
in modern times from year to year, and even from week to week,
these basically rational and persuasive political assumptions of the
thirties, created by the domestic and international crises of the times,
tend to be forgotten, or, at best, viewed as youthful aberrations which
new times and new problems have made obsolete. But exist they did,
and it is important to recall how pervasive and unexceptional such
views were at the time. Many years later, Eric Williams would twit
an opposing Trinidad politician for having paid tribute, during World
War II, to the Soviet system and the Red Army — hardly exceptional
views for those times, among labor politicians especially. Thus, one
finds, too, in Learie Constantine's book, *Colour Bar*, that despite
vigorous disclaimers as to any advocacy of Soviet politics, he nonethe-

[29] Personal interview with Mr. James.
[30] Kwame Nkrumah, *The Autobiography of Kwame Nkrumah*, Edinburgh:
Thomas Nelson and Sons, Ltd., 1957, p. 44. Padmore's account of the education
of future nationalists, his own career and related topics, will be found inter-
spersed through his *Pan-Africanism or Communism?*, London: Dennis Dobson,
1956.
[31] *New Statesman* (Jubilee Number), April 19, 1963, p. 543.

less is convinced that Soviet racial policies could serve as a model for other nations.[32]

When C. L. R. James became a Trotskyist in the thirties, therefore, he went against the prevailing currents of the British Left. Instead, he joined forces with a group of Marxist, anti-Stalinist radicals within the Independent Labour Party which was presided over by a fiery M.P. from Glasgow, James Maxton. The I.L.P. had been a ginger group within the Labor Party for many years before it withdrew to form a small, separate organization which published an influential weekly newspaper, *The New Leader*. Among the best known of the British members during the thirties were Fenner Brockway and Aneurin Bevan's wife, Jennie Lee, and author George Orwell. Among the colonials there were James, Kenyatta and Padmore. Fenner Brockway (now Lord Brockway) performed valuable services for the young colonials, providing them with entrée into the left-wing politics of the period and assisting them in various ways. In the first installment of Brockway's autobiography, *Inside the Left*, there is a glimpse of James in the thick of an I.L.P. factional fight, moving a resolution "in a typically torrential speech" in which he "appealed as a black worker for help for the black population of Abyssinia" on an issue which would nearly split the organization within which "The Marxist Group" was continually prodding its labor officials and parliamentary members from the left.[33]

For political activists and writers interested in reaching a wide audience, the climate of receptivity to radical authors in British publishing circles was obviously important and requires brief mention here. In publisher Frederic Warburg's autobiography the political climate of the time and the place of anti-Stalinist writers like James and Orwell within it is vividly portrayed at first hand. Left-wing publishing in the thirties was dominated by Victor Gollancz, a leader in the pro-Soviet United Front against fascism and founder of the highly popular and influential Left Book Club. From 1933 until 1939 Gollancz held a virtual monopoly on this section of the book trades. But in the mid-thirties Warburg inaugurated the house of Secker and Warburg on a shoestring, and challenged the prevailing pro-Soviet tendency in the Gollancz publications. The circumstances are interesting: Fenner Brockway had approached Warburg and suggested that some of the I.L.P. writers would be interested in bringing their works to him. The publisher realized that he would be running a considerable risk in view of the unfashionable anti-Soviet bias of the group. "If

---

[32] Learie Constantine, *Colour Bar*, London: Stanley Paul and Co., 1954, p. 68.
[33] Fenner Brockway, *Inside the Left*, London: George Allen and Unwin, 1942, p. 326.

Brockway's proposal was tempting, it was also double-edged. Despite my association with him over a book on the Routledge list a year before, he would never, I felt, have approached me, had he been able to place the work of his members and friends with a stronger and better established house."[34] However, Warburg decided to make the plunge – not so much out of ideological affinity with the I.L.P. writers, whose libertarian doctrines he viewed with tolerant skepticism – but because "my little firm needed authors as an army needs banners," and because his wife (their conversation on the subject consumes four pages of the autobiography!) strongly and wittily reinforced his feelings of unease over what he viewed as the uncritical and unprincipled support in British intellectual circles of the Soviet Union.

Warburg decided to gamble on Brockway's proposition and the returns formed an important chapter in British publishing history. He picked up Orwell on the road back from his Gollancz-sponsored trip to *Wigan Pier* and sent him to Spain, out of which came the classic anti-Stalinist study of the Spanish Civil War, *Homage to Catalonia.* Moreover, once embarked on this policy, Warburg published André Gide's account of his observations of the U.S.S.R. (whither he had been invited on the assumption that this apparently pro-Soviet dean of French letters would pen another one of those paeans of praise to socialist construction which became almost a literary *genre* in itself during the thirties). Gide, however, wrote a brief, spare, account of his observations and related his surprise and dismay at the social pretentiousness and privileged status which he encountered among the Stalinist leadership and bureaucracy. He opined that, "I doubt whether in any other country in the world, even Hitler's Germany, thought be less free." This statement, according to Warburg, "spread consternations and rage through the Communist ranks. Members of the Left Book Club, carefully shielded by their committee from the truth, must have rubbed their eyes in astonishment if they happened to light on these lines of Gide. Blasphemous, treacherous, reptilian. . . . the futile outpourings of a decaying homosexual, such were the anathemata launched against Gide's pamphlet."[35]

This was the bitterly controversial climate of political opinion which the biographer of an obscure West Indian politician entered during the early thirties. "One of the first authors introduced to me by Brockway," Warburg relates, "was C. L. R. James, and his book, *World Revolution,* became a kind of Bible of Trotskyism. We published it in 1937. It was dedicated to the Marxist Group. How many members

[34] Frederic Warburg, *An Occupation for Gentlemen,* London: Hutchinson and Co., 1959, p. 326.
[35] *Ibid.,* pp. 217-218.

composed this group at the time I don't know, probably less than fifty, for it was a quality of Trotskyist groups to break in two, like an amoeba when reproducing itself, and to continue doing so until the fission process had reduced the group to a mere handful . . ."[36] The Trotskyists, and James foremost amongst them, believed in the wickedness of capitalism and regarded Nazism as simply capitalism gone rotten. They loved the U.S.S.R. like children love their mother, he perceived, but they regarded Stalin as a wicked father who had debauched her and produced a miscarriage. They therefore felt free to criticise the U.S.S.R. for Stalin's crimes, while loving it for the beautiful thing it might have become — providing Lenin and Trotsky had survived in power to create the Utopia that was just around the corner. But, continued Warburg:

> Despite the atmosphere of hate and arid dispute in his writings, James himself was one of the most delightful and easy-going personalities I have known, colourful in more senses than one. A dark-skinned West Indian Negro from Trinidad, he stood six feet three inches in his socks and was noticeably good-looking. His memory was extraordinary . . . Immensely amiable, he loved the fleshpots of capitalism, fine cooking, fine clothes, fine furniture and beautiful women without a trace of the guilty remorse to be expected from a seasoned warrior of the class war . . . Night after night he would address meetings in London and the provinces, denouncing the crimes of the blood-thirsty Stalin until he was hoarse and his wonderful voice a mere croaking in the throat. The Communists who heckled him would have torn him limb from limb, had it not been for the ubiquity of the police . . .
>
> If politics was his religion and Marx his god, if literature was his passion and Shakespeare his prince among writers, cricket was his beloved activity. He wrote splendid articles on county matches for the *Manchester Guardian* during the summer. Indeed, it was only between April and October that he was in funds. Sometimes he came for the week-end to our cottage near West Hoathly in Sussex and turned out for the local team. He was a demon bowler, and a powerful if erratic batsman. The village loved him, referring to him affectionately as 'the black bastard.' In Sussex politics were forgotten. Instead, I can hear today the opening words of Twelfth Night delivered beautifully from his full sensitive lips: 'If music be the food of love, play on; give me excess of it.' Excess, perhaps was James' crime, an excess of words whose relevance to the contemporary tragedy was less than he supposed.[37]

James did not, however, limit his productivity to Trotskyist polemics. He had published a perceptive short novel on Trinidad, *Minty Alley*,

[36] *Ibid.*, p. 211.
[37] *Ibid.*, pp. 214–215.

and in 1938 Warburg published his classic study of the San Domingo slave revolt led by Toussaint Louverture, *The Black Jacobins*. Research for this brilliant work had taken James to the archives at Bordeaux where he discovered that another Trinidad scholar, Eric Williams, had been before him during the course of examining documents in preparation for the doctoral thesis he was writing at Oxford. For the Trinidad Island Scholarship winner, the England of the thirties did not afford such strong inducements to political engagement as had characterized the careers of Padmore and James. Williams' niche was not in the urban, radical milieux of the metropolitan country, but rather in the more serene traditional atmosphere of the British university. At Oxford he was chiefly motivated by the determination to continue in the prodigious feats of scholarship which had marked his educational career from the beginning. In a published fragment of his yet unpublished autobiography, Williams has described the environment and dominant concerns of "A Colonial at Oxford." It is a dramatic account of scholarly discovery and of the widening of intellectual horizons.

Williams arrived in Oxford in October, 1932, just after his twenty-first birthday (celebrated at sea) and fresh from "a few days' bewilderment in the vast metropolis of London." He described the institution around which his life centered for over seven years in these terms:

> Awed but exhilarated I was, for seven years, to be a part, however small, of the noble and inspiring traditions which have no equal anywhere in the world. Carfax, the tower of Christ Church and Magdalen, the Bodleian and the Radcliffe Camera, the several colleges, the Parks, the meadows of Christ Church, the towpath along the river — buildings and gardens, architecture and nature, all enthralled. But it was the human interest, the literary, religious and political traditions, Man, in short, which fascinated me most. It was not the Oxford of the tourist or the antiquarian which most attracted me but the Oxford of scholarship, the Oxford of the Reformation, the Civil War and the British Empire.[38]

The history and literature he had studied in Trinidad came to life at Oxford as he trod through the same corridors which Gladstone, Peel, Fox, Canning, Cecil Rhodes, and a host of other historic figures had walked. In a Welsh clergyman named Trevor Davies he acquired not only a tutor, but a guide, philosopher, and friend who counselled him during his three undergraduate years. In discussions with his tutor, Williams wrote, he took a "very independent line" — arguing that Aristotle was a "dyed-in-the-wool reactionary," and that Hobbes had a "fascist mentality." Although at Oxford he was not insulated from

[38] Eric Williams, "A Colonial at Oxford," *The Nation Christmas Annual*, 1959, p. 89.

the ideological fervor of the time, his actual participation seems to have been very limited. James later recalled having attended a meeting with Williams in which the latter, during question period, had challenged the speaker, G. D. H. Cole, on some point or other.[39] After Williams and James fell out in 1960, however, James wrote of Williams' political activities in the thirties that his former pupil had associated with him and Padmore, had criticised and taken positions, but that he had never joined any organizations.[40] This appears to have been roughly the case — with one near exception. When Williams, on the verge of entering nationalist politics in Trinidad many years later, felt compelled to give himself an ideologically clean bill of health, he stated: "I had never had any connection whatsoever with any political organization at all, except that at Oxford I had attended regularly meetings of the Indian nationalist students in their club, the Majliss."[41]

Williams was, it seems fair to say, only incidentally involved in the political struggles of the period; the primary objective to which he directed most of his energies was to graduate from Oxford with a top degree. In aiming for a First, he later wrote, he had the advantage of the necessary personal discipline, for which the ordeal of the Island Scholarship was admirable preparation.

> . . . I worked steadily throughout the entire period . . . and in the excessively long vacations . . . I made it my practice to spend three weeks at Christmas, three at Easter, six in the summer in Oxford, which was at those times almost like a dead city, reading steadily in my rooms and in the college and university libraries . . .[42]

The image of the solitary young West Indian scholar, working diligently through major portions of vacations in the deserted university, is strikingly similar to the image of olympian determination and effort which would become a legend in the early years of his P.N.M. government in Trinidad: "You could drive by his office late, late, at night," Trinidadians would repeat with awe and admiration, "and see the lights still burning." Given his diligence and native ability, Williams easily cleared his final exams at Oxford and was awarded the coveted First Class degree, placing first, with two other students, in that class. His *viva voce* examination was a mere formality, but in his recollection of the brief exchange with his examiner, Williams

---

[39] James, "Dr. Eric Williams, P.N.M. Political Leader — A Convention Appraisal," *op. cit.*
[40] James, *Party Politics in the West Indies,* San Juan, Trinidad: Vedic Enterprises, 1962, p. 158.
[41] Eric Williams, *My Relations with the Caribbean Commission, 1943-1955,* pamphlet published by Dr. Eric Williams, July 5, 1955, pp. 33-34.
[42] Williams, "A Colonial at Oxford," *op. cit.,* p. 91.

indicated that despite his love of cloistered Oxford he had developed
a pragmatic attitude toward knowledge and had retained his colonial
roots:

> The chairman of the board of examiners . . . asked me where I came
> from, and then what subject had interested me most in my course.
> I replied it was my special subject in colonial history. He stated that
> this was borne out in my marks and asked me why; I answered, in some
> surprise, 'Well, I am a colonial. . . . and I replied that I could not see
> the value of study unless there was that connection with the environ-
> ment.' His reply was: 'That is one of the most interesting answers I
> have ever heard.'[43]

WHO FREED THE SLAVES?

Williams then embarked on research for his doctoral dissertation,
which, after some further research, would be published in 1944 as
Capitalism and Slavery — his *magnum opus,* and the work on which
his reputation as an historian chiefly rests. In this study Williams
attacked, and sought to disprove, the accepted theory in British
historical circles concerning the reasons underlying the abolition of
slavery in the British Empire in 1833. The theory which he attacked
was the notion that emancipation had been due to the humanitarian
agitation and propaganda of the British abolitionists. The thesis
which he advanced was, in a nutshell, that although the West Indies
plantation economy, and its slave labor force, had been responsible for
the development of mercantilist capital in the metropolitan country,
the rise of the industrial bourgeoisie in the early nineteenth century
brought into being new forces whose interests were at variance with
those of the older capitalist group, and that their support of anti-slavery
measures was but a part of their general economic self-interest and
was the decisive factor in the emancipation of the slaves. Where did
Williams obtain this thesis? In a bibliographical footnote he cites
James' *The Black Jacobins* and states that "On pages 38–41 the thesis
advanced in this book is stated clearly and concisely and, as far as I
know, for the first time in English."[44] In examining *The Black Jacobins*
at the pages specified James is indeed found discussing precisely the
process which Williams so thoroughly documented. But a full reading
of *The Black Jacobins* leads to the rather surprising conclusion that
this was not James' thesis; rather, it was only one-half of the Trotskyist
writer's theory as to the causes of the abolition of slavery in the Caribbean colonies.

Both Williams and James agreed that the end of slavery represented

[43] *Ibid.,* p. 92.
[44] Eric Williams, *Capitalism and Slavery,* New York: Russel and Russel, 1961,
p. 268.

Kingston, the capital of Jamaica. *Courtesy of Jamaica Tourist Board.*

Port of Spain, Trinidad and Tobago. *Courtesy of Public Relations Division, Office of the Premier, Whitehall, Trinidad.*

Sugar cane fields in Antigua. *Courtesy of Alcoa Steamship Co.*

Before the collapse of the West Indies Federation. *Courtesy of the Jamaican Information Service.*

THE WEST INDIES
A PICTURE PLAN OF FEDERATION

TERRITORIES	Capital	Area sq.mis.	Population Census 1960	Distance from Trinidad Air Mls.	Sea Mls.	Government Revenue £(Local) 1960	Representatives House	Senate
Antigua	St. John's	170½	54,354	413	388	£1,342,917	2	2
Barbados	Bridgetown	166	232,085	212	207	4,522,292	5	2
Dominica	Roseau	305	59,479	302	283	626,875	2	2
Grenada	St. George's	133	88,617	109	90	1,143,958	2	2
Jamaica	Kingston	4,411	1,606,546	1211	1025	52,841,250	17	2
Montserrat	Plymouth	32½	12,157	373	362	194,375	1	1
St. Lucia	Castries	233	86,194	372	213	888,542	2	2
St. Kitts-Nevis-Anguilla	Basseterre	152	56,644	411	402	1,138,958	2	2
St. Vincent	Kingstown	150	80,005	185	156	744,375	2	2
Trinidad & Tobago	Port-y-Spain	1,980	825,700	—	—	54,950,853	10	2

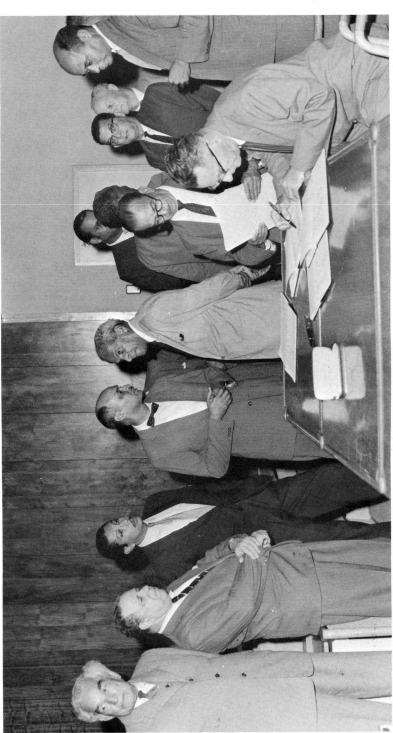

Mr. Vernon L. Arnett signing the Report of the Committee of the Legislature which prepared proposals for a Constitution to take effect on Jamaica's Independence, at Gordon House on January 17, 1962. *Courtesy of the Jamaican Information Service.*

The Prime Minister, Sir Alexander Bustamante escorts Her Royal Highness the Princess Margaret to the flag raising ceremony at the National Stadium during Jamaica's Independence celebrations.

Gleaner photo.

Then Vice President of the United States Lyndon B. Johnson being welcomed to Jamaica's Independence celebrations by Sir Alexander Bustamante.

Courtesy of Jamaican Information Service.

The People's National Movement formed the Government prior to Independence in Trinidad and Tobago. *Courtesy of People's National Movement.*

Midnight ceremonies on Independence eve in Trinidad, August 31, 1962. Front row: Dr. Eric Williams, Dr. Patrick Solomon, The Princess Royal, Governor Sir Solomon Hochoy and Mrs. Hochoy. At the microphone: the Roman Catholic Archbishop. *Courtesy of the Trinidad Guardian; British Information Services photo.*

Jamaica's first Governor General, Sir Kenneth Blackburne reads the throne speech and opens Parliament after Independence, August 1962. Sir Kenneth, whose term of office expired in November 1962, was the last of a long line of British Governors of Jamaica. *Gleaner photo.*

Gordon House, which is named after the once-traitor and now Jamaican national hero, is the home of the Parliament of Independent Jamaica.

Courtesy of the Jamaican Information Service.

Interior of Gordon House.   *Courtesy of the Jamaican Information Service.*

clash between supporters of the Jamaica Labour Party and the People's
ational Party in August 1961.

Courtesy of the Jamaican Information Service.

Forbes Burnham ad-
esses a Guyanese meet-
g in 1962. Others are
rom l.) Claude Merriman,
hn Carter, and Richard
hmael. *Courtesy of Peo-
e's National Congress.*

West Indian leaders (from left) Dr. Cheddi Jagan (Guyana), Sir Alexander Bustamante (Jamaica), Mr. Errol Barrow

Another side of West Indian nationalism. L. Forbes Burnham of British Guiana is led away by London Bobby during demonstration.

London Express News photo.

Mr. Peter D'Aguiar, leader of the United Force Party in British Guiana during a press conference in 1962.
Courtesy of Trinidad Guardian; AP photo.

Mr. V. C. Bird, Chief Minister of Antigua.
Courtesy of the Trinidad Guardian.

Mr. Donald B. Sangster, Acting Prime Minister of Jamaica.
Courtesy of Spotlight.

Trade unionist and a political leader of Grenada, Mr. Eric Gairy.
Courtesy of the Trinidad Guardian.

Mr. Edwin O. Le Blanc, Chief Minister of Dominica, discussing the possibility of a federation of the Little Eight in 1962.
Courtesy of the Trinidad Guardian.

Trinidadian intellectual and nationalist, Mr. C. L. R. James (center), returns to Trinidad in 1958. At left, Mr. Eric James, at right, Mr. Carlton Comma, Port of Spain chief librarian. *Courtesy of the Trinidad Guardian.*

Trinidadian political leader, Albert Gomes, at a reception given in London for West Indian leaders. *Courtesy of the Jamaican Information Service; official British photo.*

Dr. Cheddi Jagan, leader of the Opposition in Guyana, and his wife, Janet. *Courtesy of Newday.*

the ascendancy of the industrial middle-class interests without which, as James put it, abolitionists like Wilberforce and Clarkson would have preached themselves as black in the face as any Negro. For Williams, in *Capitalism and Slavery*, this was the key point: slavery was abolished because it happened to have been in the interest of the most powerful economic faction in the British ruling class; moreover, he argued in his conclusion, the process had been substantially the same in the French colonies, hence the justification of the general title that he had given to the study. For James, however, the ascendancy of the industrial interests appears to have been viewed as only a necessary *precondition* for the abolition of slavery, the primary cause of which was not to be found in the divided interests of the strong, but in the revolt of the weak. "The Haytian revolution," he concluded, ". . . killed the West Indian slave-trade and slavery."

> It is true that abolition was but one stage in the successive victories of the industrial bourgeoisie over the landed aristocracy . . . Those who see in abolition the gradually awakening conscience of mankind should spend a few minutes asking themselves why it is that man's conscience, which had slept peacefully for so many centuries, should awake just at the time that men began to see the unprofitablenesss of slavery as a method of production in the West Indian colonies.
>
> But the process worked itself out blindly . . . Had the British held San Domingo and started to exploit that colony, the slave-trade and slavery in the West Indies might have lasted another half-century. As it was, driven out of the West Indies, the English were so disgusted with their own half-bankrupt colonies that they stopped the slave trade in 1807 to prevent cultivation of new lands.[45]

Moreover, wrote James, even the European working class had played a significant role in the final liquidation of slavery: "One of the first things that the revolution of 1848 achieved was the abolition of slavery, the workers completing the good work of their ancestors; and so weak were the slave-holding interests that when the revolution was crushed emancipation was not reversed."[46] And, on the positive side, James insisted, the Haitian revolution gave the impulse to and subsidized the first national revolutions in Spanish America; Simón Bolívar came twice to Haiti for respite, encouragement and supplies. Thus for James, considerable moral credit had to be given to the active struggle of the oppressed in significantly accelerating and maintaining the changes *made possible by* the shifting distribution of power in the European ruling class, and thus effecting historical progress. In Williams' study, however, there were no historical bouquets for anyone;

[45] *The Black Jacobins: Toussaint Louverture and the San Domingo Revolution.* London: Martin Secker & Warburg, 1938, pp. 311–312.
[46] *Loc. cit.*

while conceding that some of the abolitionists were sincere in espousing the abolitionist cause and that slave revolts had, by 1833, produced an acute crisis in the maintenance of the slave system, the slave revolts had not triggered the emancipation: they might have, but the British industrial elite beat them to the punch.

In these differing approaches Williams and James seem to exemplify two divergent social philosophies which can be found in the works of many theorists on social change since the Enlightenment, and even before. In his interpretation of slavery James expressed a highly sophisticated version of what might be termed radical populism; a belief in the morally progressive, the historically necessary and effective role of the class struggle between rulers and ruled. This was not only an integral part of his interpretation of the abolition of slavery, but also consistent with his current contributions to Trotskyist critiques of Stalinist Russia. Only mass revolt could end the tyranny of the betrayed revolution. Williams, on the other hand, presented what was basically an economic interpretation of history and his one-sided borrowing from Marx assigned no major role to the exploited classes, in this instance, the slaves, from the making of the historical events he analyzed. The side of Marxism implicitly adopted in *Capitalism and Slavery* was the *historicist* strain in Marxist thought; namely, an emphasis on the notion that history, like Thrasymachus' theory on the origins of justice, is a product of the interests of the strong; the historicist idea, moreover, that tends to view the spontaneous, voluntaristic, moral impulses of men (like those of the abolitionists) as essentially epiphenomenal to the real business of making history, the major thrusts of which result from interests and social forces over which men can exercise but little control.[47]

[47] Karl R. Popper, *The Poverty of Historicism*, London: Routledge and Kegan Paul, 1961. Popper's formulation of "historicism" contains many elements with which I disagree; nonetheless, his discussion of certain determinist tendencies are telling and relevant to this discussion, e.g.: "Those who desire an increase in the influence of reason in social life can only be advised by historicism to study and interpret history, in order to discover the laws of its development. If such interpretation reveals that changes answering to the desire are impending, then the desire is a reasonable one, for it agrees with scientific prediction. If the impending development happens to tend in another direction, then the wish to make the world more reasonable turns out to be entirely unreasonable; to historicists it is just a Utopian dream. Activism can be justified only so long as it acquiesces in impending changes and helps them along." Popper, pp. 50–51. According to James ("A Conventional Appraisal," *op. cit.*), he and Williams had extensively discussed the latter's thesis for *Capitalism and Slavery* and he noted that Williams had concluded that if emancipation had not taken place from above, it would have taken place from below by a slave revolt. This was true, but the point remains that for James it *did* take place primarily from below; for Williams, primarily from above. I would not split hairs on this issue except for the fact that it was precisely this question which split James and Williams in Trinidad politics 25 years later.

Please note that the above distinctions were called *tendencies* in the thought process of the two Trinidad scholars. *Capitalism and Slavery* was a work with obvious anti-imperialist implications, which Williams did not hesitate to spell out in his 1942 study, *The Negro in the Caribbean*, in which he praised the rise of working-class leaders in the West Indies, and exhorted the traditionally aloof colored middle class to join in the struggle. Moreover, although he took an economic determinist tack in *Capitalism and Slavery* (a school of historiography with respectable antecedents, in contrast to the Marxist dialectic of class struggle which, being so closely identified with an organized, radical point of view, would never achieve such measure of academic acceptance) — despite this expression of economic determinism in one work, it would be doing Williams an injustice to regard him as being narrow in his intellectual range as this term suggests. In his Oxford reminiscences, for example, he wrote, "I began to see . . . history as the supreme intellectual discipline, comprehending all others: scientific progress determining technology and economic organization, religion influencing politics, the political struggle manifested itself in the literature and art of the period . . ."[48]

Nonetheless, while taking account of these qualifications and overlapping tendencies in the thought of Williams and James, one important distinction stands out in their life and work: James' commitment to a radical populism was based, as will be shown in a moment, on years of exhaustive theoretical work, speculations which would take him back to the source of the Marxist dialectic in Hegel in order to formulate anew the theory and method of the revolutionary organization. Williams, though he identified with the aspirations of the underprivileged, and though he realized that militant action on the part of the lower class, particularly in the colonies, was necessary in achieving social progress, never developed a conception of the compelling *theoretical necessity* of a high degree of spontaneous popular action in order to achieve historical objectives, which for James — as for such earlier radical populists as Rosa Luxemburg — became the key method, purpose, and index of a liberated humanity.

AFTERMATH OF THE THIRTIES

As World War II descended on England, both James and Williams were in the United States. Williams had accepted a post at Howard University; James came to deliver a set of lectures but was overtaken by illness and then the war. Padmore and Constantine stayed on in London, the latter working as a social welfare officer in the Ministry of Labor, services for which he would be awarded an M.B.E. During

---

[48] Williams, "A Colonial at Oxford," *op. cit.,* p. 91.

the war years, and immediately after, it seems that Williams and James kept in touch, although Williams was an aspiring young academic (Associate Professor at age 35 in 1946 — when academic rank was not so easily achieved) while James diligently stuck out the life of the independent radical writer and philosopher in a political atmosphere which was, in the early days of the Cold War, becoming increasingly hostile to the social ideas and politics which he represented.

The atmosphere of persecution, political frustration and grandiose revolutionary designs which afflicted the American Left in the immediate post-war period did not leave James unscathed. He was an active figure in the sectarian wars which appear so futile and sterile in retrospect. But the serious intellectual work which somehow managed to get carried on in the midst of the endless polemics and sectarian splits should not be overlooked despite the exotic political assumptions and behavior of many in these groups. Dwight MacDonald, whose *Memoirs of a Revolutionist* amusingly relates some of these struggles, produced a one-man radical magazine, *Politics*, which helped to first bring the attention of intellectuals to such later-famous social scientists as C. Wright Mills, Bruno Bettleheim, and Hannah Arendt.[49] The history of the Trotskyist factional wars out of which came James Burnham with his superficial, but influential, work on *The Managerial Revolution*, can be found detailed in the collection of polemical exchanges between the exiled Trotsky in Mexico, and his New York cohorts. James, or as he was then called, J. R. Johnson, led his dedicated band of followers out of, and then back into, and then out of again, the orthodox Trotskyist Socialist Workers' Party.[50] His American followers were as much impressed with the Trinidad radical as the British sectarians had been: "Here was a guy," one of his former American disciples said during an interview "who not only claimed to be the theoretical successor of Marx, Lenin, and Trotsky — but could give you a hell of a good argument that he was!" The Johnsonites returned to the source of the dialectic in Hegel and developed a theory of social change and proletarian organization which is one of the most remarkable in a long tradition of innovative thought. The theory of change cannot be dealt with here; but the system of organization which the sect developed is so singular in its unswerving practical commitment to the theory of radical populism as to warrant brief mention.

[49] Dwight MacDonald, *Memoirs of a Revolutionist*, New York: Farrar, Straus and Cudahy, 1957.
[50] Leon Trotsky, *In Defense of Marxism*, New York: Pioneer Publishers, 1942. For a concise guide through the American micro-left see Walter Goldwater, "Radical Periodicals in America, 1890–1950," *Yale University Library Gazette*, 1964.

Jimmy developed the theory [in the words of the former disciple] that all proletarian parties had suffered from one fatal defect; namely, the intellectuals were always telling the workers what was going on in the world. This, he argued, was completely cockeyed, because it was obviously the workers who, being closest to the system of production, were first exposed to the imminent social changes developing in connection with changing patterns of production. Therefore, he maintained, the intellectuals should shut up and listen to the workers for a change. He firmly believed that that was the only way we could find out what was going on. So the group was divided into what we called 'layers'; the real proletarians were put in the first layer; people of mixed status, like housewives, in the second; and the intellectuals were put in the third layer. Our meetings consisted of the now highly-prestigeful first layer spouting off, usually in a random, inarticulate way about what they thought about everything under the sun. The rest of us, especially we intellectuals in the third layer, were told to listen.

The writer asked the disenchanted former Johnsonite what the leader's function was in the organization. The answer: "Well, Jimmy, you see, made the assignments to the various layers . . . the group was built on him; we gave years of our life, a sizeable percentage of our income and a good share of our love to him and his ideas. Not that he lived well — he didn't; practically all of our money went into publications and political work. An amazing man."

Somewhere in the course of his American sojourn, James discovered Herman Melville, and he lectured widely on the social meaning of the novelist's works. Perhaps James' fervent and poetic view of the world is best summarized in a passage from the introduction to his Melville study, *Mariners, Renegades and Castaways:*

> The totalitarian madness which swept the world first as Nazism and now as Soviet Communism; the great mass labor movements and colonial revolts; intellectuals drowning in the incestuous dreams of psychoanalysis — this is the world the masses of men strive to make sense of. This is what Melville co-ordinates — but not as industry, science, politics, economics, or psychology, but as a world of human personalities, living as the vast majority of human beings live, not by ideas, but by their emotions, seeking to avoid pain and misery and struggling for happiness.[51]

[51] C. L. R. James, *Mariners, Renegades, and Castaways: The Story of Herman Melville and the World We Live In,* New York: C. L. R. James, 1953, "Introduction," n.p. For a statement of James' mature views as a radical sectarian, see *State Capitalism and World Revolution,* originally published in 1950 and republished in 1956. (Current address of publisher uncertain). James was co-founder of the so-called "Johnson-Forest Tendency," the orientation of which was given as follows: "The only serious theoretical opposition to Stalinism was provided over the years by Leon Trotsky. But by the end of World War II, it was obvious that Trotsky's

In 1952 James was caught in the very totalitarian madness which he thought Captain Ahab had foreshadowed and was sent to Ellis Island for deportation back to England. Williams, in the meantime, had left the United States in 1948 under more auspicious circumstances. From his position as consultant on Caribbean affairs while he was at Howard, he was drawn into full-time work for the Anglo-American Caribbean Commission, and thus, so he later wrote, was given an opportunity to be of practical service to the area and community of his origin. He soon became Deputy Chairman of the Commission, in charge of the research division in Port of Spain. There, in 1952, Lloyd Braithwaite was completing his field study of the class system of his native island and noted that the traditional attraction of the Trinidad middle class to a charismatic leader was well-exemplified in the way that Dr. Eric Williams was being lionized.[52]

It was an astute observation. Three years later Dr. Williams, discharged by the Caribbean Commission, took over Cipriani's tribune, founded the "University of Woodford Square," and delivered a series of lectures on the steps to be taken toward the political and economic modernization of Trinidad and the West Indies. In 1956 his People's National Movement, with Learie Constantine as party chairman, attained office and propelled the colony toward independence in 1962. These were turbulent years in Trinidad's evolution. Although some of Williams' earliest and strongest supporters were teachers dissatisfied with the ancient system of Dual Control, a Concordat had to be reached between the secular educators and the Church. Nor was the author of *Capitalism and Slavery* entirely successful in his major contest with the imperial powers: for three years he attempted to wrest control of the de-activated U.S. naval base at Chaguaramas, a relic of the World War II destroyers-for-bases deal between Roosevelt and Churchill. In this struggle he summoned C. L. R. James from London

---

theories no longer had any relation to reality. In the United States, the Johnson-Forest Tendency, a minority of the Trotskyist Socialist Workers Party, decided to present to the 1950 Convention of the Party, not a political resolution of the traditional type, but a long overdue statement of Marxism for our day." *Ibid.,* p. 3. This re-evaluation of Marxism led James and his associates to reject the very notion of a Vanguard Party as a proper or feasible agent for social change under present historical circumstances: "The great organizations of the masses of the people and of workers in the past were not worked out by any theoretical elite or vanguard. . . . the new organizations will come as Lilburn's Leveller Party came, as the sections and popular societies of Paris in 1793, as the Commune in 1871 and the Soviets in 1905, with not a single soul having any concrete ideas about them until they appeared in all their power and glory." *Ibid.,* p. 4. From this radical populist theory followed the organized status-inverson of the Johnsonites and a series of grass-root publications entirely written by workers.

[52] Lloyd Braithwaite, "Social Stratification in Trinidad," *Social and Economic Studies,* Vol. 2, Nos. 2 and 3 (October, 1953), p. 119.

to act as editor of the party newspaper, *The Nation*. James' editorship ushered in a brief golden era of political journalism in the West Indies but, inevitably it appears in retrospect, when the time came for negotiation and compromise — James would charge capitulation — he and his former protegé came to an acrimonious parting of ways, with James himself launching an opposition party in 1965. Oxford, it seemed, had bred a "pragmatic" gradualist wary of socialist shiboleths and suspicious of impractical schemes involving mobilization of the masses. James, frail but undaunted in his sixties, retained, against all odds, in a strongly "neo-colonial" political climate, his faith in the capacity of the masses for spontaneous action on their own behalf. As Marx and Engels had predicted, the intellectual creations of the European Left — complete with their unresolved conflicts and ambiguities — had become common property in Trinidad, as in the world.

SUMMARY

The foregoing account of the development of the educational system of a single colonial society suggests several key processes, the general relevance of which could serve as a basis for a comparative study of the ideological bases of the disestablishment of modern colonial empires. In the Trinidad case the following points seem of most crucial importance:

1. At the outset, British colonial administration in Trinidad initiated investments in a formal system of education very largely on the basis of administrative necessity; once established, the formal educational system was useful in producing a limited number of secondary and university-educated colonials to serve in the local civil service and in the professions.

2. Attainment of middle-class status in urban occupations thus became highly correlated with individual intellectual achievement on the part of colored colonial students. The explicit universalistic value-orientation of the educational system itself, the rational-legal basis of the civil service and the professions coupled with broad exposure to modern science produced men who were conscious of a contradiction between the old colonial ethics allocating status chiefly on the basis of ascribed characteristics such as race, and the achievement-orientation stressed in the educational and occupational sphere.[53]

[53] For an examination of the role of the contemporary West Indian educational system in shaping the social values of students see James T. Duke's Egalitarianism and Future Leaders in Jamaica," Chapter Seven of this volume. I think that a useful distinction is to be made between the *content* of the social values taught in the schools and the *structure* of the school system. The Victorian schoolmaster

3. Colonial university students in the metropolitan country were attracted by those social milieux which both stimulated and sympathized with their grievances against the colonial social and political order. These milieux and ideologies were not, however, homogeneous. Various radical and reformist social theories advanced competing ethical and actionist claims and the differential socialization of colonial students to such theories in the metropole laid the basis for the potential transfer of such issues to the emergent nationalist movements. This process, in the main, has yet to be described and analyzed.

In Trinidad, as this chapter has briefly suggested, religious authorities were frequently among the most important leaders and teachers in the educational system. The power of the denominational boards of education was established in the last quarter of the nineteenth century so that the impact of the formal educational system in diffusing predominantly secular philosophies was checked. The intellectual authority of the Roman Catholic Church, in particular, remained very strong. The mixture of a secular world-view with the traditional religious rhetoric and outlook of Trinidad society helped in creating a millenarian flavor for the nationalist movement headed by Dr. Eric Williams. As will be seen in a forthcoming study, the Christian faith in revival and renewal through the dramatic emergence of a Messiah would ironically become one of the most important supports that the traditional culture of the colony would provide for the exclusively earthly concerns of the charismatic leader of the nationalist movement.[54]

---

and priest may or may not have disseminated democratic values but they did manage a system of rewards in which objective, universalistic criteria for recognizing merit and granting advancement were supposed to be in force. The fact that these ideal formal criteria were often violated — or, at any rate, were often thought to be violated, by local students and teachers — was of great importance in undermining the legitimacy of the colonial regime.

[54] *Black Intellectuals Come to Power: The Rise of Creole Nationalism in Trinidad & Tobago*, by the present writer, in preparation for this series.

CHAPTER 3 Attitudes Toward
Political Independence

CHARLES C. MOSKOS, JR.*

INTRODUCTION

West Indian demands for a greater measure of self-government
associated with ill-defined aspirations for national independence can
be traced back to the nineteenth century. After Canada was federated
in the 1860's there was considerable popular discussion in the British
Empire regarding the possibility of establishing an Imperial Federation
complete with an imperial parliament – the forerunner of sentiments
leading to the establishment of the Commonwealth – and these notions
reached the West Indies. When a staunch imperialist and anti-reform
Oxford Professor of History arrived for a visit in Trinidad in the
late eighties he was dismayed to find that popular orators, newspaper
writers and some of the leading merchants in Port of Spain had discovered, as he put it, that they were living under what they called a
"degrading tyranny." "The speakers," he reported, "did their best to
imitate the fine phrases of the apostles of liberty in Europe, but they
succeeded only in caricaturing their absurdities."[1] After his arrival in
Jamaica the same visitor had a pamphlet thrust in his hand advocating,
among other sweeping reforms, Home Rule, and he noted caustically
that Mr. Gladstone's government had recently revived representative
government in the colony and had placed the franchise so low ". . . as
to include practically every negro peasant who possessed a hut and a
garden." "It is therefore assumed and understood," he wrote with

* It should be noted that I have occasionally followed the text of Wendell Bell's
and Ivar Oxaal's summary of my research in *Decisions of Nationhood: Political
and Social Development in the British Caribbean*, Denver, Colo.: Social Science
Foundation, University of Denver, 1964, pp. 15–24.

[1] James Anthony Froude, *The English in the West Indies*, London: Longmans,
Green, and Co., 1888, p. 76. The British Governor in Trinidad at the time was
more sympathetic, and Froude discovered that "responsible government" was an
open topic for table talk at Government House.

considerable exaggeration of the sentiment for self-government present at that time, "to have been no more than an initial step towards passing over the management of Jamaica to the black constituencies. It has been so construed in the other islands, and was the occasion of the agitation in Trinidad which I observed when I was there."[2]

Although things would not move so quickly, "the fine phrases of the apostles of liberty in Europe" had indeed taken root in the West Indies and, along with the implications of ultimate self-government contained in the British doctrine of colonial "trusteeship," continued to stir the nationalist imaginations of at least a few local apostles of liberty. These were chiefly middle-class men, some of whom came into their own after World War I in Trinidad where a revered local white man of Corsican descent, Captain Andrew A. Cipriani, emerged as the colony's foremost labor leader and elected politician. By 1932 an area-wide conference had been held by West Indian political reformists on the island of Dominica and a program for constitutional progress toward self-government and federation was announced. This generation of middle-class gradualists, operating on a limited franchise and without benefit of large-scale, organized, lower-class support, was overtaken by the dramatic social convulsions which rocked the West Indies in the 1930's. A fiery immigrant from the nearby island of Grenada named Uriah Butler led labor demonstrations in the Trinidad oilfields and staged a hunger march on Port of Spain. Rioting broke out on the sugar estates in British Guiana and spread up the Leeward and Windward chains. Powerful trade unions and a new set of nationalist militants appeared almost overnight in Jamaica, where Alexander Bustamante and Norman W. Manley emerged as powerful leaders. It was a time of warning from the West Indies to the Colonial Office.

The Colonial Office began to heed that warning. Although the Second World War delayed action, the end of the war emergency and the accession of Labour to power in Britain placed Dominion status for a federated West Indies within reach. As was shown earlier, the road to independence which began with the 1947 Montego Bay conference was a long one and has led — up to the present — not to political federation but to the emergence of four new nations and some uncertain "orphans" in the Leewards and Windwards.

It is by no means obvious why the major political thrust in the West Indies since the late 1930's should have been in the direction of self-government. The West Indies had been under British rule for so long, and exposed to Britain's cultural penetration to such an extent, that

---

[2] *Ibid.*, p. 179.

even such militant early nationalists as Cipriani frequently coupled their demands for political reform with sincere expressions of fealty to the Crown. There was little hatred of the British in the West Indies; indeed, many of the educated colored colonials acquired the air, manner, and accents of cultivated British gentlemen — and so they were. These celebrated "black Englishmen" who emerged in the West Indies may have struck the experienced (and biased) observer as caricatures of the real article, but they did not view themselves as such.

The black Englishman, however, was only one manifestation of a long historical process that exposed and acculturated the descendants of slaves and indentured laborers to European values. The emergence and meaning of West Indian nationalism can be traced precisely to the increasing diffusion of the European libertarian "absurdities" lamented by the writer quoted above. As will be shown here, Enlightenment values in the form of an interesting and felicitous mixture of bourgeois liberalism and labor radicalism had become the ideological and political master trend in the West Indies. These were the societal values which impelled the independence movement in the West Indies.[3] Moreover, these values were the motivating force not only of the independence movement *per se*, but were of the utmost importance in the discussions and calculations underlying the other big decisions of nationhood. They frequently tended to set narrow limitations on the range of policy alternatives which could be seriously entertained by the West Indian nationalists in power. That is to say, the goal of national independence was part of a general system of values which included conceptions of what constituted a proper form of government, its relationship to other institutions, the nature of a just society, and so forth.

Men and groups differ in the degree of clarity, commitment and consensus with which they adhere to such values, and it is my purpose in this chapter to show how differences in the commitment to national independence for the West Indies were correlated with differences in individual attitudes toward Enlightenment values as well

[3] Space does not permit an examination of the historical process that led to the state of affairs described here. In the following discussion attention is focused on the value *outcomes* of that process. Two studies conducted by Fellows of the West Indies Study Program deal with aspects of the process: Ivar Oxaal, "West Indian Intellectuals Come To Power: A Study of the Colonial Heritage and Nationalist Action in Trinidad," unpublished Ph.D. dissertation, University of California, Los Angeles, 1964, traces the political socialization of several later-prominent Trinidad nationalists; and James T. Duke, "Equalitarianism Among Emergent Elites in a New Nation," unpublished Ph.D. dissertation, University of California, Los Angeles, 1963, shows how the correlation between the Jamaican educational process and favorable attitudes toward equality holds in the present and may be expected to continue in the future. The Oxaal volume will appear in revised form as a separate book in this series, and Duke summarizes his thesis in Chapter Seven of this volume.

as social background characteristics. I examine in this chapter, then, the factors that led certain members of a colonial society to question the old order and eventually to take steps that would bring about a dismantlement of an empire, and others to look on with alarm at this course of events, and still others to accept the changing order without being personally committed to it.

BASIC DATA

The data reported here are from interviews with 112 top leaders in Jamaica, Trinidad and Tobago, (then) British Guiana, and in a sample from the smaller islands: Barbados, Grenada, and Dominica.[4] All told, these six territories account for well over 90 per cent of the population and land area of the British West Indies. The leaders who were interviewed constituted, with a few exceptions, the most important decision-makers in their respective territories.

To locate such national leaders, a modified "snow ball" technique was used. Initially, persons in a cross-section of institutional sectors were selected who, on the basis of their formal roles or institutional positions, were likely to be top leaders. They were asked to identify individuals whom they considered to wield national influence. As the nominations of the national leaders accumulated, the most frequently mentioned persons were in turn asked to identify other influentials. In this way, the original positional approach gave way to a reputational approach, and the list of reputed national leaders was increasingly refined. The same procedure was used in each of the territories, so that comparability between the units was insured.

None of the West Indian leaders so selected and identified refused to be interviewed and, when the field research had been completed, each leader had been questioned at some length about, among other things, the issues discussed in this chapter. These leaders were interviewed during late 1961 and early 1962, and included in each territory the Premier, the most influential Cabinet members, top leaders of the opposition party(ies), heads of labor unions, wealthy merchants, large plantation owners, and newspaper editors. Also interviewed were leading members of the clergy, educationists, leaders of voluntary organizations, prominent professionals, and high-ranking civil servants.

Although the West Indies Federation disintegrated and there are now four new or emergent nations in the British Caribbean instead

---

4 This section constitutes in part a brief summary of some of the data collected by Moskos, "The Sociology of Political Independence: A Study of Influence, Social Structure, and Ideology in the British West Indies," unpublished Ph.D. dissertation, University of California, Los Angeles, 1963. A revised version of this will also appear as a separate book in this series.

of one, a similar pattern runs through them and the meanings of their "nationalisms" are much the same. Thus, West Indian nationalism here is viewed as turning upon the question of the desire for political independence *per se*, rather than upon the size of the unit — the entire West Indies or some particular territory within it — for which independence was desired. In other words, the issue of political independence, regardless of the scope of the geographical area involved, was used as the crux of West Indian nationalism. This is not to say the *incidence* of support or opposition to independence was the same in each of the territories. In fact, as will be shown shortly, there were important differences between some of the West Indian territories as to their leaders' behavior toward political independence.

A NATIONALIST TYPOLOGY

As might have been expected, there was considerable disagreement among these West Indian leaders over the desirability of political independence, and while that disagreement to a great extent was correlated with the basic cleavages in the social structure, it was more closely associated with the broader values of individuals regardless of social position. From a content analysis of the respondents' attitudes and activities regarding political independence, three basic types were identified: *colonialists, acquiescing nationalists*, and *true nationalists*.

Colonialists were those leaders who opposed political independence for the West Indies in the present or future and favored an indefinite continuation of colonial rule. Usually, however, they did not express such sentiment publicly because of their belief that theirs was a lost cause, that independence was inevitable and that the climate of opinion was hostile to such views. There were exceptions to this posture of colonialist political disaffiliation, particularly in British Guiana where colonialists openly espoused an anti-independence position.

Acquiescing nationalists were differentiated into three sub-types. Some were found to be *reluctant nationalists* because, while they expressed a desire for political independence as a long-range goal, they disavowed it for the near future. They temporized by saying, for example, that the West Indies were not ready for independence, that economic development should come first and that the people lacked political maturity. They were not prepared, however, to form an open opposition to the nationalist movement but expressed the notion that events were moving too quickly. Another acquiescing group were the *dutiful nationalists*, leaders motivated to aid the nationalist movement out of a sense of *noblesse oblige*. Some of these men were mavericks from the traditional upper classes who did not view political independence as desirable but who nonetheless were willing to bend with the "inevitable" by using their skills and influence to alleviate the strains of the transition from colony to independent nation-state. A third acquiescing type was identified, the *opportunistic nationalists* who, although privately opposed to independence, publicly engaged in pro-independence activity in the belief that they would gain personally by doing so.

True nationalists were defined as those leaders who favored immediate independence and who backed their expressed convictions by open support of the nationalist cause, including such activities as membership in nationalist parties, public speaking, and pamphleteering in favor of independence.

The distribution of these types among the top West Indian leaders was as follows:

Nationalist Types		Percentage
True nationalists		39
Acquiescing nationalists		25
reluctant	11	
dutiful	5	
opportunistic	9	
Colonialists		36
Total (112 cases)		100

Slightly more than one-third each of the West Indian leaders were either true nationalists or colonialists. The remainder, one-fourth of the total, were acquiescing nationalists. These findings can be viewed in either of two ways. From one perspective, much less than a majority of the West Indian elites were genuinely committed to political independence. But the apparently low number of true nationalists may be a result of the narrow definition of this type which involved private as well as open support for immediate political independence. Thus, by keeping in mind the acquiescing nationalists, it can be said that close to two-thirds of the leaders exhibited some amount of pro-independence sentiment.

REGIONAL EFFECTS

Before examining the relation between the nationalist typology and the leaders' social characteristics and views, a brief comment is needed concerning the territorial context of West Indian nationalism. As reported in Table 1, the distribution of the nationalist types varied between the territories. The smaller territories, when compared to the larger ones, contained relatively fewer leaders who favored immediate independence and more leaders who opposed it. True nationalism

Table 1. NATIONALIST TYPES BY TERRITORY

	Percentages of West Indian Leaders Who Were:			
Territory	*Colonialists*	*Acquiescing Nationalists*	*True Nationalists*	*Total*
British Guiana	38	7	55	100 (13)
Jamaica	21	29	50	100 (24)
Trinidad	36	23	41	100 (22)
Grenada	28	33	39	100 (17)
Barbados	43	28	29	100 (21)
Dominica	47	26	27	100 (15)
Total Six West Indian Territories	36	25	39	100 (112)

Number of cases on which percentages are based given in parentheses.

among the leaders was most characteristic of British Guiana, followed by Jamaica, Trinidad, Grenada, Barbados, and Dominica. It was also found, however, from analysis not shown here, that the individual configurations of background traits, attitudes, and activities relating to political independence were markedly similar among the West Indian leaders regardless of locality. For this reason, we treat the West Indies as a whole and group the various territories together in the presentation of the remainder of the findings.

EFFECTS OF SOCIAL BACKGROUND CHARACTERISTICS

As one would expect, variation in three nationalist types were correlated, although never perfectly, with the social backgrounds of the West Indian leaders. The relative frequency of selected social characteristics among the nationalist types is given in Table 2.

The colonialists were generally very well-off economically, being found chiefly among the more prosperous planters and merchants. Because economic status — as discussed earlier — is associated with skin color in the West Indies, most whites and near whites were also found to be colonialists. In contrast to the true nationalists, colonialists were statistically likely to be older, to adhere most closely to Anglo-European styles of life, and to have been educated to the secondary-school level rather than having received more or less education. True nationalists, on the other hand, were younger, tended toward a more provincial middle-class West Indian variant of European life styles, and were likely to have either a university degree or an education not extending beyond elementary school. Moreover, the true nationalists were typically dark brown or black (and East Indian in British Guiana) and leaders of mass-based organizations such as trade unions or political parties. The true nationalists, therefore, included relatively few mem-

Table 2.   TYPES OF NATIONALISTS BY SELECTED SOCIAL
BACKGROUND CHARACTERISTICS

Selected Characteristics	*Percentages of West Indian Leaders Who Were:*			
	Colonialists	Acquiescing Nationalists	True Nationalists	Total
Age				
60 and over	54	34	12	100 (24)
50 to 59	47	23	30	100 (36)
40 to 49	23	23	54	100 (35)
39 and under	12	23	65	100 (17)
Education				
College or higher	32	19	49	100 (37)
Secondary school	38	32	30	100 (57)
Elementary only	28	22	50	100 (18)
Personal Wealth				
Wealthy	66	21	13	100 (39)
Not wealthy	20	27	53	100 (73)
Color and Ethnicity				
White	59	23	18	100 (39)
Light brown	35	35	30	100 (20)
East Indian and Chinese	42	33	25	100 (12)
Dark brown and black	12	20	68	100 (41)
Institutional Sector				
Political or labor	6	25	69	100 (48)
Economic	76	18	6	100 (34)
Mass media	25	50	25	100 (8)
Civil service	13	50	37	100 (8)
Other*	57	14	29	100 (14)
Life Style				
Anglo-European	42	32	26	100 (62)
West Indian	27	16	57	100 (49)

* Includes religious personages, free professionals, educationists, and heads of voluntary organizations.

Number of cases on which percentages are based given in parentheses.

bers of the traditional white oligarchy but at the same time their numbers were not overly reflective of a basically lower-class origin.[5]

Acquiescing nationalists tended to have intermediate background characteristics, although they were notably persons who occupied important positions in governmental service or in the mass media. Many of the opportunistic nationalists among the acquiescing type were old-style colonial politicians who apparently were not leading

[5] Interestingly, this was not true of the early leaders of the nationalist movement in Trinidad. Cipriani, as true a West Indian nationalist as there has been, was born into the local white elite. Uriah Butler, who came after Cipriani as the prophet of independence, was incurably proletarian in behavior and outlook. Fragmentary reports indicate, however, that most of their lieutenants were not generally unlike the profile of contemporary nationalists reported here.

so much as they were following the crowd down the path toward independence.

EFFECTS OF ECONOMIC IDEOLOGIES

More highly correlated with the nationalist types than the above social background characteristics were the economic ideologies of the leaders. We classified the leaders into five categories according to their views on the proper role of the government in the economy of their territories: *reactionaries* — those who thought the state's role should be about what it was before the rise of the nationalist movements and should not extend beyond providing basic services such as a postal system, roads, police and fire protection; *conservatives* — those who wished to maintain the present situation, with the state in addition to providing basic services also being responsible for welfare schemes for the ill, aged, and unemployed, for public works, and for a general educational system, but with the reservations that taxation should be less discriminatory against the entrepreneurial class and that government should be less protective of labor union interests; *populists* — those who lacked long-range economic policies, and who were pragmatically concerned with immediate bread and butter issues, although accepting a belief in a market economy geared to the demands of labor unions or mass-based political organizations; *liberals* — those who wanted greater intervention of the government in the economy, but who did not foresee radical changes beyond the achievement of modern welfare capitalism; and the *radicals* — those who advocated fundamental changes in the present system so that the state would become the major factor in determining local economic life, with the extreme radicals seeking the abolishment of all private property.

The distribution of these economic ideologies among the nationalist types is reported below.

Economic Ideologies	Percentages of West Indian Leaders Who Were:				
	Colonialists	Acquiescing Nationalists	True Nationalists	Total	Number of Cases
Reactionaries	86	14	0	100	(22)
Conservatives	58	42	0	100	(33)
Populists	18	36	46	100	(11)
Liberals	0	28	72	100	(25)
Radicals	0	0	100	100	(21)

The above table shows an unmistakable connection between nationalist behavior and economic ideologies. Among West Indian leaders, "Left" economic ideologies went with true nationalism and

"Right" economic ideologies went with support for the colonial system: all of the radicals were true nationalists, and none of the reactionaries or conservatives were. Moreover, the acquiescing nationalists tended to be concentrated in the intermediate economic ideologies.

These data illustrate what was quite evident in the interviews with the West Indian leaders: the nationalists wanted political change not so much as an end in itself, but as a means to greater economic growth and to distributional reforms by governmental action — to be controlled by the new elite. From its onset, the independence movement had been motivated not simply by a desire for political independence, but by the desire and demand for economic and social progress as well. And it was seen that this progress could not be achieved without a substantial departure from the narrow economic horizons and aspirations of the planter and merchant.

It was true, as conservative critics of the independence movement had argued, that political change in itself would not alleviate the poverty and stagnation of the West Indies economy, but for the nationalists this meant that political power had to be exercised to stimulate economic development. The only way in which the complacency of the traditional colonial economic oligarchy could be ended, it was believed, was by mass political action and by winning control of local governmental machinery. Political change and economic reform were intimately linked in the minds of the nationalists and, once they had achieved power during the terminal phases of colonial rule, they discovered that their promises of economic progress could be discharged — at least to a considerable degree. In the 1950's Jamaican nationalists under Norman W. Manley stimulated a tremendous increase in economic growth, and economic indicators under the new nationalist government launched by Dr. Eric Williams in Trinidad in 1956 showed a similar sharp rise. Moreover, once in power, nationalist politicians found practical reinforcement for their electoral claims that greater local political autonomy would breed greater economic opportunities. "We became increasingly eager to end colonial rule," a Trinidad nationalist politician said, "after we had gotten into office. We repeatedly found that so many of the things we wanted to do were hampered by our political status as a colony." Thus, the West Indian nationalist movement in power found that political power was indeed instrumental to the achievement of its overall economic objectives and this provided an important fillip to bringing independence aspirations to their culmination.

EFFECTS OF ENLIGHTENMENT VALUES

It would be a mistake, however, to view the preceding table as suggesting that adherence to programmatic economic philosophies in the narrow sense was the ideological mainspring of the independence movement. For the goals of the true nationalists went far beyond increasing the role of government in the economy. In fact, the most distinctive trait among the nationalist leaders was their overwhelming commitment to reorganize West Indian society in such a far-reaching fashion as to achieve many of the higher ideals of Western civilization. Indeed, the course of nationalism in the West Indies seems to have recapitulated some of the ideological currents that brought about the rise of nationalism in Western Europe and that underlay the ethical principles of the French, American, and Russian revolutions.

To document this thesis, we use as points of reference attitudinal items which, although having roots deep in the past, were specific outgrowths of a common philosophical tradition — the Enlightenment.[6] There were, of course, many strains in the Enlightenment, not all of which were necessarily consistent, but the principal feature of the Enlightenment was its radical approach to what constituted the Good Society. Basically, the thought of the Enlightenment consisted of a belief in the possibility of progress, the use of reason, skepticism of the old order, the equality of man, the removal of inherited privilege, and a faith in men collectively to govern themselves under democratic procedures.

This general intellectual movement culminated politically in the *rights of man* embodied in the French Revolutionary slogan: *liberté égalité, fraternité*. These ideals were codified in such documents as the American Declaration of Independence, the Bill of Rights in the Constitution of the United States, and the French Declaration of the Rights of Man and of the Citizen. Three of the items covered in the interviews with the West Indian leaders — attitudes toward political democracy, egalitarianism, and social inclusiveness — can be paired with their equivalents embodied in the rights of man. That is, "liberty" corresponds to political democracy, "equality" is egalitarianism, and "fraternity" comes close to our meaning of social inclusiveness.

[6] Since the realization that the attitudinal measures used were tapping Enlightenment values came rather late during the data collection, it was not possible to obtain data on other facets of these value patterns. Thus, the present Index of Enlightenment is limited to the rights-of-man dimension of the Enlightenment. Other dimensions could have been included such as measures of belief in progress, in the efficacy of reason, and in the potentiality of man to transform and develop himself. However, another Fellow in the West Indies Studies Program, James A. Mau, centered his entire study on the belief in progress and collected data which show that attitudes toward equality and the belief in progress are in fact intercorrelated in the anticipated way. See "Social Change and Belief in Progress: A Study of Images of the Future in Jamaica," University of California, Los Angeles, 1963, which will also appear as a separate book in this series. A summary of his thesis is given in Chapter Ten of this volume. For a recent interpretation of the French Enlightenment, see Peter Gay, *The Party of Humanity*, New York: Alfred A. Knopf, 1964.

Attitudes toward political democracy were measured by asking the leaders if they thought the democratic form of government was the best suited for their territory, the referent being a British parliamentary type of government based on universal adult suffrage with guarantees for the maintenance of civil rights. Of all the leaders interviewed, half said that they did not think the democratic form was desirable, or else expressed major misgivings about it. They were termed "non-democrats," while leaders who believed that the democratic form was most suitable for their home territories without qualification were called "democrats."

The concept of equality used here refers primarily to equality of opportunity, to the desire for a society within which each individual would be able to advance according to his capabilities. The measurement of attitudes toward equality was based on responses to a probe following the question concerning attitudes toward democracy. If the leaders revealed that equality of opportunity or the classless society were part of their images of the Good Society, then they were classified "egalitarian." If no such images, or if contrary images, were expressed, then the leaders were classified "inegalitarian." Thus, democrats and non-democrats could be either egalitarian or inegalitarian.[7]

The concept of social inclusiveness or fraternity refers to the attitudes persons have toward interaction with other persons. It is akin to notions of low social distance and comradeship, the social inclusivist favoring contact between groups and individuals that transcend whatever barriers there may be, such as those based on racial, religious, or class differences. Social inclusiveness was operationalized by measuring the attitudes of West Indian leaders toward reducing social barriers between groups *within* their societies as compared to their attitudes toward increasing their contact with persons *outside* of the West Indies. Leaders who placed high priority on eliminating internal social barriers were termed "inclusivists." Contrariwise, persons who placed secondary emphasis on reducing internal social barriers or who favored the perpetuation of such social distinctions within their societies were designated "exclusivists."

On the basis of these three indicators of the rights of man, an Index of Enlightenment was constructed by adding together attitudes toward political democracy, egalitarianism, and social inclusiveness. Each of these attitudes was dichotomized in such a way as to separate out the most intense commitment to the Rights of Man. Democrats included

[7] Studies of the correlates and causes of attitudes toward equality in Jamaica are given in Wendell Bell, "Equality and Attitudes of Elites in Jamaica," *Social and Economic Studies,* 11 (December, 1962), pp. 409–432; and James T. Duke in Chapter Seven of this volume.

only those who expressed no reservations on the suitability of parliamentary democracy and public liberties for their territory; egalitarians affirmed their desire for a society based on equal opportunities in an open-ended question; and social inclusivists gave higher priority to reducing social barriers among members of their own societies than they did to increasing external contact. Thus, a maximum score of three on the Index of Enlightenment was possible only if a West Indian leader was a democrat, an egalitarian, and an inclusivist. Similarly, a leader would obtain a score of zero on this Index if he was a non-democrat, an inegalitarian, and an exclusivist.

The data reported in Table 3 support the contention that West Indian nationalism was a manifestation of the desire to transform West Indian society into one which conformed more closely than before to some of the basic values of Western civilization, as symbolized by the Rights of Man derived from the Enlightenment.[8] As is obvious from Table 3, there is a direct relationship between adherence to Enlightenment values and true nationalism among the West Indian leaders.

Table 3. TYPES OF NATIONALISTS BY AN INDEX OF ENLIGHTENMENT

	Percentages of West Indian Leaders Who Were:			
*Index of Enlightenment**	*Colonialists*	*Acquiescing Nationalists*	*True Nationalists*	*Total*
High 3 (enlightened)	0	0	100	100 (29)
2	0	22	78	100 (18)
1	25	71	4	100 (24)
Low 0 (unenlightened)	83	17	0	100 (41)

*Based on attitudes toward political democracy ("liberty"), reducing social barriers ("fraternity"), and egalitarianism ("equality").

Number of cases on which percentages are based given in parentheses.

At this juncture the more tough-minded reader might interpose the objection that these findings are "merely" ideological correlations and therefore do not reveal very much about the social dynamics of the independence movement. These high-flown ideals, it could be objected, might be merely altruistic rationalizations for private interests and that the individuals here identified as "true nationalists" may be nothing more than clever and articulate brothers of the "opportunistic nationalists."

[8] The 1961–62 study of West Indian nationalism reported here confirms and elaborates the findings of an earlier study done among Jamaican leaders in 1958. See Wendell Bell, *Jamaican Leaders: Political Attitudes in a New Nation*, Berkeley and Los Angeles: University of California Press, 1964.

Space here does not permit a full refutation of such objections. In a sense, they are really irrelevant to the demonstration at hand, which has to do with a description of what types of societal values were voiced in connection with the independence movement in the West Indies. It is difficult to see how the societal values just analyzed can be regarded as any less real in a causal sense than the undoubtedly wide range of personal rewards obtained by nationalist leaders through participation in the independence movement. The nationalist leaders were not always paragons of virtue immune to the temptations of seizing some personal advantages as these may arise from their participation in nationalist politics. All that has been attempted here is to show that those West Indian leaders who demonstrated the greatest commitment to the cause of national independence — regardless of whether some among them might be vain, alcoholics, status seekers, wife beaters, or had authoritarian personalities — were the same men who manifested the strongest belief in the ideals of the Enlightenment.

EFFECTS OF ROMANTICISM

But before commenting further on the implications of Enlightenment values and nationalist behavior in the West Indies, let us look at another set of attitudinal items seeking to measure a different intellectual tradition. Overlapping with the end of the Enlightenment period, though generally occurring somewhat afterwards, a counter-movement arose in Europe. This movement, Romanticism, reached its apogee among certain nineteenth-century writers and musicians, who, unlike the *philosophes* of the eighteenth century, stressed the importance of emotion, the uniqueness of the folk, and the historical and legendary past of a people. Though operating from different premises, Romantic notions, like Enlightenment thought, were also used to serve as rationales for national independence.

Indicators of West Indian Romanticism were drawn from three items covered in the interviewing of the West Indian leaders. These questions sought to measure whether the leaders thought West Indian culture and the West Indian people were and should be unique from other cultures and peoples. The first item examined attitudes toward the slave or indentured labor background in the teaching of West Indian history. The responses of the leaders were divided into two categories: one group favoring more emphasis on the non-European and indigenous aspects of the West Indian experience, the other group supporting the customary way in which history had been taught, a history focusing on the "mother country," Great Britain. The second item dichotomized the leaders into those who preferred future cultural development to take a West Indian form as contrasted to those who wished to see Anglo-European aspects predominate. The third item dealt with whether the leader's paramount personal identification was with the West Indian population at large or with persons of his same ethnic or racial background in other countries (e.g. English, Hindu, Moslem, African, Jewish, Chinese).

The dichotomized responses to these items were used to construct an Index of West Indian Romanticism. Thus, a leader who favored emphasis on a uniquely West Indian history, desired a purely West Indian cultural development in the future, and identified himself more with West Indians than with groups outside of the West Indies would score three on the Index. Conversely, a leader who opposed emphasis on West Indian history, desired a cultural development within an Anglo-European framework, and identified himself more closely with a non-West Indian group than with West Indians would receive a zero on the Index of West Indian Romanticism.

As shown in Table 4, there is a strong relationship between West Indian Romanticism and true nationalism among the West Indian leaders. This association, however, is not as strong as that observed previously between the nationalist types and the Index of Enlightenment. In fact, when we examine these two Indices simultaneously, from a tabular breakdown not shown here, it was found that Enlightenment is a much better predictor of true nationalist attitudes and activities than is West Indian Romanticism.

Table 4. TYPES OF NATIONALISM BY AN INDEX OF WEST INDIAN ROMANTICISM

| Index of West Indian Romanticism* | *Percentages of West Indian Leaders Who Were:* | | | |
	Colonialists	Acquiescing Nationalists	True Nationalists	Total
High 3 (most Romantic)	6	14	80	100 (35)
2	26	26	48	100 (27)
1	52	38	10	100 (29)
Low 0 (least Romantic)	76	24	0	100 (21)

* Based on attitudes toward West Indian history, future cultural development, and identification with West Indian population at large.

Number of cases on which percentages are based given in parentheses.

AN EXPLANATION OF THE RISE OF WEST INDIAN NATIONALISM

It is always a difficult task in social science to make causal inferences concerning human behavior. And this task is even more complex when we deal with large-scale societal issues involved in the decisions of nationhood. As has been apparent in the arrangement of the tabular data in this chapter, the nationalist behavior of the West Indian leaders has been conceived as being a "dependent" variable or "effect" of the diverse background characteristics and attitudinal items that have been presented. The following explanation of the development of West Indian nationalism is based on the logical and temporal priorities of the variables examined, the historical context of the British Caribbean setting, and a qualitative analysis of the West Indian leaders' own assessments of the origins of their views toward political independence.

The political independence movement in the British Caribbean was an outcome of the economic discontent of the depressed segments of West Indian society being linked with the introduction of Enlightenment values to which many middle-class West Indians had been exposed in their higher education abroad. Thus, the inchoate demands of the traditionally underprivileged social groups to improve their positions and the long-range goals of individuals adhering to Western Enlightenment values became articulated in terms of the Rights of Man. To attain these ends, it was held that the colonial order would have to be terminated. Through the establishment of a new and independent political order with enlarged control over the rest of society, it was believed, the power to achieve the desired changes could be instituted. Metaphorically, we can liken the indigenous unrest of the West Indian masses to a dry tinder which was ready to be set aflame by the spark of a Western-derived ideology.

This sociological overview of West Indian nationalism, supported by empirical evidence, leads us to interpret the bases of the drive for political independence as centering on collective efforts to attain the Rights of Man. In the words of a prominent labor union leader, "I began to realize that political independence was the only means to bring about a society with no discrimination and equal opportunity for all. I had just come back from the university in England and was filled with all those notions of social justice. After a while, I knew that real changes were possible only in an independent nation where we could control our own destiny."

Concurrently, a large number of the West Indian leaders who desired a society dedicated to liberty, equality, and fraternity saw this as being achievable only through a radical change in the existing economic order. In terms of its intellectual content and its role in the history of ideas, a radical or "socialist" economic ideology concerns instrumentalities toward structuring an economy in such a way as to facilitate the establishment of a certain kind of egalitarian society. Thus, like the desire for political independence, we regard a Left economic ideology as a "dependent" variable, while the Rights of Man have more of an "independent" nature. This line of reasoning is also supported by the interviews with the West Indian leaders. For the socialist leaders themselves explicitly regarded their economic ideology as a means to attain a more generalized version of their images of the Good Society. Hence, economic radicalism is seen here as an associative rather than a causal factor of West Indian nationalism.

In the wake of the West Indian political independence movement, which was engendered by egalitarian beliefs and supported by democratic and social inclusivist principles, our findings indicate there has arisen a new awareness of the region's local qualities and its past. That is, this new consciousness of West Indian culture and history — what can be called the West Indian Romantic movement — although a consequence of the independence movement has in turn become another aspect of West Indian nationalism alongside the original Enlightenment values. In brief, the initial political nationalism has begun to merge with a later cultural nationalism. This interpretation of the feedback nature of West Indian Romanticism is supported by statements from the true nationalists who regarded their Romanticism as emerging from their prior political motivations. As a barrister from Grenada put it, "Once I became convinced of the need for political independence, I began to take a great interest in the history of my people. This was difficult in the early days because the text books always talked about Mary Jane with flaxen hair. Now we are learning to be proud of ourselves." Moreover, the conscious attempt to create a West Indian cultural identity in recent years — itself a decision of nationhood — was demonstrably preceded by the agitation for political independence in the various territories.

This capsule assessment of the development of West Indian nationalism is diagrammatically presented in Chart 1.

SUMMARY

The West Indian nationalist movement, reflecting its Enlightenment origins, was in its fundamental meaning a combination of both nineteenth-century, middle-class liberalism and twentieth-century, working-class radicalism. (The more recent cultural nationalism, an outcome rather than a precipitating feature of the drive for political independence, could — if carried to extreme — result in an exclusive circularity and undermine the initial values of the nationalist movement.) The desires of the West Indian nationalist leaders to reshape their societies to conform more closely with the principles symbolized by the Rights of Man were able to materialize into major social action because the economic discontent of the West Indian masses was largely directed into support of the nationalist movement. Toward this end

Chart 1.   DIAGRAM OF THE CAUSAL RELATIONSHIPS OF MAJOR VALUES
AND STRUCTURAL CONDITIONS IN WEST INDIAN NATIONALISM

Enlightenment Values
of Western Europe

Structural Location
of Persons in Middle
Classes of West
Indian Society

Structural Location
of Persons in Lower
Classes of West
Indian Society

Introduction of
Rights-of-Man Ideals
in West Indies

Articulation of
Rights-of-Man Ideals

Conception of Ways to
Achieve Rights-of-Man
Ideals

Radical Economic
Ideology

Desire for Political
Independence

West Indian
Romanticism
(cultural national-
ism)

West Indian Nationalism
(initially desire for
political independence,
later including cultural
nationalism as well)

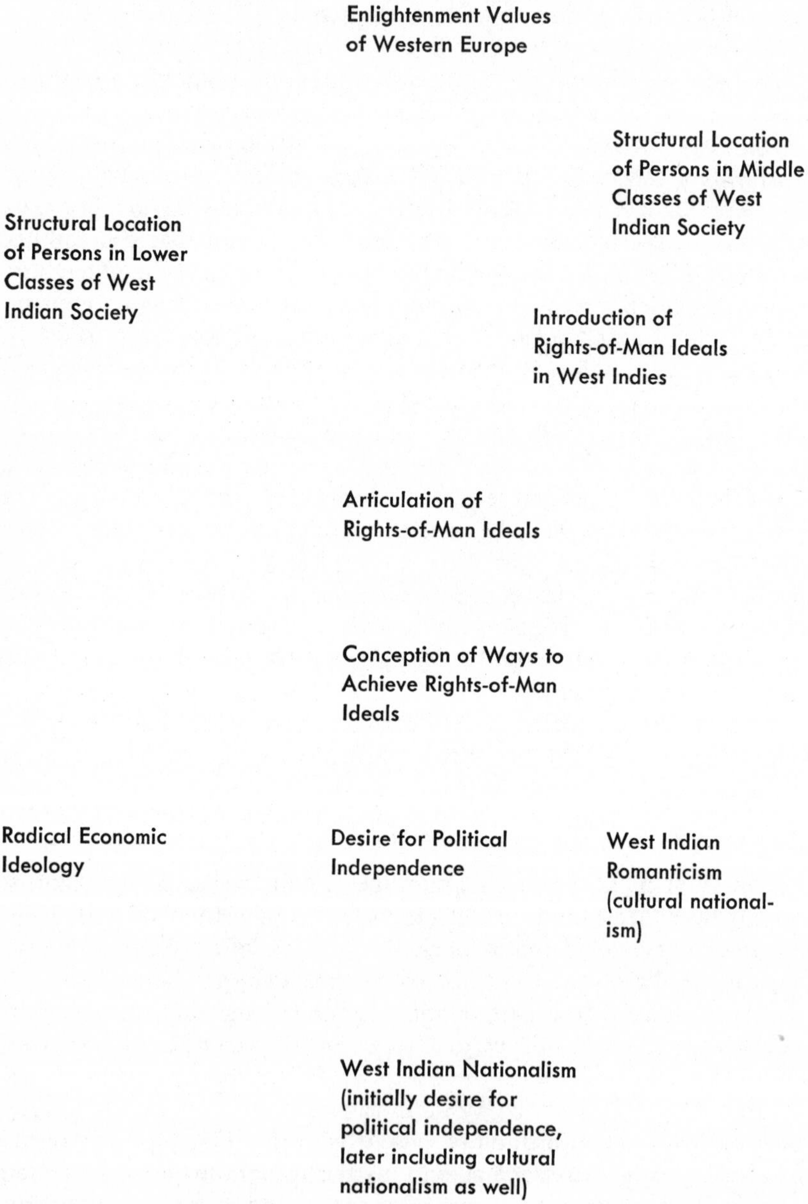

grass-root political organizations were formed and alliances with labor unions were made. Thus, with middle-class leadership and working-class support, it became possible for a social movement, engendered by humanistic ideals, to arise which was able to transform older notions of the legitimacy of the imperial order into a belief in the sovereignty of the West Indian people.[9]

It is too early to say how consistently the ideals documented here as underpinning the drive for political independence will be realized in the West Indies. Whether "massa day done" or whether new masters will replace the traditional elite is a decision yet to be determined by the leaders and citizenry of the West Indies. Without radical reform, the new nationalist leadership will be unable to bring to fruition the hopes of the independence movement. On the other hand, fulfillment of the humanistic and egalitarian promise of the West Indian nationalists would demonstrate the far-reaching changes that are possible through a democratic revolution. Given the obvious shortcomings of the more advanced societies in their progress toward these same goals, one wonders how much success can be expected of the smaller and poorer West Indian nations. But the urge to try is there, as it is for any person, group, or nation that believes in progress, reason, and the future perfectability of man.

[9] The argument underlying the causal explanation of West Indian nationalism is developed in detail in Moskos, "The Sociology of Political Independence," *op. cit.*

CHAPTER 4 Attitudes Toward Democracy

CHARLES C. MOSKOS, JR. AND WENDELL BELL

In the large majority of new nations the drive toward the establishment of a political democracy, as pointed out in Chapter Three, has worked hand-in-hand with desires for equality of opportunity and the inclusive society to motivate the nationalist movements. Likewise, beliefs in economic progress, including distributional reforms, social and cultural development, and often massive alterations in the degree of national integration, fitted in nicely with democratic beliefs of emergent nationalist leaders while colonial yokes still were attached to the nascent nations' necks.

When new nationalist leaders come to power, however, they do not always appear able to maintain their faith in democracy in the face of what appear to be incompatible demands for the achievement of other goals, especially for rapid economic development. As a result, within some of the new nations the "more advanced spirits" do not seem to be democrats by any reasonable definition of that term, but seem intent upon establishing undemocratic political systems not wholly unlike those of some of their ideological opponents among the conservatives and especially the reactionaries, although they may do so in the name of "the people." We regret that this judgment appears fundamentally sound despite the democratic rhetoric used by the new nationalist elites, some of whom by their actions can only be classified as authoritarians or totalitarians.

In this chapter, we probe still further into the democratic or authoritarian attitudes of the West Indian leaders interviewed by Moskos in 1961–62. It is our purpose to explore the attitudinal context within which the new national decision-makers will decide over the next few years what form of government their new nations should have. We are concerned with the prospects for democracy in the new states, and we are searching for the possible causes and consequences of various attitudes toward democracy by asking such questions as the following of our particular data: Leaders representing what socio-economic groups and what economic and social philosophies support democratic institutions? What leaders oppose them? Are there different appeals of democracy for such leaders? If so, what are they? Are undemocratic practices inevitable outcomes of the drive toward rapid economic progress and political modernization? How much choice does a modernizing elite in the developing areas have in selecting a type of political system? Can political democracy be salvaged within the new states?

INDICATORS OF DEMOCRATIC BELIEFS

By democracy, we mean a political system "...in which public policies are made, on a majority basis, by representatives subject to effective popular control at periodic elections which are conducted on the principles of political equality and under conditions of political freedom."[1] Operationally, we used two indicators of democratic beliefs. The first was similar to that used by Bell in his 1958 sample survey of democratic and undemocratic beliefs in Jamaica.[2] He used an Index of Political Cynicism suggested by Charles R. Nixon and Dwaine Marvick[3] and classified Jamaican elites as either "idealistic" or "cynical" with respect to political democracy. The politically idealistic leaders, according to this Index, were those who had favorable judgments of the average Jamaican voter, while the politically cynical leaders were those who had unfavorable attitudes. The former were considered democratic and the latter undemocratic.

In the present study the indicator similar to Bell's measure of political idealism or cynicism was based on the responses of the West Indian leaders to the question: "Do you feel the typical (West Indian)* voter

---

*The name of the territory appropriate to each respondent was inserted.

[1] Henry B. Mayo, *An Introduction to Democratic Theory*, New York: Oxford University Press, 1960, p. 70.

[2] Wendell Bell, *Jamaican Leaders: Political Attitudes in a New Nation*, Berkeley and Los Angeles: University of California Press, 1964, Chapter V, "Should Jamaica Have a Democratic Political System?" Although a few comparisons are made in this paper between the Jamaican results of the present study and Bell's earlier study, the two studies are not strictly comparable. Bell included middle ranks of leadership as well as upper, while the present study is confined to the *top* leaders. There are also differences in response rates and in procedures of collecting data: mail questionnaires vs. personal interviews.

[3] Charles R. Nixon and Dwaine Marvick, "Active Campaign Workers: A Study of Self-Recruited Elites," paper read at the annual meetings of the American Political Science Association, September, 1956; Dwaine Marvick, "Active Campaign Workers: The Power Structures of Rival Parties," unpublished paper, University of California, Los Angeles, mimeographed; and Dwaine Marvick, "The Middlemen of Politics," paper read at the annual meetings of the American Political Science Association, Washington, D.C., September 1962.

supports leaders who serve the long range interests of (the West Indies)? That is, how competent do you feel the average (West Indian) voter is?" The results were:

The West Indian electorate is:

	%
Competent	28
Incompetent	72
Total (111 cases)[4]	100

The second indicator of democratic beliefs was based on the leaders' answers to the question, "Do you think the democratic form of government is the best suited for (the West Indies)?", the referent being a British parliamentary type of government based on universal adult suffrage with guarantees for the maintenance of civil and minority rights. This is the question that was used in Chapter Three to measure the democratic attitudinal component of the Index of Enlightenment. The percentage distribution of responses of the 111 West Indian leaders is as follows:

The democratic form of government is:

	%
Very suitable	50
Partially suitable	10
Unsuitable	40
Total (111 cases)	100

Given in Table 1 is a political typology based on the simultaneous responses to these two indicators of democratic attitudes.[5] Twenty-two per cent of the leaders were termed true "democrats," that is, they thought that parliamentary democracy was very suitable for their home territories *and* that the voters were competent. The smallest group, 6 per cent, were labelled "authoritarian idealists," i.e. they had qualifications about the parliamentary form or believed it was unsuitable but held favorable attitudes toward the competency of the typical West Indian voter. "Cynical parliamentarians," constituting 28 per cent of the top West Indian leaders, were those who, while favoring a parliamentary system, thought that the average voter was incompetent. Finally, nearly half of the leaders were classified as "authoritarians" because

[4] The number of cases is given as 111 in this chapter while 112 was reported as the N in Chapter Three. The discrepancy is explained by the fact that one leader could not be classified with respect to attitudes toward democracy.
[5] The second measure of democratic attitudes has been dichotomized in Table 1 by combining the "partially suitable" and "unsuitable" responses.

they neither believed in the suitability of the parliamentary form nor thought the typical voter was competent. One must conclude from these overall figures alone that the foundations of democracy as reflected in the beliefs and attitudes of the West Indian elite are somewhat shaky.

Table 1.   A POLITICAL TYPOLOGY OF WEST INDIAN LEADERS

Political Types	Percentage
Democrats	22
Authoritarian idealists	6
Cynical parliamentarians	28
Authoritarians	44
Total (111 cases)	100

ELABORATION OF THE MEANING OF THE POLITICAL TYPES

Relation to economic ideologies. The significance of the political types, as well as of the analysis to follow, can be enhanced if their import is made clear at the outset. The constructed political types have direct and obvious implications for the preferred nature of the political system and for the chances of the ideals of political democracy being at least striven for and perhaps to some degree achieved in fact. But the implications of these types are not confined to the nature or processes of the political system *per se:* they also bear on some of the broader questions of the desired outcomes or end results toward which political action is directed. To document this view we examine here the relationship between the political types and a major aspect of the West Indian leaders, long-range social philosophies: their economic ideologies. The classification of West Indian leaders as reactionaries, conservatives, populists, liberals, or radicals is the same one reported in Chapter Three.

In Table 2 is shown the relationship between economic ideologies and the political types. Truly democratic attitudes were most characteristic of liberals, 50 per cent of whom were democrats, with most of the remainder being cynical parliamentarians. Almost the same proportion of populists, 46 per cent, were democrats, but over one-third of them were authoritarians. The radicals were most evenly spread over the political types: 14 per cent were democrats, 29 per cent authoritarian idealists, 38 per cent cynical parliamentarians, and 19 per cent authoritarians. Over half of the conservatives and fully 95 per cent of the reactionaries were authoritarians. Thus, excluding the radicals for the moment, there is a clear and strong relationship between the political types and economic ideologies, with the Right

Table 2. POLITICAL TYPES BY ECONOMIC IDEOLOGIES

Economic Ideologies	Democrats	Percentages of West Indian Leaders Who Were:				
		Authoritarian Idealists	Cynical Parliamentarians	Authoritarians	Total	Number of cases
Radical	14	29	38	19	100	(21)
Liberal	50	4	42	4	100	(24)
Populist	46	0	18	36	100	(11)
Conservative	9	0	33	58	100	(33)
Reactionary	5	0	0	95	100	(22)

economic ideologists having more anti-democratic or authoritarian attitudes compared to the Left economic ideologists who have more democratic views. This is consistent with data we have reported elsewhere which show that opponents of the democratic revolution in the West Indies were those persons most out of step with the nationalist movements whose progressive policies were, in contrast to the rigidly stratified social system which then existed, supportive of political, economic, and social egalitarian principles.

The tensions underlying West Indian society, however, are not to be understood solely as democratic and progressive forces combating non-democratic elements seeking to maintain their advantages or to restore the old order. For some West Indian leaders economic changes within the parliamentary system have been too superficial, as shown in the tapering off of democratic attitudes among the radicals. Yet, unlike the opponents of parliamentary democracy on the Right, some of the radicals, among whom were found nearly all of the authoritarian idealists, had a greater faith in the political competency of the West Indian citizenry. While most of the non-democratic or authoritarian West Indian leaders were conservatives or reactionaries, there was also a tendency for some of the most egalitarian leaders to be authoritarians too, but for different reasons: they regarded parliamentary processes, as currently operating, as being unresponsive to popular needs, and blamed the parliamentary system for slowness in instituting radical reform. This is a growing sentiment which contains a challenge of great significance to democratic institutions and potential threat to their survival.

Revolutionaries and counter-revolutionaries. An additional elaboration of the meaning of the political types is found in the relationship between the types and attitudes toward the overthrow of the legally constituted government. Of course, advocacy of overthrow of a government is not in itself necessarily either democratic or anti-democratic. It depends. If the government in question is thwarting the control of ordinary citizens over their leaders, then such an over-throw might be inspired by democratic beliefs and attitudes. But if the government is pursuing democratic and progressive aims, then violent opposition to it would be found among anti-democratic persons. Thus, advocates of overthrow of the government can be in this sense either revolutionary or counter-revolutionary.

Following the close of each formal interview, a time when rapport between the interviewer and respondent was generally highest, the West Indian leaders were queried about their views concerning the overthrow of the constitutionally elected governments of their terri-tories. A total of 17 per cent of the leaders indicated that they would either favor outright or acquiesce to a violent or illegal overthrow of the existing government, but there was considerable variation by political type:

Political Type	Percentage Who Condoned Overthrow	Number of Cases
Democrats	0	(24)
Cynical parliamentarians	6	(31)
Authoritarian idealists	29	(7)
Authoritarians	33	(49)

Nearly all of the leaders who condoned overthrow of the govern-ment were either authoritarian idealists or out-and-out authoritarians. Different motives tended to underlie such deep-seated opposition to the existing government: revolutionary as contrasted to counter-revolutionary sentiments. An examination of these diverse motives requires an indicator of the varying images of the Good Society held by the West Indian leaders, and we used the economic ideologies of the leaders given above as such an indicator.

The distribution was as follows:

Economic Ideologists	Percentage Who Condoned Overthrow	Number of Cases
Radicals (revolutionary)	24	(21)
Liberals	0	(24)
Populists	9	(11)
Conservatives	12	(33)
Reactionaries (counter-revolutionary)	41	(22)

Leaders having moderate economic ideologies were least likely to oppose overthrow of the constitutionally legitimate governments of their territories. All of the liberals as well as the large majority of the populists and conservatives supported orderly and stable government. The ideological extremists, particularly the Rightist variant (41 per cent of the reactionaries), were the most hostile to the existing governments, but 24 per cent of the radicals also condoned overthrow of the government.

These and other data indicate that counter-revolutionary more than revolutionary sentiments underlay the motives of the bitterest opponents of the existing governments. Furthermore, the deep-seated hostility of the reactionaries is some evidence of the basically progressive policies which the emergent Caribbean nations have been implementing. At the same time, it is important to note that the undemocratic sentiments of the conservatives were not translated into advocacy of non-constitutional means. We suggest that while most of the West Indian reactionaries had withdrawn from active political participation (only 23 per cent being high political activists overall), many of the conservatives sought to mitigate major changes in the *status quo* through involvement in the parliamentary system (46 per cent engaging in high political activity). For the conservatives, the parliamentary system, though bringing on social change, was seen as the lesser of two evils, the greater being contained in the potential threat of a radical-authoritarian regime. That the efforts of the opponents of reform were perceived as at least somewhat successful by a few leaders is reflected in the fact that some radicals also advocated overthrow of the government. Whether or not the radical authoritarians will be able to find popular support in the future depends on the capacity of the West Indian democratic revolution to meet the rising social and economic aspirations that it has engendered. That is . . . unless fairly substantial economic and social progress is achieved — including distributional reforms — under a democratic regime, the ranks of the authoritarian idealists may be markedly increased by egalitarian leaders who become disillusioned with the parliamentary system as an instrument of economic and social reform.

DIFFERENCES BY TERRITORY

As reported in Table 3, the support for democracy was highest and authoritarian sentiment was lowest in Jamaica. There, experience with the modern democratic system is most mature of all the British territories in the West Indies — the franchise was extended to all Jamaican adults in 1944 compared to similar action in the other territories in the early 1950's — and a firm base in a two-party system exists, both parties — the liberal People's National Party and the more conservative Jamaica Labour Party — having each had some time at the helm of government. Probably, the longer experience of the Jamaican leaders in the give-and-take of parliamentary life and their witnessing of the electoral behavior of the Jamaican citizenry for nearly two decades promoted a growing trust and faith in democratic processes. That is, the existence of a genuine parliamentary system well before full independence may be a major element in establishing the legitimacy of a democracy which extends into the post-independence period. Some support for this observation is given when we note that the relative number of Jamaican political idealists (i.e. democrats and authoritarian idealists) found in this 1961–62 study, 48 per cent, was greater than the 42 per cent of the Jamaican elites who could be termed idealistic in Bell's 1958 survey. Also, the fact that 65 per cent of the Jamaican leaders in the 1961–62 study believed in the suitability of parliamentary democracy for Jamaica adds weight to the conclusion that on the average there has been growing support for democracy in Jamaica in the recent past.

Table 3. POLITICAL TYPES BY TERRITORY

Territory	Percentages of West Indian Leaders Who Were:					
	Demo-crats	Authori-tarian Idealists	Cynical Parlia-mentarians	Authori-tarians	Total	Number of Cases
Jamaica	39	9	26	26	100	(23)
Trinidad	18	14	27	41	100	(22)
British Guiana	8	8	38	46	100	(13)
Barbados, Dominica, & Grenada	19	2	26	53	100	(53)

In British Guiana, 38 per cent of the leaders were cynical parliamentarians, the highest in the British Caribbean, and the number of democrats was the lowest. This reflects the internecine conflict which has marred political life in that territory in recent years: the two major political parties have come to be divided along the colony's social and racial cleavages. The Communist-led People's Progressive Party draws upon the rural East Indians, and the socialist People's National Congress is supported by the urban Negroes, and a common response among Guianese leaders has been to praise the wisdom of their respective ethnic supporters and to denigrate the electoral competency of the opposite group. The system of proportionate representation that has recently resulted in the PNC election victory undoubtedly has made attitudes toward the political system more complicated and reduced the legitimacy of the present (1966) government in the eyes of PPP's supporters.

In Trinidad, 18 per cent of the leaders were democrats, 27 per cent cynical parliamentarians, 14 per cent authoritarian idealists, and 41 per cent authoritarians. Thus, despite a communal cleavage in Trinidad similar to that of British Guiana (except that the relative number of East Indians and Negroes is reversed), there is a somewhat higher level of political idealism. This may reflect the partial success of the incumbent People's National Movement to consciously transcend racial lines. Trinidad offers itself as an example of a new nation where ethnic and racial cleavages have not resulted in breaking down parliamentary democracy, although such a breakdown remains a danger.

Among the leaders of the smaller islands, authoritarian sentiments were highest. Nonetheless, 45 per cent of the leaders interviewed in the smaller islands were either democrats or cynical parliamentarians, and it should be remembered that the political development of these islands resembles that of the larger territories a decade or more ago. Although the term "labour" is an indispensable appellation of political parties and the rhetoric of socialism is frequently used, most of the local political groups are personal vehicles with little ideology. An important exception to the low level of political party viability among the smaller islands is Barbados; and it is more than mere coincidence that Barbados has enjoyed the largest measure of self-government over a longer period than any of the other smaller islands.

SOCIAL CORRELATES OF THE POLITICAL TYPES

Although we are dealing with different emergent Caribbean nations, between which the *incidence* of the democratic attitudes varied, a similar pattern runs through all of them with respect to the correlates of democratic attitudes among their leaders, just as it does with respect to the correlates of nationalist attitudes. From partials not presented here, we found that individual configurations of attitudes, activities, and personal background characteristics relating to attitudes toward democracy were markedly similar regardless of territory. Thus we treat the West Indies as a whole and group the various territories together in the presentation of the following data.

Comparing the different age levels in Table 4, one can see that leaders aged fifty and older were more likely to be authoritarians than younger leaders, with fully two-thirds of the oldest group so classified. The youngest leaders contained the largest relative number of democrats, although they are closely followed by leaders aged 50 to 59. Cynical parliamentarians were most numerous among leaders in the 40 to 49 age group, least among the youngest leaders. Also, virtually all of the authoritarian idealists were found among the youngest leaders. This finding contrasts somewhat with Bell's 1958 data which

Table 4. POLITICAL TYPES BY SELECTED SOCIAL CHARACTERISTICS

Selected Social Characteristics	*Percentages of West Indian Leaders Who Were:*					
	Demo-crats	Authori-tarian Idealists	Cynical Parlia-mentarians	Authori-tarians	Total	Number of Cases
Age						
60 and over	17	0	17	66	100	(23)
50 to 59	28	0	22	50	100	(36)
40 to 49	14	6	51	29	100	(35)
39 and under	30	30	10	30	100	(17)
Education						
College or higher	26	8	33	33	100	(36)
Secondary school	16	5	26	53	100	(57)
Elementary only	33	6	22	39	100	(18)
Personal Wealth						
Wealthy	10	3	18	69	100	(39)
Not wealthy	28	8	33	31	100	(72)
Color and Ethnicity						
White	10	3	29	58	100	(38)
Light brown	25	5	10	60	100	(20)
East Indian and Chinese	8	8	42	42	100	(12)
Dark brown and black	34	10	32	24	100	(41)
Institutional Sector						
Political or labor	36	13	30	21	100	(47)
Economic	9	0	18	73	100	(34)
Mass media	12	0	38	50	100	(8)
Civil service	12	0	76	12	100	(8)
Religious or ethnic	0	0	14	86	100	(7)
Other	29	14	14	43	100	(7)

showed little variation in political idealism by age among the Jamaican elites. This discrepancy may be due to the fact that this study dealt only with top West Indian leaders, while Bell's survey included many Jamaicans from the upper middle ranks. Also Bell's survey was less representative of political and labor leaders, the group that constituted the largest number in the present study.

Although the data support a generally held view that aging is positively related to conservatism (undemocratic sentiment is here regarded as conservative), the historical context of the West Indian experience suggests attention should be paid to more extrinsic factors. Rather than being concerned with age *per se*, we must also look to the values and ideas which are in circulation during a particular person's generation. It must be remembered that truly democratic forms of government are of recent origin in the West Indies. The younger West Indian leaders have had more of their lives shaped during a period when political democracy was a real alternative to either Crown Colony or limited franchise rule, and they have attained their maturity in a period during which democracy was actually operating in their territories.

There was a tendency for cynical parliamentarianism to increase with level of education while the percentage of authoritarian idealists varied little by education. A more pronounced finding was the relatively high percentage of authoritarians among the West Indian leaders who had a secondary-school education only, while true democratic attitudes were most evident among leaders with either the most or least formal education. This association is in accord with Bell's earlier findings in which the least politically idealistic Jamaican elites were also in the middle educational levels.

Two different factors account for this "U" shaped distribution. On the one hand, the percentage of persons with low educational levels who are democratic is evidence of the general finding: greater relative support for democracy among West Indian leaders of lower-class origins (which is corroborated by findings reported below dealing with wealth, color and ethnicity, and institutional sector). Thus, among some of the socio-economically disadvantaged sectors of society, democracy is perceived as advancing the welfare of the lower groups and is viewed with favor by the leaders with such backgrounds either because of class interest or because of greater first-hand knowledge of and empathy for the disadvantaged groups. On the other hand, the most highly educated leaders who favored democracy relatively more than the middling educated leaders often seemed inconsistent with their class interest, *as narrowly conceived,* and reflected in their attitudes the enlightenment of a Western humanitarian ideology. They had usually been exposed to the latter during their higher education which, until the establishment of the University College of the West Indies in 1947 in Jamaica, meant an extended stay abroad, most often in the United Kingdom, the United States, or Canada.

Wealth, an important variable in any society, also served to demarcate the West Indian political types. In this study, a person was termed wealthy if he owned a large home with a permanent household staff and had an income of such an amount and nature that he would probably be able to live close to his current standard of living even if he became incapacitated. As reported in Table 4, wealthy leaders were more likely to be authoritarians than the non-wealthy, and less likely to be any of the other three political types.

Dark brown and black leaders were most likely to be democrats and authoritarian idealists, the East Indians and Chinese most likely to be cynical parliamentarians, and light-brown and white-skinned leaders were most likely to be authoritarians. Again low social status is correlated with democratic attitudes.

Because wealth and color are to some extent confounded in the West Indies, it is important to clarify their independent effects on the political types. From a table not shown here: wealth appears more important than color, especially for the authoritarians where nearly all of the total variation is accounted for by wealth and very little is accounted for by color; for the democrats, the variation due to color remains, although it is reduced more than that due to wealth.

The final social characteristic that is presented in Table 4 is the institutional sector in which the leaders exercised their national influence. Although some leaders engaged in several spheres of activity each leader was classified just once according to his primary function.

Democratic attitudes were most frequent among political and labor leaders and "other" (e.g. voluntary organizations' heads, educationists) leaders. All of the authoritarian idealists also were in these same groups. Civil servants were the most likely to be cynical parliamentarians. Authoritarians were most prevalent among economic dominants and religious personages. In general, democrats were characteristically leaders of secular, mass-based organizations that were outgrowths of the modern West Indian awakening. Contrariwise, authoritarianism was most typical of those leaders who represented the established vested interests of West Indian society. Yet, it must be emphasized that the correlates between the institutional sectors and the political types, as with the other social background variables, were not perfect and there were many exceptions to the general pattern.

CAUSES OF THE POLITICAL TYPES

The social distance hypothesis. From this brief presentation of some of the social correlates of the political types among West Indian leaders, we turn to a consideration of the underlying causes of democratic attitudes. Bell formulates three hypotheses from a *post factum* analysis of his data two of which we subject to test here. The first is given below:

Hypothesis 1. Feelings of social distance towards the subordinate socio-economic-racial groups produce cynicism about political democracy.

Converse 1. Feelings of social nearness towards the subordinate socio-economic-racial groups produce idealism about political democracy.

The social correlates presented above, although somewhat confounded by other variables, tend to support this hypothesis and its converse. That is, the most authoritarian leaders were economic dominants, wealthy, and light skinned, those who typically would be the most distant from the masses in West Indian society, and the most democratic leaders tended to be their opposites. The findings that the intermediate educated were more authoritarian than what would appear to be a more socially distant group, the highest educated, seems to be inconsistent with the hypothesis. This apparent exception is partially explained, however, by the fact that wealthy West Indian leaders were more than twice as likely to have only completed secondary school than to have completed college.

The social distance hypothesis can be directly tested by relating views toward social inclusiveness — reduction of racial, religious, or class distinctions between groups within a society — and the political types. As in Chapter Three, leaders who placed highest priority on eliminating internal social barriers were termed "social inclusivists"; conversely, persons who placed secondary emphasis on reducing internal social barriers or who favored the perpetuation of such social distinctions within their societies were designated "social exclusivists." As reported in Table 5, inclusivists compared to exclusivists were much more likely to be democrats, slightly more likely to be cynical parliamentarians, and much less likely to be authoritarians. All of the authoritarian idealists were social inclusivists. Thus, the hypothesis is supported.

Table 5. **POLITICAL TYPES BY A MEASURE OF SOCIAL DISTANCE FROM THE MASSES**

Feelings of Social Distance from the Masses	*Percentages of West Indian Leaders Who Were:*					
	Demo-crats	*Authori-tarian Idealists*	*Cynical Parlia-mentarians*	*Authori-tarians*	*Total*	*Number of Cases*
Social inclusivists (near)	39	15	31	15	100	(46)
Social exclusivists (distant)	9	0	26	65	100	(65)

The effect of social inclusiveness is particularly strong among those leaders who had a high opinion of the competency of the average West Indian voter; 54 per cent of the social inclusivists were political idealists as compared to 9 per cent of the social exclusivists. And it is the measure of democratic beliefs used by Bell in the 1958 survey.[6]

[6] The social distance hypothesis was supported further when another measure of social nearness-distance was used based on the personal life styles of the West Indian leaders, e.g. their tastes concerning entertainment, language, and consumership. *West Indian* life styles (50 cases) were contrasted with the more socially distant Anglo-European life styles (61 cases). Those with West Indian life styles were more than twice as likely to be political idealists than were leaders with Anglo-European life styles.

The powerlessness hypothesis.

Hypothesis 2. Feelings of powerlessness and the sense of losing relative power with respect to public affairs produce cynicism about political democracy.

Converse 2.   Feelings of efficacy and the sense of gaining relative power with respect to public affairs produce idealism about political democracy.

During the transition to nationhood, tutelary democracies based on universal adult suffrage were established in the West Indies, with the tutelary aspects of the systems giving way as independence approached. Formal political power was transferred during this period, passing from the hands of Crown-appointed functionaries and their official and un-official advisers among the economic dominants and other members of the local establishment into the hands of the leaders of the newly-formed mass-based organizations, the political parties and labor unions. Furthermore, the government was increasingly viewed as the instrument to bring about economic and social reforms. Thus, the transition to nationhood was also a transition from oligarchy to democracy and from *laissez-faire* to state intervention in the economy. Under such circumstances, the second hypothesis, stated above, is understandable.

The findings from the 1961—62 interviews with West Indian leaders generally support the hypothesis. Democratic sentiments were highest among the labor and political leaders, while economic dominants were more authoritarian. The greater likelihood of younger leaders being more democratic than older leaders might also be construed as being in accord with the powerlessness hypothesis, since these younger leaders were waxing while some of the older elites were waning.

A more direct measure of feelings of political efficacy was obtained by classifying the West Indian leaders according to the amount of their political activity on the issue of national independence. If a leader engaged in open activity (e.g. pamphleteering, organizational work, speech-making) either *for or against* independence he was classified as high in political activity; all others were low political activists.

As shown in Table 6, West Indian leaders who were politically active were three times more likely to be democrats than were those who were politically passive. All of the authoritarian idealists were political activists. Cynical parliamentarianism was somewhat more characteristic of the political active than the passive elite. Passives in political affairs, on the other hand, were more than twice as likely as actives to be authoritarians.

Simultaneous effects of social distance and powerlessness. Generally, feelings of social distance from the lower socio-economic-racial groups

Table 6.   **POLITICAL TYPES BY A MEASURE OF POLITICAL POWER**

	Percentages of West Indian Leaders Who Were:					
Measure of Political Power	*Demo-crats*	*Authori-tarian Idealists*	*Cynical Parlia-mentarians*	*Authori-tarians*	*Total*	*Number of Cases*
Politically active	31	11	32	26	100	(62)
Politically passive	10	0	22	68	100	(49)

and a sense of losing power in public affairs in the West Indies during the last twenty years varied together and had similar effects on democratic attitudes. But they appear to have some independent effects on attitudes towards political democracy, as is shown in Table 7. For example, the percentage differences in political types between the extremes, using both social distance and powerlessness (politically active inclusivists vs. politically passive exclusivists), are generally higher than comparable differences shown by either variable alone in Tables 5 and 6, the difference in authoritarians among the politically active inclusivists compared to the politically passive exclusivists being the largest shown (66 per cent).

Table 7.   **POLITICAL TYPES BY MEASURES OF SOCIAL DISTANCE AND POLITICAL POWER**

	Percentages of West Indian Leaders Who Were:					
Measures of Social Distance and Political Power	*Demo-crats*	*Authori-tarian Idealists*	*Cynical Parlia-mentarians*	*Authori-tarians*	*Total*	*Number of Cases*
Politically active inclusivists	39	20	33	8	100	(36)
Politically passive inclusivists	40	0	20	40	100	(10)
Politically active exclusivists	19	0	31	50	100	(26)
Politically passive exclusivists	3	0	23	74	100	(39)

Of further interest are the facts that all of the authoritarian idealists are politically active inclusivists and that with respect to the two extreme political types — democrats and authoritarians — social distance accounts for larger differences than does powerlessness.[7]

[7] Unfortunately, no data to test Bell's third hypothesis were collected in the 1961–62 survey. Accounting for the fact that political cynicism regarding political democracy developed not only among elites who opposed the political, economic, and social emergence of the lower classes that accompanied independence, but

A CONSEQUENCE OF THE POLITICAL TYPES

The weight of our knowledge of recent developments in the West Indies, including the data presented here, leads to the conclusion that democratic attitudes were fostered as a result of social nearness to the masses and a sense of political efficacy, the latter in part reflecting the belief that the historical trends were moving toward democracy and reform, as they in fact were in the West Indies.

But the democratic attitudes themselves had further consequences as shown in Chapter Three: they resulted in favorable attitudes toward nationhood and promoted actions to bring about political independence from the United Kingdom. In the biographies of the West Indian leaders, Moskos finds considerable evidence of the time priority of democratic over nationalist attitudes and behaviors. That is, the nationalist leaders were democrats before they were nationalists.[8] From Table 8, note that 79 per cent of the democrats were true nationalists

Table 8. **ATTITUDES TOWARD POLITICAL INDEPENDENCE BY POLITICAL TYPES**

| Political Types | Percentages of West Indian Leaders Who Were: | | | | |
	True Nationalists	Acquiescing Nationalists	Colonialists	Total	Number of Cases
Democrats	79	21	0	100	(24)
Authoritarian idealists	100	0	0	100	(7)
Cynical parliamentarians	42	48	10	100	(31)
Authoritarians	8	16	76	100	(49)

compared to only 8 per cent of the authoritarians; conversely, none of the democrats were colonialists compared to 76 per cent of the authoritarians. Cynical parliamentarians had an intermediate position on the question of political independence with 48 per cent of them being acquiescing nationalists and 42 per cent true nationalists. However, 100 per cent of the authoritarian idealists were true nationalists, again reflecting the overwhelming change-leading proclivities of this group.

The West Indian nationalist movements were organized within the liberal framework, with populist and radical principles being strong

also among some elites who favored, even agitated for, the changes that resulted in such an emergence, it was stated as follows: Among elites who favor progress, intolerance of recalcitrance (on the part of persons whom such progress is supposed to benefit) that is perceived to interfere with progress produces political cynicism.

[8] This is fully documented in another book in this series authored by Moskos, *The Sociology of Political Independence.*

competitors. They were also inspired by democratic ideals, which along with the other Rights of Man, fraternity and especially equality, as Moskos showed in Chapter Three, propelled the nationalist leaders toward independence. Thus, a democratic political system was not simply forced on the West Indians by the departing British, but it was an important part of the nationalist leaders' image of their own independent future.

SUMMARY

In this chapter, we have analyzed attitudes toward political democracy held by leaders with an eye to the implications for the future prospects of democracy. The overall level of democratic — as opposed to authoritarian — beliefs and attitudes was not very high, probably lower than in most Western democracies, although we know from public opinion surveys that attitudes favorable to democracy are far from unanimous even in the most mature democracies. But democratic institutions are now functioning in the West Indies, and attitudes favorable to democracy are most pronounced in Jamaica where modern democratic political institutions have been in force for the longest time. Although interracial hostility seriously blemishes the political scene in British Guiana, the experiences of Trinidad (where East Indians and Negroes also form the dominant groups) and Barbados (where a sizeable white minority exists) are evidence that internecine conflict need not necessarily mar the political development of ethnically plural new states. Furthermore, support for democracy in the West Indian territories is highest where it counts: among political and labor leaders and among the younger leaders. The threat to democracy from the reactionaries is waning, although some reactionaries still harbor hopes to effect their political views, particularly in British Guiana, to the detriment of their country's welfare, and probably of their own personal interest as well. The commitment to democracy of the liberals, radicals, and populists should continue if economic and social progress is maintained. But if progress is impeded, then democracy may be threatened, especially by the radicals who may become politically alienated while nonetheless being politically involved.

So far, the recent history of the new nations of Jamaica, Trinidad, Guyana, and Barbados and the semi-independent states of the Leeward and Windward chain, stands in contradistinction to the undemocratic trends in many of the other new states in the post-colonial era. From this history, one can conclude that the drive toward modernization and development is not necessarily achieved better under authoritarian than under democratic regimes. **In fact, the opposite may be the case.**

Thus, this study calls into question much of the recent social science literature devoted to a functional explanation of *why political democracy must fail* in many of the new states. Such functional analyses may be grossly in error. Also called into question are some recent efforts by social scientists, who, like some of the new nationalist leaders, rationalize patently undemocratic systems by altering the definition of democracy in novel and erroneous ways.[9]

Finally, the results of this chapter reveal a diversity of beliefs and attitudes, a dynamic and changing system, and a problematic future within which the hopes people have and the actions that they take can affect the future in significant ways. The particular kind of political system that a nation has is not simply the result of impersonal or inevitable forces. Instead, it is in some sense "decided upon" by the relevant actors under a given set of circumstances. And this is a decision every new nation faces. The specific political outcomes of the developing societies depend on many things, including importantly the beliefs and attitudes of the new nationalist leaders themselves.

[9] We give an analysis of these two tendencies in recent social science literature in Moskos and Bell, "New Nations and the Ideologies of Social Scientists," unpublished paper read at the annual meetings of the American Sociological Association, Montreal, Canada, 31 August–3 September 1964.

CHAPTER 5 Attitudes Toward Global Alignments

CHARLES C. MOSKOS, JR. AND WENDELL BELL

Another decision of nationhood is: What should the new nation's external affairs be? When this question was raised, the new nations faced an outside world that was global in scale and prominently divided into communist and Western blocs, locked in a worldwide struggle just short of war, and an emergent group of neutral countries whose practical weaknesses were more apparent that their strengths. How the new nations decide to align themselves has obvious implications for the nature and welfare of the international community, including the course of the Cold War itself; and it has implications for the new nations' own internal developments: the direction and tempo of political, economic, and social changes *within* the new nations are being affected, although not always in anticipated ways, by the patterns of communication, the exchanges of personnel, and the flow of aid and loans that have been set in motion by decisions regarding international relations.

Furthermore, what different individuals within the new nations think should be the proper foreign policy for their countries gives us some insight into the nature and strength of the appeals of communism — as they are perceived and judged by the peoples of the new nations. What foreign policies are preferred by persons who have different socioeconomic backgrounds, who vary in political philosophies, and who hold different social values? The answers to such questions also permit us in the West to examine ourselves, our policies, the Cold War, and the worldwide division between rich and poor countries from a fresh perspective. This perspective may be based upon the subjective definitions of the situation held by others, but it is a major thesis of this book that such definitions are consequential for historical action.

In this chapter we ask the question about global alignments. We seek an answer in the attitudes and beliefs of the 112 top leaders interviewed by Moskos in 1961–62; we relate variations in foreign policy attitudes to the social differentiation of leaders; and we explain the attitudes held by different leaders by showing that they are manifestations of basic ideals or values. Although we have not here studied the process of decision-making itself, we view these data primarily as a contribution to the decision-making approach to foreign policy in that we describe and analyze the context of elite attitudes — including attitudes of the decision-makers themselves — within which decisions regarding global alignments are being made and constantly reviewed.[1]

FINDINGS

What should the new nation's global alignments be? West Indian leaders were much more likely to recommend that their new nations align with the Western than with the communist countries, although nearly one-fifth preferred neutrality. They were asked: "When (Jamaica)* becomes fully independent, with which group should (Jamaica) align itself, the Western nations, the communist countries, or the neutralist countries?"

Western Nations	77%
Neutralist countries	19
Communist countries	4
Total	100%
Number of cases	(112)

There is some evidence to suggest that between 1958 and 1962 there was a slight shift of opinion away from the West, although neither the data nor the sample of leaders are strictly comparable. In 1958 Bell's questionnaire survey of Jamaican leaders showed that 83 per cent thought the United States had been morally right more often than the Soviet Union as an actor on the world scene compared to 16 per cent who thought both were about the same and only one per cent who said the Soviet Union was more often right than the United States.[2] These figures can be compared to the results among the Jamaican leaders in the present study: 70 per cent preferred alignment with the West, 25 per cent preferred neutrality, and 5 per cent preferred alignment with the East.

---

* The name of the territory appropriate to each respondent was inserted.

[1] For a discussion of the decision-making approach to foreign policy, see Richard C. Snyder, H. W. Bruck, and Burton Sapin (editors) *Foreign Policy Decision-Making*, New York: The Free Press of Glencoe, 1962.

[2] Wendell Bell, "Images of the United States and the Soviet Union Held by Jamaican Elite Groups," *World Politics*, 12 (January, 1960), pp. 225–248; also see Bell, *Jamaican Leaders: Political Attitudes in a New Nation*, Berkeley and Los Angeles: University of California Press, 1964.

Who is winning the Cold War? In spite of the overwhelming preferences of the top leaders in the West Indies for alignment with the
West, many leaders had grave doubts about the ability of the United
States to cope with the Soviet challenge. When asked, "Which do you
think is winning the Cold War, the Soviet Union or the United States?",
the leaders responded:

United States	34%
Neither	25
Soviet Union	41
Total	100%
Number of cases	(112)

Again a rough comparison with the 1958 Jamaican data is possible.
If one can rely on the approximate comparability of the data, Jamaican
leaders were somewhat less pessimistic about the efficacy of the United
States in 1962 than in 1958. Fifty-six per cent of the Jamaican leaders
in 1958 thought that the Soviet Union was more effective in winning
over to its point of view the people living in the so-called underdeveloped countries of the world, 20 per cent said both were about the
same, and 24 per cent said the United States was more effective in this
way. In 1962, 46 per cent of the Jamaican leaders said the Soviet Union
was winning the Cold War, 17 per cent said neither, and 37 per cent
said the United States was winning.

Similar patterns of responses can be noted for both the 1962 West
Indian data and the 1958 Jamaican data: high levels of preferences for
the United States and the West on the one hand and considerable appre-

Table 1.   **ATTITUDES TOWARD GLOBAL ALIGNMENT BY BELIEFS ABOUT
WHO IS WINNING THE COLD WAR**

The new nation should align itself with:	*Which do you think is winning the Cold War?*		
	United States (per cent)	*Neither (per cent)*	*Soviet Union (per cent)*
Western nations	95	71	65
Neutralist countries	5	29	24
Communist countries	0	0	11
Total	100	100	100
Number of cases	(38)	(28)	(46)

ciation or fear of Soviet effectiveness on the other. The correlation
between these two variables, shown by comparing the percentages in
Table 1, reveals that leaders who believed that the United States was
winning the Cold War were more likely to desire alignment with the

Western nations than were those who believed that the Soviet Union was winning, with those who thought neither was winning having an intermediate position. But this correlation leaves considerable unexplained variance in attitudes toward global alignments. Thus, the desire to be on the "winning side" appears to explain relatively little of the variation in foreign policy preferences.

Effects of territory. Anyone familiar with the turbulent political developments that have occurred in British Guiana will find no surprise in the fact that British Guianese leaders least favored alignment with the West when compared to the other West Indian leaders (see Table 2). Furthermore, from data not shown here, 77 per cent of them believed that the Soviet Union was winning the Cold War, a larger percentage than in any other territory.

Each of the three political parties in Guyana advocates a somewhat different foreign policy. The PPP definitely sees Guyana's fortunes lying with the communist bloc. Under its sponsorship (when it was in power before independence), trade missions from Eastern Europe and geological survey teams from the Soviet Union came to the country. During an anti-Jagan strike in the spring of 1963, the PPP government called upon personnel from Communist Cuba to staff the local airline. The United Force stands in complete opposition to the foreign policy

Table 2. **ATTITUDES TOWARD GLOBAL ALIGNMENT BY TERRITORY**

	The new nation should align itself with:				
Territory	*Western Nations (per cent)*	*Neutralist Countries (per cent)*	*Communist Countries (per cent)*	*Total (per cent)*	*Number of Cases*
Jamaica	71	25	4	100	(24)
Trinidad	77	23	0	100	(22)
British Guiana	46	23	31	100	(13)
Barbados	86	14	0	100	(21)
Grenada	88	12	0	100	(17)
Dominica	87	13	0	100	(15)

of the PPP and is resolutely in the Western camp; the PNC, now sharing power with the United Force, takes a middle path between these two extremes and advocates a policy of non-alignment, considering itself to be in the mainstream of Asian-African neutralism.

Except for one leader in Jamaica, no West Indian leaders in any of the territories other than British Guiana favored alignment with communist countries. Although the most striking finding in Table 2 is the difference between British Guiana and the other territories, another difference, although relatively small in percentage terms, is worth noting. The top leaders of Jamaica and Trinidad were slightly less likely to favor alignment with the West, and slightly more likely to favor alignment with the neutralist countries, when compared to the top leaders from the three smaller islands. This finding reflects a very real difference in elite opinion in the different territories.

Since independence, Jamaica has followed a pro-Western foreign policy for the most part. Indeed, minutes after his election victory in 1962, Bustamante was on the air offering Jamaican territory to the United States as a military base. Although the offer has not been taken up, Jamaica has signed a military aid pact with the United States for a small air and sea defense force. Jamaica's voting record in the United Nations shows generally a pro-Western pattern, although on questions involving colonialism it goes with the neutralist countries. But the opposition PNP and other elements have criticized the foreign policy that Bustamante has established as being too unreserved in its Western alignment, and there has been considerable support in the Jamaican Senate, from members of both political parties, in favor of Jamaica's alignment with the international policies of the African nations. The latter action was viewed by some, if carried out, as an expression of the "fight for man's equality throughout the world" and a reflection of the fact that 95 per cent of the Jamaican people are of African descent.[3]

Trinidad's record in the U.N. is similar to that of Jamaica's, although somewhat closer to the neutralist countries and strongly anti-colonialist. Also, Trinidad abstained from the vote on the admission of Communist China, while Jamaica voted against seating the Peking regime. Nonetheless, Trinidad too is more attracted to the Western than to the communist camp, although Dr. Eric Williams, being critical of some Western actions, was initially less outspoken in his pro-Western attitudes than Bustamante of Jamaica.

The single most important issue in Trinidad's formulation of a foreign policy was a carry-over from the colonial past: the existence of an American naval base on the island at Chaguaramas. The base was obtained by the United States from the United Kingdom during World War II in exchange for lend-lease. Williams has insisted that the status of Chaguaramas be renegotiated with now-sovereign Trinidad. Currently, the dispute has subsided due to an agreement between the United States and Trinidad to reopen the entire Chaguaramas question at a later date (which established U. S. recognition of Trinidad's right to negotiate the issue) and for Trinidad in the meantime to receive U. S. aid (which has become the subject of further differences of

[3] *The Jamaican Weekly Gleaner*, Friday, June 28, 1963, pp. 3–4.

opinion and negotiation). Like Jamaica, Trinidad remains part of the British Commonwealth and avidly seeks the investment of Western capital.[4]

In many ways, the political development of the smaller islands seems to resemble that of the larger territories a decade or so ago, and their commitment to the West is quite strong (see Table 2). There are emotional ties to the "mother country" of England and little hostility toward the imperial power. Some leaders in the Leewards and Windwards, as pointed out earlier, favor a "Puerto Rico-like arrangement" with the United Kingdom.

Effects of social characteristics of leaders. Attitudes toward global alignments by selected social characteristics of the top West Indian leaders are given in Table 3. The oldest leaders were most likely, and the youngest leaders least likely, to prefer alignment with the West. College graduates were somewhat less likely to support alignment with the West than leaders with less education; wealthy leaders tended to prefer the West more frequently than leaders who were not wealthy. Alignment with the West was favored by the economic dominants, but less so by political and labor leaders. The elites falling into other occupational categories (such as civil servants, mass media personages, and clergymen) were highly in favor of Western alignment. However, leaders classified as "other" (heads of voluntary organizations, free professionals, and educationists) were least in favor of a Western alignment. It is noteworthy that the elites with mass followings, the political and labor leaders, were among the least favorable to alignment with the West. With respect to color and ethnicity, Table 3 shows that dark brown or black leaders were least favorable to the idea of Western alignment, closely followed in their views by the East Indians. The light brown and white leaders were more favorable to Western alignment than the East Indians or darker-skinned persons, and each of the three Chinese leaders favored the Western nations.[5]

Effects of economic ideologies. More highly correlated with attitudes toward global alignments than the above social characteristics were the economic ideologies of the national leaders.

Among West Indian leaders, the more Right the economic ideologies,

---

[4] A detailed discussion of some aspects of Trinidad's foreign policy is given by Ivar Oxaal in *Black Intellectuals Come to Power: The Rise of Creole Nationalism in Trinidad & Tobago,* which will be published in this series.

[5] Although we ran partials on combinations of wealth, education, and color and ethnicity, we can add little more than to say that the relationships shown in Table 3 tend to remain. The small number of cases and the complete absence of cases in some cells make any further specification risky.

Table 3. ATTITUDES TOWARD GLOBAL ALIGNMENTS BY SELECTED SOCIAL CHARACTERISTICS

Selected Social Characteristics	*The new nation should align itself with:*				
	Western Nations (per cent)	*Neutralist Countries (per cent)*	*Communist Countries (per cent)*	*Total (per cent)*	*Number of Cases*
Age					
60 and over	96	4	0	100	(24)
50 to 59	89	11	0	100	(36)
40 to 49	60	29	11	100	(35)
39 and under	59	35	6	100	(17)
Education					
College or higher	68	27	5	100	(37)
Secondary school	82	14	4	100	(57)
Elementary only	78	17	5	100	(18)
Personal Wealth					
Wealthy	90	8	2	100	(39)
Not wealthy	70	25	5	100	(73)
Color and Ethnicity					
White	87	8	5	100	(39)
Light brown	85	15	0	100	(20)
East Indian	67	22	11	100	(9)
Chinese	100	0	0	100	(3)
Dark brown and black	63	32	5	100	(41)
Institutional Sector					
Political or labor	56	33	11	100	(48)
Economic	97	3	0	100	(34)
Mass media	87	13	0	100	(8)
Civil service	100	0	0	100	(8)
Religious or ethnic	100	0	0	100	(7)
Other	43	57	0	100	(7)

the more likely alignment with the West was preferred (see Table 4). All of the reactionaries and conservatives were supporters of the West. Among the populists, as well, nearly all, 91 per cent, favored the West. Even among the liberals, neutralist sentiments were held by only 20 per cent, the large majority of liberals, 80 per cent, advocating Western alignment. Looking at the responses of the radicals, however, one finds by far the largest percentage, 71, preferred a policy of neutralism. Also, the percentage of radicals favoring a policy of association with the communist countries, 24 per cent, exceeds the five per cent supporting Western alignment.

It is clear from these relationships that those leaders who opposed change or who desired relatively little change in the local economic order, *an order pervaded by great maldistribution of wealth and welfare*, were the staunchest supporters of Western alignment. But

Table 4. ATTITUDES TOWARD GLOBAL ALIGNMENTS BY ECONOMIC IDEOLOGIES

Economic Ideologies	*The new nation should align itself with:*				
	Western Nations (per cent)	Neutralist Countries (per cent)	Communist Countries (per cent)	Total (per cent)	Number of Cases
Reactionaries	100	0	0	100	(22)
Conservatives	100	0	0	100	(33)
Populists	91	9	0	100	(11)
Liberals	80	20	0	100	(25)
Radicals	5	71	24	100	(21)

we think it important to stress that, although all those desiring alignment with the communist camp had radical economic ideologies, the large majority of radicals, nonetheless, favored neither the East nor the West.

The effects of attitudes toward independence. As was shown in Chapter Three, there was considerable disagreement among West Indian elites concerning the desirability of political independence, and such disagreement reflected basic cleavages in the society which, even after independence, represent some of the major conflicts in the struggle of different groups to control the future of the nations. From an analysis of the leaders' attitudes and behavior regarding political independence, Moskos identified three basic types: *colonialists, acquiescing nationalists,* and *true nationalists.*

Table 5 shows attitudes toward global alignments by these types. One hundred per cent of both the colonialists and the acquiescing

Table 5. ATTITUDES TOWARD GLOBAL ALIGNMENTS BY ATTITUDES AND BEHAVIOR TOWARD POLITICAL INDEPENDENCE

Attitude and Behavior Toward Political Independence	*The new nation should align itself with:*				
	Western Nations (per cent)	Neutralist Countries (per cent)	Communist Countries (per cent)	Total (per cent)	Number of Cases
True nationalists	41	48	11	100	(44)
Acquiescing nationalists	100	0	0	100	(28)
Colonialists	100	0	0	100	(40)

nationalists preferred alignment with the Western nations compared to 41 per cent of the true nationalists. Forty-eight per cent of the true nationalists preferred a neutralist role, and eleven per cent preferred alignment with the communist countries. Thus, the desire for nationhood and for the elimination of political domination by the

United Kingdom was related to the preference for a foreign policy based upon neutralism. Some of the basic values explaining this co-variation are discussed below.

The effects of enlightenment. In this section, we examine the relationship between West Indian leaders' foreign policy preferences and their ideas about what constitutes the "Good Society." We ask "What are the leaders' basic ideals as these are expressed in their images of the future of their societies?" and "How are these ideals for the future of their own societies related to their preferences regarding foreign policy?"

We use as a point of reference the Index of Enlightenment composed of measures of attitudes toward democracy, equality, and social inclusivism reported in Chapter Three. A maximum score of three on the Index of Enlightenment was possible only if a leader was a democrat, an egalitarian, and an inclusivist, and a minimum score of zero would result only if a leader was a non-democrat, inegalitarian, and exclusivist.

The relationship between the Index of Enlightenment and attitudes toward global alignments is presented in Table 6. It may come as a surprise to the casual reader from the Western democracies, if not to the student of the politics of new nations, to see that the enlightened West Indian leaders were much less likely to favor alignment with the West than the unenlightened leaders. In fact, 100 per cent of the most unenlightened leaders preferred a Western alignment compared to only 50 per cent of the most enlightened leaders. *The West Indian leaders most committed to Western ideals and values were least likely to favor alignment with the Western nations!*

Table 6. ATTITUDES TOWARD GLOBAL ALIGNMENTS BY THE INDEX OF ENLIGHTENMENT

| Index of Enlightenment | The new nation should align itself with: | | | | Number of Cases |
	Western Nations (per cent)	Neutralist Countries (per cent)	Communist Countries (per cent)	Total (per cent)	
3 (enlightened)	50	43	7	100	(30)
2	41	47	12	100	(17)
1	96	0	4	100	(24)
0 (unenlightened)	100	0	0	100	(41)

From Table 7, where foreign policy attitudes are given by each of the attitudes toward the Rights of Man separately, note that attitudes toward equality and toward social inclusiveness are considerably more highly related to variations in foreign policy preferences than are attitudes toward political democracy. Nonetheless, even though 73 per cent of the democrats preferred alignment with the West, still more, 80 per cent, of the non-democrats did so.

But this latter fact is a consequence of the intercorrelations between attitudes toward democracy, egalitarianism, and inclusiveness. From tables not shown here, the democrats, when comparing just egalitarians and controlling for inclusiveness, were considerably more favorable toward alignment with the West than were the non-democrats. Among the inegalitarians, however, since 100 per cent of them preferred alignment with the West, there was no difference between the democrats and non-democrats. Thus, variation in foreign policy attitudes due to independent variation in attitudes toward political democracy, when egalitarianism and inclusiveness are controlled, shows the democrats more inclined to the West than the non-democrats, reversing the original relationship shown in Table 7. Inclusiveness and egalitarianism with each of the other variables simultaneously controlled, retain the direction of their original relationships with preferences for global alignments, egalitarianism showing by far the stronger relationship of the two.

Table 7. **ATTITUDES TOWARD GLOBAL ALIGNMENTS BY THREE ATTITUDES TOWARD THE RIGHTS OF MAN**

| Attitudes Toward the Rights of Man | The new nation should align itself with: | | | | |
	Western Nations (per cent)	*Neutralist Countries (per cent)*	*Communist Countries (per cent)*	*Total (per cent)*	*Number of Cases*
Political democracy (liberty)					
Democrats	73	23	4	100	(56)
Non-democrats	80	14	6	100	(56)
Equality					
Egalitarians	41	48	11	100	(44)
Inegalitarians	100	0	0	100	(68)
Social inclusiveness (fraternity)					
Inclusivists	48	44	8	100	(48)
Exclusivists	98	0	2	100	(64)

Two facts help to explain these findings. The first involves the interrelationships between enlightenment, attitudes toward political independence, and foreign policy preferences. The nationalists among the West Indian elites were committed to the ideas of self-determination for their territories and of freedom from the political domination of the United Kingdom. Such commitments carried over into their foreign policy attitudes and led them to prefer the more "independent" posture of neutralism rather than following along after the United States, the United Kingdom, and the other nations of the West, or for that matter after the nations of the communist bloc either. To them, neutralism involved the least dilution of their countries' newly achieved or soon hoped-for national sovereignty. At the same time, nationalists' hopes and ambitions were in fact inspired by Western ideals, by the commitment to the Rights of Man — especially by the desire for equality.

At the other extreme, the colonialists among the West Indian elites were non-democrats, inegalitarians, and social exclusivists. The same combination of factors which produced their anti-independence attitudes also produced their 100 per cent preference for Western alignment. Their fear of what the nationalists would do in the years after independence and their hope for policies which would not undermine their generally well-established socioeconomic positions in the society were linked to their desire for Western alignment, their opposition to nationalist movements, and their preferences for the conservative or reactionary versions of the Western models of polity, economy, and society. They opposed progressive change, they represented the status-quo, and they found the basic values of Western Civilization, as expressed in the three Rights-of-Man variables we have selected, abominations. According to them, such "abominations" characterized the communist countries to a much greater extent than the Western nations.

A second fact that helps to explain these findings involves the positive appeal of the communist model, or at least some aspects of it. Among the forty-four nationalists, there were ten who were non-democrats. These leaders were egalitarians and social inclusivists; they were change-leaders dedicated to economic development, distributional and social reforms, and the welfare of the West Indian peoples. But they believed that the changes necessary for the significant betterment of the lives of the mass of West Indians could not take place under a democratic political system. They believed that some kind of a dictatorship was needed to create the singleness of purpose, the social mobilization, and the large-scale planning necessary to develop and transform their societies into modernity.[6] Eight of these leaders preferred a neutral role for their new nations, two preferred alignment with the communist countries, none wanted their countries to align with the West.

---

[6] Although this belief is widely shared by many leaders in various new nations and by many intellectuals, both in the West and in the East, it should not go unchallenged. As logical and rational as it may appear to some, it may be — probably is — incorrect. If so, the West Indian people may find themselves, if this false view were to dominate future political changes, without many of the civil and political rights which they now enjoy and no closer to the achievement of their hopes for economic and social progress.

SUMMARY

We have analyzed attitudes toward one of the decisions of nation-hood, "What should the new nation's global alignments be?" Such elite attitudes constitute the context within which the foreign policies of these emergent nations are being formulated and reviewed by new national elites, as they face the outside world on their own for the first time. We have described these attitudes, related them to the social differentiation of elites, and tried to explain them by showing how they are manifestations of basic values or ideals.

We have not stressed the theoretical implications of our findings, but we see two relevant lines of theoretical development which we can but briefly suggest in conclusion. The first represents at least a partial, although modest, answer to a recent accusation of Barrington Moore, Jr., who has said:

> For quite some time there has been a concerted effort to bar the terms 'progressive' and 'reactionary' from any discussion of human affairs that claimed to be objective or scientific. In the academic disciplines of political science, sociology, and history the attempt has enjoyed a large measure of success. . . . The main argument against their use is that the terms carry with them ethical and factually incorrect judgments to the effect that the course of history has been, in general, an advance toward greater freedom of the individual.[7]

Throughout this book, as in this chapter, we freely use such terms as "reactionary, liberal, and radical," "progress," "the Good Society," "images of the future," "Enlightenment values," "Western ideals," "social reform," "freedom," "the Rights of Man," and "liberty, equality, and fraternity." Yet we have done so while trying to meet the standards of modern social research. Our purposes are to help bridge the gap between empirical techniques and the great philosophical and moral traditions and to probe the latter for theoretical insights.

Secondly, the "theory" that has resulted, and that is briefly sketched in this book does not have quite the same features as that which is currently regarded in sociological circles as theory, but it does embrace an image of society and a theory of progress. It is not uncongenial to empirical research. Far from it, the theory seems to offer that happy circumstance where social significance, personal values, and scientific rigor can coalesce in the same approach.

This chapter illustrates the general proposition linking values, dynamics, and problematics. We have shown how certain fundamental

---

[7] "On the Notions of Progress, Revolution, and Freedom," *Ethics*, 72 (January, 1962), p. 106.

values, identified as the Rights of Man of the Age of the Enlightenment, held by new nationalist leaders result in particular foreign policy preferences. Social reality — in this case foreign policy — is viewed as changing and problematic, as in the process of *becoming*. But what it is becoming is to some extent uncertain. It depends on what men do, and what they do reflects in part men's purposes and hopes, their images of the future as defined by the values and beliefs that they hold.

Finally, it is with some diffidence that we ponder the possible implications of these findings for the policies of the Western democracies toward the new nations. We are too well aware of the fact that the most difficult decisions in formulating such policies are often day-to-day exigencies rather than long-term ideals or objectives. Yet there are times when the most practical, effective, and expedient thing to do is that which is guided by basic values and ideals. We are inclined to think that on this issue such a time has come.

From our data, we know that many of the pro-Western leaders in the West Indies were truly enemies of the West (and of the East) in the sense that they were deeply opposed to basic Western values (and to some extent — omitting liberty from the trilogy — communist values too if we grant the obvious truth that the Marxist idea of progress is also a variant of Western Enlightenment values). Pro-Western leaders opposed liberty, equality, and fraternity. Conversely, many of the leaders who supported neutralist foreign policies — even some who wished communist alignment — were among the best friends of the Western democracies in that they were deeply committed to the Rights of Man.

Problems of national defense and of deterrence, of containing the spread of communism, and of protecting and promoting American interests abroad are real enough, but the fixation on them has resulted in giving Americans a badly distorted image of what is going on in the world and has frequently made a mockery of American efforts to promote genuine political, economic, and social progress in the depressed areas of the world.

For the emerging nations, the option is less and less a choice between the communist or Western alternatives. Rather we are witnessing the formation of a sense of common cause among the world's poor nations (and here we include many older independent nations as well) resulting from the growing gap between the poor three-quarters of humanity and the relatively rich peoples of the industrially-advanced nations, a gap which is widening within *both* the communist and the non-communist world.

In the United States, as in the other Western democracies, there exists the danger of viewing the ascendancy of the higher ideals of

Western Civilization in the emerging nations as threats to national security and international order. These ideals have driven the new national movements, have shaped the modern images of the future, and have led some of the new national elites to prefer neutralism to Western alignment. Through failure to translate their own revolutionary values into global policy, Americans find themselves in the ironic position of looking with alarm at the foreign policies that result from the implementation of the Rights of Man by change-leaders in other societies. Yet these rights are inherently part of the Western tradition and they are now becoming the heritage of all humankind.

CHAPTER 6 Attitudes Toward Equality

CHARLES C. MOSKOS, JR. AND WENDELL BELL

The democratic revolution, as we use the term in the broad sense to describe the spread of certain ideas about the Good Society and the extension of certain political and social movements from eighteenth-century Western Europe into the twentieth-century world society, connotes much more than simply a desire for representative government and public liberties. The formation of republics and democracies, of representative systems, and of guarantees for the establishment and maintenance of equal civil and political rights was a chief aim to be sure, but most especially is a commitment to a more general ideal of equality. The latter encompasses the notion of an enlarged and redefined society into which more and more persons within any given territory would be brought until at the extreme every adult would be included as a member on the same basis of equality as everyone else. For example, in the newly formed United States not everyone was at first included: Amer-Indians and Negroes were excluded from many of the new rights that independence had won for "fullfledged" American citizens. But the concept of equality, through expansion of its generally agreed upon criteria of application, has been providing a larger and larger umbrella to cover more and more persons and groups within the United States as it has in other older nations as well. The enlarged and now nearly universal conception of equality is what has been generally applied by new nationalist leaders to the emergent citizenries during their transition to nationhood since World War II. The usual exception, of course, is that representatives of the imperial power who may be living within the boundaries of the nascent nations are usually defined out of the new national polities since such persons are citizens of another nation, although in some cases even they have had an opportunity to opt for citizenship in the emergent country.

Furthermore, the concept of equality has been widening not only in that it has increasingly been presumed to apply to more and more individuals and groups within given populations, but also it has been broadened to include as relevant more and more different social situations and institutional settings. Thus, to the desire for civil and political freedom that dominated the older independence movements have been added with new emphasis and meaning in the twentieth century the rights to economic, social and cultural equality as well, and not just within nations but between nations too. Different priorities placed upon the various goals of increasing minimums of civil, political, economic, social, or cultural rights; different perceptions as to the achievement of which of the rights constitutes the main and immediate challenge to the change leaders; disagreement over how fast it is practical to demand change; what consequences for rapid change are acceptable; and what compromises should be made to keep the ship of progress from being scuttled are among the factors that help produce some of the ambiguities mentioned by Ivar Oxaal in Chapter Two.

After our years of research in the emergent nations of the British Caribbean, we are convinced that, of all the Enlightenment values, equality is the key element in the images of the future that are shaping the new nations. We generalize: "Within the conditions characteristic of colonial political, economic, social and cultural settings, if a person holds egalitarian attitudes then he will desire political independence." There are, of course, some obvious exceptions. At least, the converse does not hold for white South African and white Rhodesian nationalism, based as they are on sectional interests and socially exclusive principles. But for the vast majority of the new nations of the twentieth century, it is our conclusion that it holds, as it does also, we believe, for most of the nations formed in the eighteenth century (where domination of some classes over others often provided conditions similar to the colonial subordination) and in the nineteenth century as well.

Furthermore, it is our conclusion that attitudes toward equality not only constitute an important part of the ideology that has given rise to nationalist movements, but also they significantly influence the value premises of decision-making after the nationalist leaders come to power. In fact, such attitudes constitute the value context most relevant to the answers given by new national leaders to the question: What type of social structure should the new nation have? Some of the data on which our conclusions are based are presented in this chapter.

Here we first describe and analyze attitudes toward equality held by the 112 top West Indian leaders interviewed by Moskos on the eve of political independence in 1961–62. The analysis of these data is of practical significance by revealing some of the sources of support or opposition to the spread of equality; and it is of theoretical significance by showing the ways in which the distribution of attitudes toward equality are related systematically to the social differentiation of West Indian leaders.

Second, and most importantly, we examine the relationship between egalitarian attitudes and political, economic, social and cultural development. We ask, what are the implications of attitudes toward equality for images of the future? What are the implications for the emergent polity, economy, society and culture that West Indian leaders are in the process of creating? The answers to these questions permit us to make some further observations on the meaning and character of these emergent Caribbean nations, and by cautious generalization perhaps on the future prospects of some other new states as well.

AN INDICATOR OF EGALITARIAN ATTITUDES

A classic and succinct definition of the philosophy of egalitarianism, that is generally reflected in the attitudes of West Indian leaders, has been given by R. H. Tawney:[1]

> It is to hold that while (man's) natural endowments differ profoundly, it is the mark of a civilized society to aim at eliminating such inequalities as have their source, not in individual difference, but in its own organization, and that individual differences, which are a source of social energy, are more likely to ripen and find expression if social inequalities as far as practicable, are diminished.

The measurement of egalitarian attitudes among the West Indian leaders was based on their responses to an open-ended question. As described in Chapter Three, immediately prior to the item in the interview dealing with egalitarian attitudes, the respondent was asked what he considered the best form of government for his territory. Persons who favored political democracy were asked what they considered the essence of democracy. Persons who did not favor political democracy were asked what they considered the best alternative form of government. In either case, if features such as equality of opportunity, the classless society, or related notions were mentioned, the leaders were called "egalitarians." This is a rather stringent test with the egalitarians being highly egalitarian and the remainder including both highly and mildly inegalitarian attitudes. Thirty-nine per cent of the 112 interviewed West Indian leaders were classified as egalitarian, the remaining 61 per cent, those who did not explicitly affirm egalitarianism as part and parcel of their social ideology, being termed "inegalitarians."

DIFFERENCES BY TERRITORY

The percentage distribution of egalitarian attitudes among the West Indian leaders, as shown below, differed between the territories.

[1] R. H. Tawney, *Equality*, London: George Allen and Unwin, Ltd., 1962, p. 49.

·Territory	Per Cent Egalitarian	Number of Cases on Which Per Cent Is Based
British Guiana	55	(13)
Jamaica	50	(24)
Trinidad	41	(22)
Barbados, Dominica, and Granada	32	(53)

The percentage of egalitarian leaders was highest in British Guiana where in 1950, as will be recalled, a left-wing nationalist movement was formed that has since split into the two current dominant political parties: the Communist-influenced People's Progressive Party and the socialist People's National Congress. In Jamaica, where egalitarian attitudes characterized half of the leaders, it will be remembered that a viable two-party system has been operating since 1944.[2] Political mobilization in Trinidad did not gain real momentum until the formation of the People's National Movement in 1956. The level of political mobilization in the smaller islands, where the lowest percentage of leaders were egalitarians, seems to resemble that of the larger territories a decade or so ago. Only in Barbados have the local political parties advanced beyond being personal vehicles.

As before, the data from the different territories are lumped together in the remainder of the analysis.

ELITE DIFFERENTIATION AND EGALITARIAN ATTITUDES

Obviously, some elites are more strategically placed than others to voice and represent economic and social interests and some are more strategically placed than others to make and execute policies designed to bring about economic and social change. Also, the location of structural support for, or against, the spread of equality is of theoretical interest.

[2] As a point of reference, we note that in a 1958 survey of Jamaican elites conducted by Wendell Bell, over 70 per cent of the respondents were "pro-equalitarian," dividing his scale at the midpoint. This is considerably higher than the 50 per cent of the Jamaican leaders in this study having egalitarian attitudes. See Bell, *Jamaican Leaders: Political Attitudes in a New Nation*, Berkeley and Los Angeles: University of California Press, 1964, Chapter IV, "What Kind of a Social Structure Should Jamaica Have?" Bell's earlier study and this one, however, are not strictly comparable. He included middle ranks of leadership as well as upper, while the present study is confined to the top leaders. There are also differences in the measures used and in procedures of collecting data, e.g., a 7-item Index of Egalitarianism vs. an open-ended question, mail questionnaires vs. personal interviews. Undoubtedly, the more than 20 per cent difference in the two studies is mostly due, if such comparison is valid, to the fact that a more stringent test of egalitarianism was used in the later study where the leaders had to "volunteer" their egalitarianism.

Table 1 shows the percentage of West Indian leaders who were egalitarians by selected social characteristics. Starting with the first characteristic given, one can see that egalitarianism decreases with age. Young leaders are more than five times as likely to have egalitarian attitudes than the oldest group of leaders, with the middle-age groups falling in between. Perhaps, this merely reflects the increasing "conservatism" that develops with increasing age, or perhaps new and more liberal generations are being added to the age distribution at the bottom, each generation retaining certain characteristic habits of belief and attitude throughout its life. In any event, this correlation between age and egalitarianism may augur well for the continued spread of equality, since new younger leaders have been entering the scene.

Table 1.   PERCENTAGE OF WEST INDIAN LEADERS WHO ARE EGALITARIANS BY SELECTED SOCIAL CHARACTERISTICS

Selected Social Characteristics	Per Cent Who Are Egalitarians	Number of Cases on Which Per Cent Is Based
Age		
60 and over	12	(24)
50 to 59	30	(36)
40 to 49	54	(35)
39 and under	65	(17)
Education		
College or higher	49	(37)
Secondary school	30	(57)
Elementary only	50	(18)
Personal Wealth		
Wealthy	13	(39)
Not wealthy	53	(73)
Color and Ethnicity		
White	18	(39)
Light brown	30	(20)
East Indian and Chinese	25	(12)
Dark brown and black	68	(41)
Institutional Sector		
Political or labor	69	(48)
Economic	6	(34)
Mass media	25	(8)
Civil service	37	(8)
Religious or ethnic	0	(7)
Other	57	(7)

Looking at the relationship between attitudes toward equality and amount of formal education, we find egalitarian sentiments most typical of the highest and lowest levels. Leaders with intermediate education levels were the least likely to be egalitarian. The same two factors may account for this "U" shaped distribution as accounted

Members of the Jamaica Regiment. *Courtesy of the Jamaican Information Service.*

Then Prime Minister of the West Indies Federation, Sir Grantley Adams (left), arrives in Florida for a tour of the U.S. Air Force Missile Test Center in August 1961. He is greeted by U.S. Air Force Brigadier General Harry J. Sands, Jr. (center) and Group Captain L. D. Dadswell, Royal Air Force Assistant to General Sands. *Cortesy of Newday.*

Members of the Jamaica Regiment. *Gleaner Photo*

A parade at the Police Training School in Jamacia. *Gleaner photo.*

Mr. Errol Barrow, Premier of Barbados, addressing the opening session of the Conference of Heads of Government of Commonwealth Caribbean Countries in Jamaica in January 1964. *Courtesy of the Jamaican Information Service.*

The Prime Ministers or their Deputies of the 15 member countries of the British Commonwealth—Britain, Canada, Australia, New Zealand, India, Pakistan, Ceylon, Ghana, Malaya, Nigeria, Cyprus, Sierra Leone, Tanganyika, Jamaica, and Trinidad and Tobago—attend the opening session of their conference in Marlborough House, London, in September 1962. *Courtesy of Jamaican Information Service; British Information Services photo.*

The Prime Minister of Trinidad and Tobago, Dr. Eric
Williams, chats with President Nasser of the United Arab
Republic in the Presidential palace in Cairo during No-
vember 1962. *Courtesy of the Trinidad Guardian.*

Emergent Jamaica begins foreign affairs. Former Premier of
Jamaica, Norman Washington Manley, visits the late U. S. Presi-
dent John F. Kennedy. *Courtesy of the Jamaican Information
Service; from Wide World Photos.*

A new Science Block of the Morant Bay High School in Jamaica which was built partly with Government funds and partly with contributions from the Methodist Church. *Courtesy of the Jamaican Information Service.*

A new primary school at Port Antonio, Jamaica. *Courtesy of the Jamaican Information Service.*

Aerial view of the campus of the University of the West Indies at Mona, Jamaica. Science buildings in left foreground; teaching hospital in left background. Library, administrative buildings in center; halls of residence to the right and behind the circle. The University has two other branches, one in St. Augustine, Trinidad, and the other in Bridgetown, Barbados. Guyana has its own separate institution, The University of Guyana, in Georgetown. *Photo by Amador Packer.*

U. Thant, the Secretary General of the United
Nations, on a visit to Jamaica pauses to talk with
a laboratory technician at the University of the
West Indies. *Gleaner photo.*

Students at the University of the West Indies in Mona,
Jamaica. *Courtesy of the Jamaica Tourist Board.*

A worker in the Central Cotton Ginnery in Antigua. *Courtesy of the Trinidad Guardian.*

Stowing bananas in railway cars in Jamaica. *Courtesy of Jamaica Banana Board.*

Inter-island trade is conducted by sailing boats such as these unloading in Port of Spain, Trinidad. *Photo by Paul Rupp Associates.*

An oil worker in Trinidad. *Photo by Paul Rupp Associates.*

Bauxite mining operations near Ewarton in Jamaica.
Courtesy of the Jamaica Tourist Board.

Bauxite is processed into alumina at the Ewarton works of Alumina Jamaica Ltd. *Courtesy of the Jamaica Industrial Development Corporation.*

Loading bauxite at Ocho Rios on Jamaica's north coast. *Courtesy of the Jamaica Tourist Board.*

A fishing fleet in Bathsheba, Barbados. *Photo by W. E. Alleyne.*

Sand, sea, and sun make tourism a major industry in much of the West Indies. *Courtesy of the Jamaica Tourist Board.*

Sunbathing, swimming, waterskiing, and sailing on Jamaica's north coast. *Courtesy of the Jamaica Tourist Board.*

Rice Cultivation is a major food source and provides supplemental income for East Indians in Trinidad's sugar belt. *Photo by Noel P. Norton, Trinidad Photographers Ltd.*

for the similar relationships between age and democratic attitudes: (1) greater relative support for equality among West Indian leaders of lower socio-economic origins, and (2) the most highly educated leaders reflected in their attitudes the enlightenment of Western humanitarian philosophy.[3]

Wealth, an important variable in any society, also served to demarcate the West Indian leaders' views toward equality. As reported in Table 1, non-wealthy leaders were four times more likely to be egalitarians than were wealthy persons.[4]

There was a strong correlation between skin color and attitudes toward equality among the West Indian leaders. Over two-thirds of the dark brown or black leaders were egalitarians as compared to 18 per cent of the whites. Falling between these two groups, but somewhat closer to the white leaders, were East Indians, Chinese, and persons of light brown complexion.

Because wealth and color are to some extent confounded in the West Indies, it is important to clarify their independent effects on egalitarianism as we did in the last three chapters. From a table not shown here, wealth appears to be more important than color. Non-wealthy whites were twice as likely to be egalitarian as were the wealthy non-whites. Class rather than color is the more important variable.

The final social characteristic presented in Table 1 is the institutional sector in which the leaders exercised their national influence. Egalitarian attitudes were much more frequent among political and labor leaders than any other group, and least typical of economic dominants and religious or ethnic leaders. More egalitarian than the economic dominants, but much less so than the political and labor leaders, were persons involved in the mass media, civil service, and in other areas of activity such as heads of voluntary organizations, free professionals, and educationists.

In general, then, egalitarians, like democrats, were characteristically leaders of secular, mass-based organizations who held legitimate change most directly in their hands. Contrariwise, inegalitarians tended to

---

[3] For a discussion of the ideological effects of the Jamaican educational system and an analysis of the function of higher education in changing attitudes toward equality in Jamaica, see James T. Duke, "Equalitarianism Among Emergent Elites in a New Nation," unpublished Ph.D. dissertation, University of California, Los Angeles, Calif., 1963. One part of the study is reported in Chapter Seven of this volume.

[4] As mentioned before, the relatively high number of inegalitarians with a completion of no more than a secondary-school level of education may reflect the typical academic pattern of most West Indian economic dominants during the period under consideration. Of the 39 leaders who were termed wealthy in this study: 12 were college graduates; 26 had an educational level of completion of secondary school only; and one had not gone beyond elementary school.

be leaders who represented the established vested interests of West Indian society. In a study of Warsaw students, Nowak found attitudes toward equality to be related to perceived self-interest.[5] Most West Indian economic dominants also thought — probably erroneously — that they had most to lose by the spread of economic and social equality. Yet, it must be emphasized that the relationship between the institutional sectors and egalitarianism, as with the other social background variables, was not one-to-one; there were exceptions to the general pattern.

IMPLICATIONS FOR POLITICAL DEVELOPMENT

The following pages of this chapter are a modest effort to bring some empirical data to bear on the implications of egalitarian attitudes for a few of the major political, economic, social and cultural issues concerning the emergent nations under discussion.

Political Independence. Forty-four of the West Indian leaders were egalitarians, and from Table 2 note that all of them were true nation-

Table 2.   PERCENTAGE OF WEST INDIAN LEADERS HAVING CERTAIN POLITICAL ATTITUDES BY EGALITARIANISM

Political Attitudes	Egalitarian	Inegalitarian
Attitudes toward political independence:		
True nationalist	100%	0%
Acquiescing nationalist	0	41
Colonialist	0	59
Total	100%	100%
Number of cases	(44)	(68)
Attitudes toward political democracy:		
Democrat	44%	7%
Authoritarian idealist	16	0
Cynical parliamentarian	30	27
Authoritarian	10	66
Total	100%	100%
Number of cases	(43)	(68)

alists; also all of the true nationalists were egalitarians. None of the egalitarians were either acquiescing nationalists or colonialists. That political independence was fostered by an egalitarian ethic, and opposition to it by inegalitarian values is, of course, a sub-proposition of the more general statement presented earlier that Enlightenment values fostered nationalist sentiments. Here we show, more specifically, that attitudes toward equality are highly correlated with the nationalist

[5] Stefan Nowak, "Equalitarian Attitudes of Warsaw Students," *American Sociological Review*, 25 (April, 1960), pp. 219–231.

types. Historically, attaining political independence was one step, and a crucial one, toward obtaining the political power thought necessary by some leaders to transform the British West Indies into new, more egalitarian societies.

Political Democracy. Reported in Table 2 is the relationship between egalitarianism and attitudes toward political democracy (as the latter were typed in Chapter Four). In general, egalitarians were more likely to be democrats, and less likely to be authoritarians, than were the inegalitarians. But the correlation between attitudes toward political democracy and attitudes toward equality is less than that discussed earlier between nationalist types and egalitarianism: there is some disagreement — especially among the egalitarians — concerning the most desirable political system. A warning signal may be found in the fact that all of the authoritarian idealists were egalitarians. This group regarded the parliamentary process as it was currently operating as thwarting the egalitarian desires of the masses. We predict that the authoritarian idealists represent a type that is more numerous among leaders in many of the new states other than in the Caribbean countries considered here; but even though they constitute only a small group among West Indian leaders, they are significant in that they tend to be among the youngest leaders engaged in political activity and they may be increasing in numbers. Furthermore, still more egalitarians may fill the ranks of the authoritarian idealists, or even those of the out-and-out authoritarians, unless the democratic system in these countries can effectively realize the egalitarian promise of West Indian nationalism — a promise that is part of the same web of basic values as democracy.

We cannot entirely agree with Tocqueville's dictum that when societies are confronted with the choice of either freedom or equality they "at all times habitually . . . prefer equality to freedom";[6] we do, however, have some support from these data for the inverse: inegalitarians are most likely to be opposed to freedom. Unlike our conclusion that commitment to the value of equality in some sense caused the desire for political independence, we regard attitudes toward equality and political democracy operating in tandem. Not only is it difficult to causally relate equality to democracy in any unilinear fashion in the modern history of ideas, but there is also no evidence of temporal priority of one or the other of these two notions in the intellectual development of the West Indian leaders.[7]

[6] Alexis de Tocqueville, *Democracy in America,* New York: New American Library, 1961, p. 190.
[7] Tocqueville, on the other hand, holds "the taste and the ideal of freedom" is a "consequence of . . . equality." Tocqueville, *op. cit.,* p. 192.

IMPLICATIONS FOR ECONOMIC DEVELOPMENT

As we have seen, a major justification for political independence was that it would bring an end to economic exploitation resulting from colonial imperialism, and would permit economic growth and a more equal distribution of economic benefits to the citizenry. Thus, nationhood was viewed not only as a means of achieving equality of opportunity and as being consistent with democratic theory, but also as conferring new and proper economic rights on the general population. The drive toward economic development, under the conditions of the underdeveloped new states, required many changes in the old economic system and led, among other things, to another decision of nationhood, "How large a role should the government play in the economy?"

To bring documentation to this decision of nationhood, we examine here the relationship between egalitarianism and the economic ideologies of the West Indian leaders, one important aspect of this decision. The classification of economic ideologies is the same as that introduced in Chapter Three. One might expect the egalitarians to be more Left in their ideologies, that is more committed to greater government intervention in the economy, than the inegalitarians. This is precisely what the data in Table 3 show. Forty-eight per cent of the egalitarians were radical compared to none of the inegalitarians; 41 per cent were liberal compared to 10; 11 per cent were populist compared to 9; and none of the egalitarians were either conservative or reactionary compared to 81 per cent of the inegalitarians.

Table 3.   PERCENTAGE OF WEST INDIAN LEADERS HAVING CERTAIN ECONOMIC IDEOLOGIES BY EGALITARIANISM

Economic Ideologies	Egalitarian	Inegalitarian
Radical	48%	0%
Liberal	41	10
Populist	11	9
Conservative	0	49
Reactionary	0	32
Total	100%	100%
Number of cases	(44)	(68)

This evidence supports the notion that most egalitarians perceived a reordering of the economy as a prerequisite for the attainment of equality of opportunity. It must be noted, however, that egalitarian attitudes were not an exclusive preserve of radical economic ideologists. In fact, slightly over half of all the egalitarians were either liberals or populists. The data reported in Table 3 are consistent with findings we have reported earlier: if a person was an opponent of the democratic revolution in the West Indies then the chances were that he was also out of step with the progressive policies of the nationalist movements.

Like the desire for political independence, we regard a Left economic ideology — what we will now loosely refer to as socialist beliefs — as a "dependent" variable, while equality has more of an "independent" nature. Egalitarians in the colonial circumstance wanted to gain control of their governments by means of political independence and to enlarge the role of government after doing so. Both actions were means of getting the power necessary to transform their societies, the first by taking legitimate governmental power into their hands and the second by increasing the total power from that source.

Another implication of equality for economic development can only be mentioned in passing here. The realities of economic growth are such, that, as new wealth develops, it may grow faster in the hands of the few than the many, thus contributing to increased incomes of those groups who already have large incomes, unless government intervenes in the process of distribution. This may result in economic inequalities offsetting some of the relative gains of the spread of a minimum set of economic rights to all members of the society, but it does not offset the absolute gains thereby achieved. In addition, it is by no means agreed among economists that economic inequalities necessarily contribute to economic growth and that economic equalities retard it, although some contend that this is so. In fact, in a discussion of underdeveloped areas Myrdal goes so far as to suggest the opposite:[8]

> If we seek to learn from what has actually happened in the richer countries which during the last half-century have proceeded far in the direction of greater equality of opportunities we reach . . . a dynamic theory: that the realisation of more equal opportunities has been needed to spur and sustain economic progress as well as to make good the assumptions of social democracy. A corollary to this is the important fact that in a progressive society — characterised by both redistributional reforms and economic growth as the two types of social change mutually support each other by circular causation — the improvement of the lot of the poor can often be won without substantial sacrifices from those who are better off and is sometimes not only compatible with, but a condition for, the attainment of higher levels in all income brackets, including the higher ones.

[8] Gunnar Myrdal, *Economic Theory and Underdeveloped Regions*, London: Gerald Duckworth and Co., Ltd., 1957, p. 121.

IMPLICATIONS FOR SOCIAL AND CULTURAL DEVELOPMENT

Along with the problems of political modernization, foreign affairs, and economic growth, there are also decisions to be made setting the direction and tempo of social and cultural development in the new states. Our hypothesis is that the distribution of egalitarian attitudes is consequential for this decision-making process. It is tested below by relating attitudes toward equality to a sample of three attitudes toward social and cultural development.

Complementing the ideals of liberty and equality in the triad of the Rights of Man is the desire for fraternity — the reduction of racial, religious, and class distinctions between groups and individuals within a society. With fraternity, like political democracy, we again are dealing with an associative trait or correlate of egalitarianism rather than one of its effects. To measure attitudes toward fraternity we use here attitudes toward social inclusivism introduced in Chapter Three. Leaders who placed highest priority on eliminating internal social barriers were termed "social inclusivists"; conversely, persons who placed secondary emphasis on reducing internal social barriers or who favored the perpetuation of such social distinctions within their societies were designated "social exclusivists."

As shown in Table 4, the correlation between favorable attitudes toward equality and social inclusivism is very high. Eighty-nine per cent of the egalitarians are social inclusivists compared to only 13 per cent of the inegalitarians.

The interviews revealed that the exclusivists were acutely conscious of the institutionalized color and class distinctions of West Indian society and saw the reduction of such distinctions as a peril to their own social status. The inclusivists, on the other hand, thought the realization of the West Indian democratic revolution required an equal access to and equal treatment within public facilities and institutions for all West Indians. In 1961, the nationalist and then-Premier of Jamaica, Norman W. Manley, addressing a convention of teachers, spoke of this concern:[9]

> Let the voice of reason in this country remember that all has not yet been won in Jamaica, let it be understood what we can contribute to the future as a nation that can show the world how black, brown, white, Chinese, Indians — all the races of the world — can dwell together in harmony . . . We must fight against all traces of discrimination which in fact do exist in this country, but fight always for one purpose —

[9] Norman W. Manley, "Address by the Premier to the Jamaican Union of Teachers," April 12, 1961.

that we will make our contribution to the purpose of God and the purpose of History that created all men equal in the land.

Table 4. **PERCENTAGE OF WEST INDIAN LEADERS HAVING CERTAIN
ATTITUDES TOWARD SOCIAL AND CULTURAL DEVELOPMENT BY
EGALITARIANISM**

Attitudes Toward Social and Cultural Development	*Egalitarian*	*Inegalitarian*
Priority of concern with social inclusiveness		
Greatest need for reducing social barriers at home (inclusivist)	89%	13%
Greatest need for increasing social contact abroad (exclusivist)	11	87
Total	100%	100%
Number of cases	(44)	(68)
Teaching of West Indian history (Africa and slavery)		
Favors more emphasis	95%	16%
Opposes more emphasis	5	84
Total	100%	100%
Number of cases	(44)	(68)
Desired direction of future cultural development		
Uniquely West Indian	82%	31%
Basically Anglo-European	18	69
Total	100%	100%
Number of cases	(44)	(68)

Related to the issue of social inclusivism, with its *leitmotif* of popular
participation in all aspects of the new society, is the question of the
cultural development of the West Indies. A popular theme of West
Indian fiction and social commentary deals with the question of
cultural identity, and in recent years it has taken the form of a growing
consciousness of the unique qualities of the West Indian people. A
mood is reflected in this where the proper credentials of nationhood
are seen as including an impressive "indigenous" cultural tradition.

Two items in this study measure the leaders' views toward West
Indian cultural development. The first is the attitude toward teaching
the African and slave history of the West Indies in the schools, or as
modified in Trinidad and British Guiana for the appropriate respondents, the teaching of the history of the indentured laborers from
India. A second item measuring attitudes toward future cultural development concerned a rather direct question about the leaders'
preferences for Anglo-European as opposed to West Indian cultural

forms. The answers were simply dichotomized as being primarily West Indian or basically Anglo-European. These are described in greater detail in Chapter Three.

Another implication of equality, as indicated in Table 4, is shown in the distribution of attitudes toward the teaching of West Indian history and future cultural development. Ninety-five per cent of the egalitarians compared to only 16 per cent of the inegalitarians favored teaching West Indian history with an emphasis on African origins and slavery — or the Indian origins and indentured labor; and 82 compared to 31 per cent desired a distinctively West Indian future cultural development.

In the wake of the West Indian political independence movements that were engendered by egalitarian beliefs and supported by democratic and social inclusivist principles, our findings indicate there has arisen a new pride in the region's background and local qualities. That is, this new consciousness of West Indian history and culture, what we have called the West Indian Romantic movement, although a consequence of the independence movements has in turn become another aspect of West Indian nationalism alongside the original Enlightenment — especially egalitarian — values.

For West Indians, such a cultural nationalism may become an honest and accurate counter-balance to the imperial versions of history and cultural forms with their implicit denigration of the backgrounds of the vast majority of West Indians. But if carried to extreme, it may lapse into another kind of chauvinism, or into what Barrington Moore has termed "nativistic egalitarianism."[10] This would be a perversion of the doctrine of equality. It might start by denying an out-group's claim to superiority by emphasizing similarities within the in-group, and might end with the in-group regarding itself as superior to everyone else and a rejection of everything — no matter how intrinsically worthy — that was not "indigenous." For example, some aspects of incipient West Indian Romanticism stress common racial identity as a source of social cohesion, and this leads to invidious comparisons with nations of predominantly fair-skinned peoples and a heightening of ethnic and racial cleavages between citizens in the emergent Caribbean nations themselves. Nonetheless, we wish to emphasize, although notice must be paid to potentially deleterious strains in the modern West Indian awakening, that the major current of West Indian nationalism at the time of this field research was definitely within the humanitarian tradition and strongly motivated by its egalitarian underpinnings.

[10] Barrington Moore, Jr., *Political Power and Social Theory*, Cambridge: Harvard University Press, 1958, pp. 12–13.

SUMMARY

In this chapter, we have described and analyzed attitudes of top national leaders toward equality, and we have shown some of the implications for attitudes toward political, economic, social and cultural change, attitudes that constitute important aspects of the images of the future that are shaping the actual future in the emerging Caribbean nations under study.

Elsewhere, we have shown that there has been a long-term trend toward equality throughout much of West Indian history.[11] Thus, the egalitarian-sponsored drive to nationhood represents a continuity with the past. Furthermore, an important process underlying the spread of equality has been the resolution of questions of legitimacy concerning particular institutions: certain ideas have led to the questioning of structural arrangements, and ideas held by elites have been of particular importance. Thus, the distribution and interrelationships of attitudes of modern-day West Indian leaders, the new national elites, are important indicators of the chances for future structural changes toward more equality, and the manner — planned change or violent revolution or static oligarchy — of their accomplishment or retardation.

The over-all level of egalitarianism among West Indian leaders was not overwhelmingly high, but 39 per cent, on a rather stringent test, were definitely favorable to the spread of equality. There was variation by country with the percentage of egalitarians among national leaders being 55 in British Guiana, 50 in Jamaica, 41 in Trinidad, and 32 in the sample of the three smaller islands.

Some of the variation in egalitarian attitudes was explained by the social differentiation of elites: egalitarians tended to be young; either highly (college or higher) or lowly (elementary only) educated, but not middling (secondary school only) educated; dark brown or black in skin color; not wealthy; and leaders of secular, mass-based organizations — specifically political parties or labor unions. But these correlations were not perfect and there were exceptions to the general pattern — exceptions that the self-interest hypothesis could not explain (as illustrated by the U-shaped correlation with education).

The implications of attitudes toward equality for political, economic and social development appear to be far-reaching and highly significant. Some of them have been documented here. For *political development* the egalitarian ideal fostered the independence movements as a means to achieve the image of a new, egalitarian society, and it tended

[11] Bell, *Jamaican Leaders, op. cit.;* Moskos and Bell, "Some Implications of Equality for Political, Economic, and Social Development," *International Review of Community Development*, 13–14 (1965), pp. 219–246.

to work along with the ideal of political democracy in doing so. Also egalitarianism generally supports democratic values, and even more clearly inegalitarianism supports authoritarian values. Should the inegalitarians be successful in stalling the trend toward equality by manipulation of the democratic process, however, then the egalitarians may be forced to recommend non-democratic methods — such as the authoritarian idealists already do.

For *economic development* favorable attitudes toward equality result in Left economic ideologies and unfavorable attitudes toward equality result in conservative or reactionary economic ideologies. The egalitarians generally favor a large role of government in the affairs of the economy for the purpose of reordering the economy for the benefit of the masses of the people. Also, it was suggested that distributional and other reforms could be beneficial to economic growth.

For *social and cultural development* egalitarianism is linked with the desire to create a socially inclusive society, to break down ascribed social barriers. Furthermore, it produces a drive toward the West Indianization of cultural traditions and of the teaching of a new version of social and cultural history in the schools. The latter could be an important corrective to some of the deleterious aspects of cultural domination by the imperial power, but it contains the danger of being perverted into an exclusivist movement in contradiction to the underlying egalitarian drive.

Finally, through the analysis of these attitudes we have tried to reconstruct a small piece of social reality by looking through the eyes of elites. It is, after all, their perceptions and motivations, their judgments and involvements, which importantly determine for such elites, as for anyone, the stimulus to which they respond, the goals they try to reach, and the meaning they attach to the actions they decide to take. But leaders, by definition, shape the future more than ordinary men and therefore shape both the present and the past. Their ideas about political, economic, social and cultural equality — especially such ideas since they have been the driving force behind much of modern man's history — have obvious and important implications for major aspects of development. This is true not only of the West Indies, but also of other nations, both old and new.

7 Egalitarianism and Future
Leaders in Jamaica

JAMES T. DUKE

In the foregoing chapters, we have seen the importance of attitudes
toward equality in shaping and giving direction to the nationalist
movements and in influencing other attitudes that may have significant
implications for political, economic, social and cultural development.
The important point, of course, is that a group's attitude toward
equality is basically an attitude toward the kind of future society
the group would like to have come into being. Egalitarianism
as an ideology is thus a crucial variable as it enters into national
decisions that determine the social structure of the future. The
strength and distribution of egalitarian or inegalitarian attitudes in
any particular nation are indicators of the direction future developments may go.

In this chapter, I try to project the probability of the spread of
egalitarian attitudes into the future by a study of Jamaican youth.
It should be pointed out at the outset that the concept of equality
has many different, though related, connotations, even as used by
the authors of the related studies reported in this book: Moskos stresses
equality of opportunity, though his concept of social inclusivism is
similar to social equality or brotherhood; Mau in Chapter Ten emphasizes brotherhood in his concept of social equality; and I have to
some extent used both notions in the Index of Egalitarianism that I
construct and test in this chapter using standard scaling techniques.
The reader is by now aware that the concept in one or more of its
connotations comes up again and again in this book. Our studies should
be read with the explicit understanding that the importance of the
ideal of equality in forming and shaping the new nations is one of our
major conclusions and that we have devoted much of our research
energies exploring the various meanings, consequences, and conditions
of equality. Much more, of course, remains to be done.

Here I analyze questionnaire data for over 200 Jamaican university students and over 2,000 Jamaican secondary-school students, persons who by Jamaican levels of education are already elite and from whose ranks many, if not most, of the future leaders of Jamaica will be drawn. The questions that I seek to answer are: How high is the overall level of egalitarianism among these future leaders? How much variation in attitudes toward equality characterizes them? How can differences in attitudes toward equality be explained? What implications can be drawn for a more egalitarian social structure in the future?

LEADERSHIP AND EGALITARIANISM

Leaders reflect the values and hopes of the people they lead and, at the same time, give scope and direction to them. The persons who hold important positions in the key institutions of the nation — government, education, industry, commerce, religion, agriculture, etc. — are influential in shaping the masses' attitudes toward equality, and their attitudes toward equality help to determine both the rate at which structural change toward equality progresses and the nature of the means — violent or peaceful.

Wendell Bell has recently said,

> If the leaders generally favor the extension of equality, if they believe that the present structures which give rise to and maintain the present inequalities are no longer legitimate . . . , then structural changes may be achieved extending equality still further without violence and other debilitating disruptive effects . . . However, if the . . . leaders feel that the present inequalities are right and fair, if they feel that the trend toward equality has already gone far enough, if they believe present inequalities should remain, then the trend toward equality may not continue at all or it may continue only at the expense of social integration and with violence and the use of force.[1]

EDUCATION AND LEADERSHIP

Education as a prerequisite for leadership is becoming increasingly important in both developing and industrialized nations. For example, by 1961 an advanced education was "indispensable for most people who want to be considered for high positions in the government, in large businesses, in politics, and in the professions."[2] Education is most important among the top levels of the occupational system, and relatively few elite positions can be achieved without higher education. The level of education required, of course, varies from one society to another,

---

[1] "Equality and Attitudes of Elites in Jamaica," *Social and Economic Studies*, 11 (December, 1962), pp. 415–416.

[2] Seymour M. Lipset and Reinhard Bendix, *Social Mobility in Industrial Society*, Berkeley and Los Angeles: University of California Press, 1959, p. 100.

but as a general rule, access to high status positions depends upon access to higher education.[3]

According to Yale sociologist, Burton R. Clark:

> The contest among men and ideas over the nature of society is reflected throughout the educational institution in modern times, as the formal agencies of cultural transmission and socialization enter ever more intimately and decisively into economic, political, and social affairs. The demands on education range from the mounting of morality to the making of technicians, from the maintenance of the small community to the exploration of space. The effects of education on other institutions and society, large as they currently appear, are undoubtedly more complex and substantial than has yet been imagined. Social science has attended little to education, and rapid change has moved empirical reality out of reach of perspectives brilliantly applicable to the societies and social problems of 1850 or 1900 . . . [The] society characterized by technology and expertness is an educative society, a place where man is to be conceptualized as Educational Man as well as economic and political man. So, too, in the case of the traditional society undergoing industrialization, attention swings toward man in his educational aspects and to society in its educational forms. The sociological imagination has long grasped the general idea that he who forms the child and dispenses cultural funds also maintains and changes society and culture. That imagination is now moving closer to the astonishing implications of locating much cultural transmission and socialization in a separate major institution, there to be shaped by different processes and forces, there to pose distinctive problems of performance and function . . . Who says society, says education.[4]

Furthermore, Edward Shils says that intellectuals have played a more important part in recent years in the formation of new states than at any other time in history.[5] They were active in the process

---

[3] Data from the present study may be illustrative of the Jamaican situation. A total of 381 students reported that their fathers held a highly ranked occupation (1 or 2 on the Warner occupational scale). Of these persons, 10.5 per cent had received only a primary education, 10.8 per cent had received a teacher training education (head teachers in primary schools or teachers in secondary schools are rated as 2 by Warner), 49.6 per cent had received a secondary education, and 29.1 per cent had received a university education. Approximately ten per cent of the fathers of secondary and university students in Jamaica had achieved a highly ranked occupation without obtaining significant education — education past the primary level. Channels for mobility other than education were present, but the attainment of the proper education was still highly important.

[4] "Sociology of Education," in Robert E. L. Faris (editor), *Handbook of Modern Sociology*, Chicago: Rand-McNally, 1964, pp. 765–766.

[5] "The Intellectuals in the Political Development of the New States," *World Politics*, 12 (April, 1960), pp. 329–368. Shils defines intellectuals in new states as "all persons with an *advanced modern education* and the intellectual concerns and skills ordinarily associated with it." *Ibid.*, p. 332. (Italics are Shils'.) Although this definition is more general than that for Western industrial nations, it is useful for developing nations and is particularly applicable to the Jamaican situation.

of protest which led to independence, and filled the vacuum of leadership that resulted from the colonial experience, such as the lack of
locally-owned business, a local army, and the lack of indigenous civil
servants and statesmen. Intellectuals occupied important positions in
the civil service, the professions, teaching (particularly college and
university teaching, but also secondary school teaching), journalism
and law. Many of the elected political leaders in newly independent
nations were drawn from the small portion of the population who
were well educated.

Students in these nations, although they often did not occupy positions of power in the nation, had considerable prestige, and it was
expected of them that in the future they would hold positions of
power and influence in public affairs of the nation. Also, they had
more of a role, even as students, in the intellectual and public life of
the nation than most other groups.

> In advanced countries, students are not regarded as ex-officio intel-
> lectuals; in underdeveloped countries, they are. Students in modern
> colleges and universities in underdeveloped countries have been treated
> as part of the intellectual class . . . and they have regarded themselves
> as such.[6]

Speaking of the future, Shils states that intellectuals will constitute an
important part of the elite in new nations, and will be extremely important in the decision-making process.

Thus, studying students in a country such as Jamaica permits us to
get some insight into the kinds of attitudes the new educational system
is engendering and to estimate the extent to which certain values — in
this case egalitarianism — are present among the emergent leaders of
the new society.

BASIC DATA[7]

University and higher secondary students in Jamaica were chosen
for study because they represent the pool from which future Jamaican
leaders will be chosen. Also, the attitudes of present Jamaican leaders
have already been studied by others including Bell, Mau, and Moskos,
but we know relatively little about the attitudes of students in the top
levels of the Jamaican educational system. Such students are already
elite in an educational sense, and are considered as intellectuals.
Many will enter the top levels of government, education, the professions
and business in the next few years. As a group, their attitudes will
in all probability have an important influence on the level of egalitarian-

[6] *Ibid.*, p. 336.
[7] For an extended discussion of the methodology of this study, see James T. Duke,
"Equalitarianism Among Emergent Elites in a New Nation," unpublished Ph.D.
dissertation, University of California, Los Angeles, 1963, pp. 42–89.

ism in Jamaica and on the policies which future governments will follow.

Over 2,600 questionnaires were administered to university students at the University of the West Indies in Kingston and to all students in the Fifth and Sixth Forms (equivalent to high school seniors and college freshmen in the United States) in a select sample of 21 secondary schools throughout Jamaica in 1961. Non-Jamaican students were eliminated for analysis purposes, leaving 2,197 usable questionnaires. This represents 51 per cent of the Jamaican students at the University of the West Indies and approximately 60 per cent of secondary students in the Fifth and Sixth Forms in all of Jamaica. Since a related purpose of the study was to examine the recruitment process of leaders, all of the highest status secondary schools on the island were included in the sample. Most of the middle status schools were included, and relatively few of the low status schools were included, the latter for comparative purposes. The sample is thus non-random and over-weighted with students from high status schools. This allows more effective generalization regarding future leaders, but does not allow valid generalizations to all Jamaican students.

The sample of university students was representative of all university students on known variables. Not enough information was available on secondary students to check the representativeness of the secondary student sample.

The major part of the study was focused on egalitarianism as a dependent variable. The relative weights of various factors were examined as explanatory variables. The last part of the chapter, which is not strictly empirical, but rather seeks to generalize from the data obtained, treats egalitarianism as an independent variable and looks at the possible consequences for the future of Jamaica.

AN INDEX OF EGALITARIAN ATTITUDES

The index used here was first developed as the Index of Status Attitude by Melvin Seeman to measure the extent to which people feel that status differences are acceptable and desirable.[8] The index focuses on

---

[8] Melvin Seeman, *Social Status and Leadership: The Case of the School Executive*, Columbus, Ohio: Bureau of Educational Research and Service, Ohio State University, 1960; Melvin Seeman, with the assistance of Richard T. Morris, *A Status Factor Approach to Leadership*, Columbus, Ohio: Personnel Research Board, Ohio State University, no date (multilithed). See also Paul W. Hiatt, "An Investigation of Status Attitudes," M.A. Thesis, Ohio State University, 1959. Other recent works on status attitudes include the following: Stuart Adams, "Social Climate and Productivity in Small Military Groups," *American Sociological Review*, 19 (August, 1954) pp. 421–425; H. M. Blalock, Jr., "Status Consciousness: A Dimensional Analysis," *Social Forces*, 37 (March, 1959) pp. 243–248; and Walter C. Kaufman, "Status, Authoritarianism, and Anti-Semitism," *American Journal of Sociology*, 62 (January, 1957), pp. 379–382.

Table 1.   PERCENTAGE DISTRIBUTION OF RESPONSES FOR THE ITEMS
OF THE INDEX OF EGALITARIANISM, JAMAICAN UNIVERSITY
AND SECONDARY STUDENTS AND JAMAICAN LEADERS.

Response Category*	Males			Females			Bell's Leaders
	Fifth Form	*Sixth Form*	*University*	*Fifth Form*	*Sixth Form*	*University*	

1. Differences in rank among people are acceptable since they are chiefly the result of the way individuals have made use of the opportunity open to them.

1	38	33	12	33	31	16	45
2	29	32	27	32	29	25	30
3	16	6	9	14	8	9	4
4	7	13	18	10	16	22	11
5	10	16	34	11	16	27	10
Total	100	100	100	100	100	100	100
Number	(629)	(313)	(117)	(667)	(306)	(95)	(228)
No Ans.	(22)	(2)	(4)	(29)	(12)	(10)	(1)

2. Social clubs which restrict membership on a racial basis ought to be considered as being against Jamaican principles.

1	69	81	87	61	70	86	80
2	8	5	5	10	10	5	6
3	8	3	2	9	3	1	2
4	6	4	2	8	3	1	3
5	8	7	4	12	5	6	9
Total	99	100	100	100	100	99	100
Number	(644)	(315)	(119)	(678)	(314)	(95)	(233)
No Ans.	(7)	(2)	(0)	(18)	(4)	(1)	(5)

3. High social or economic position in Jamaica is a pretty good sign of an individual's superior ability or efforts.

1	31	16	13	28	18	18	20
2	27	24	16	28	20	12	18
3	11	7	3	14	11	8	6
4	17	27	21	13	21	17	21
5	14	26	47	17	30	45	35
Total	100	100	100	100	100	100	100
Number	(640)	(313)	(119)	(668)	(308)	(95)	(231)
No Ans.	(11)	(4)	(0)	(28)	(10)	(1)	(7)

4. Differences in prestige among the various occupations should be reduced.

1	34	39	34	37	35	41	39
2	20	22	23	18	18	28	24
3	25	13	12	24	18	13	13
4	10	11	12	11	15	7	10
5	11	15	19	10	14	11	14
Total	100	100	100	100	100	100	100
Number	(629)	(311)	(117)	(644)	(303)	(94)	(230)
No Ans.	(22)	(6)	(2)	(52)	(15)	(2)	(8)

(concluded on next page)

Table 1. (concluded)

Response Category*	Males			Females			
	Fifth Form	Sixth Form	University	Fifth Form	Sixth Form	University	Bell's Leaders
5. People of about the same social or economic position ought to pretty much mingle with their own kind.							
1	25	21	9	24	18	9	21
2	20	24	16	22	22	14	21
3	11	8	9	9	7	15	8
4	18	22	26	17	24	26	17
5	26	24	40	28	30	35	33
Total	100	99	100	100	101	99	100
Number	(634)	(312)	(117)	(657)	(311)	(91)	(225)
No Ans.	(17)	(5)	(2)	(39)	(7)	(5)	(13)
6. The incomes of most people are a fair measure of their contribution to human welfare.							
1	15	6	3	16	12	3	3
2	18	9	11	18	10	6	7
3	21	10	7	22	16	11	8
4	19	19	13	17	18	15	20
5	27	56	67	28	44	65	62
Total	100	100	101	101	100	100	100
Number	(637)	(314)	(117)	(658)	(314)	(94)	(229)
No Ans.	(14)	(3)	(2)	(38)	(4)	(2)	(9)
7. We should not be too concerned if there are many people in low positions in Jamaica since most of them do not want the responsibility of higher positions.							
1	13	12	5	14	6	7	12
2	11	10	8	12	7	7	15
3	9	6	3	6	5	5	4
4	19	20	19	17	19	15	24
5	48	51	65	51	62	65	45
Total	100	99	100	100	99	99	100
Number	(647)	(317)	(117)	(679)	(314)	(95)	(227)
No Ans.	(4)	(0)	(2)	(17)	(4)	(1)	(11)

* Response categories are as follows:
  1. Strongly agree
  2. Somewhat agree
  3. Undecided or in between
  4. Somewhat disagree
  5. Strongly disagree

the way individuals relate to each other and on equality of economic and social rights. Bell recently utilized a shortened version of the index in his study of Jamaican leaders,[9] but reversed the scoring of each item

[9] Bell, *op. cit.* Also see, Bell, *Jamaican Leaders: Political Attitudes in a New Nation*, Berkeley and Los Angeles: University of California Press, 1964.

and of the total scale, calling the resulting scale the Index of Egalitarianism. The index as utilized in the present study generally follows the usage of Bell.

The index, which contains seven questions with Likert-type response categories, is given in Table 1. It focuses on equality of economic and social rewards and on interpersonal interaction. As such, it measures only some of the factors which have often been included in the concept of equality. The index has no items which are directly concerned with political or civil rights. While it is true that inequalities existed in Jamaica in these spheres, the battle for agreement on the propriety of civil and political equality had for all intents and purposes already been won in Jamaica at the time the data were collected in 1961. Further, equality in political and civil rights was generally supported in Jamaica because of the assumption that these rights would lead to equality in the social and interpersonal spheres. The index thus measures the core values of equality, but does not specifically include items regarding equality of civil and political rights.

The index is concerned with general values of equality in the social and economic spheres, but is not concerned with any specific action-oriented programs for the increase or reduction of status differences. As such the respondent must react to the general value of equality rather than to the effectiveness of specific programs or policies.

A strength of the index is that respondents with inegalitarian values are provided with ready-made rationalizations for the maintenance of status differences. The questions are not phrased with "loaded" phrases in support of egalitarianism. On the contrary, the respondent is given ample opportunity to respond in an inegalitarian manner with socially acceptable rationalizations for the maintenance of an inegalitarian structure.

SCALING PROCEDURES

To test empirically the unidimensionality of the attitude universe, the responses of students to the seven items were analyzed using the Guttman technique.[10]

[10] Louis Guttman, "The Quantification of a Class of Attributes: A Theory and Method of Scale Construction," in P. Horst, et al., *The Prediction of Personal Adjustment*, Committee on Social Adjustment, New York: Social Science Research Council, 1941, pp. 319–348; Louis Guttman, "A Basis for Scaling Quantitative Data," *American Sociological Review*, 9 (April, 1944), pp. 139–150; Louis Guttman, "The Cornell Technique for Scale and Intensity Analysis," *Educational and Psychological Measurement*, 7 (Summer, 1947), pp. 247–280; Leon Festinger, "The Treatment of Qualitative Data by 'Scale Analysis,'" *Psychological Bulletin*, 44

A random sample of two hundred respondents, both university and secondary students, was selected to serve as the scaling sample. The responses of these students to the items of the index were analyzed, using all the major criteria of unidimensionality relating to the Guttman method. The results of this analysis for the scaling sample are reported in Table 2.

The coefficient of reproducibility obtained was .86. This was lower than the criterion of .90 arbitrarily designated by Guttman. The coefficient of minimum marginal reproducibility was found to be .69. The improvement in prediction represented in the difference between the coefficient of reproducibility and the coefficient of minimum marginal reproducibility was .17.

The spread of marginal frequencies was sufficient to provide a range of scores, and the distribution of frequencies was such that most marginal frequencies were not extreme. The coefficient of minimum marginal reproducibility of .69 is considered low in this respect.

Only one of fourteen response categories contained more error than non-error, and the ratio in that category was small. Since all errors were random, it was concluded that no important second variable was present.

Only seven items were used in the formulation of the index. This is a smaller number than recommended by Guttman, but is similar to other widely used scales.[11] For five of the items, a "disagree" response was an egalitarian response, while in two items an "agree" response was an egalitarian response.

Although the coefficient of reproducibility was slightly lower than the minimum Guttman criterion, the scale was acceptable on all other criteria of evaluation and no second variable could be found. Thus, the unidimensionality of the scale was tentatively accepted.

(March, 1947), pp. 149–161; Louis Guttman, "On Festinger's Evaluation of Scale Analysis," *Psychological Bulletin*, 41 (September, 1947), pp. 451–465; Louis Guttman, "The Problem of Attitude and Opinion Measurement," Chapter Two, "The Basis for Scalogram Analysis," Chapter Three, and "The Relation of Scalogram Analysis to Other Techniques," Chapter Six, in Samuel A. Stouffer, et al., *Studies in Social Psychology in World War II*, Vol. 4, Princeton: Princeton University Press, 1950; E. F. Borgatta and D. G. Hays, "Some Limitations on the Arbitrary Classification of Non-scale Response Patterns in a Guttman Scale," *Public Opinion Quarterly*, 16 (Fall, 1952), pp. 410–416; Allen L. Edwards, *Techniques of Attitude Scale Construction*, New York: Appleton-Century-Crofts, Inc., 1957, Chapter 7–9, pp. 172–243; John McNamara, *A Bibliography of Materials Dealing with Guttman Scaling: Theory and Techniques*, unpublished paper, University of California, Los Angeles, September 30, 1957.

[11] See for example Leo Srole, "Social Integration and Certain Corollaries: An Exploratory Study," *American Sociological Review*, 21 (December, 1956), pp. 709–716. See also Allen E. Edwards, *op. cit.*, p. 177.

**Table 2. GUTTMAN SCALE CRITERIA, INDEX OF EGALITARIANISM,
JAMAICAN STUDENTS**

1. Coefficient of reproducibility: .86.
2. Range of marginal frequencies:
   (a) The extreme modal frequencies are 88% and 22%.
   (b) Ten of the fourteen response categories fall between 75% and 25%.
   (c) The spread is sufficient to provide a range of scores.
3. Minimum marginal reproducibility: .69.
4. Number of items and response categories: seven dichotomous items.
5. Pattern of error: all errors are random.
6. Error to non-error ratio:
   (a) Ratio for all items: one of fourteen answer categories has more error than non-error.
   (b) Item by item error:

	Response Category	Error	Non-error
Question #2	(1–3)	0	164
	(4–5)	9	7
Question #7	(3–5)	2	129
	(1–2)	22	27
Question #6	(3–5)	10	119
	(1–2)	14	37
Question #5	(3–5)	12	96
	(1–2)	22	50
Question #4	(1–2)	21	78
	(3–5)	22	59
Question #3	(4–5)	17	54
	(1–3)	9	100
Question #1	(4–5)	14	27
	(1–3)	0	139

OVERALL LEVEL OF EGALITARIANISM

On the basis of responses to the index, Jamaican students were classified into eight scale types. At the one extreme were individuals who gave an egalitarian response to each item, and at the other extreme were individuals who gave an inegalitarian response to each item.

Table 3 shows the distribution of Jamaican students in each scale type. Jamaican students generally were favorable toward social and economic equality. The distribution was skewed, with the median falling in scale type six. Although the greater number of cases were in the pro-egalitarian end of the scale, some students fell in each scale type.

To facilitate analysis, students were divided into two groups on the basis of their scale type. Students with scale types six, seven and eight were classified as "egalitarians," and those with scale types one through five were classified as "inegalitarians." The division was made as near

Table 3. **PERCENTAGE DISTRIBUTION OF SCALE TYPES, INDEX OF EGALITARIANISM, JAMAICAN STUDENTS**

Scale Type	Per Cent
8 (Egalitarian)	19.2
7	16.4
6	17.2
5	10.4
4	8.6
3	10.2
2	11.3
1 (Inegalitarian)	6.7
Total	100.0
Number	2,116
Non-scalable	81

the median as possible. A total of 52.8 per cent of the students were classified as egalitarians.

STRUCTURAL VARIABLES AND EGALITARIANISM

Structural sociologists emphasize the importance of social structure in determining ideas and attitudes. From this point of view, the attitudes commonly held in a group will be determined by the position of that group in the social organization of the larger society. Social statuses are treated as the building blocks of social organization. Those who have different statuses are thus likely to have different attitudes.

Table 4 shows the percentage of Jamaican students who were egalitarian according to their position in the Jamaican social structure.

Level of education. Level of education was found to be an important determinant of egalitarianism. University students were highly favorable to equality, while Fifth Form students were least egalitarian and Sixth Form students were intermediate. In multivariate analysis not reported herein, level of education was consistently related to egalitarianism when other variables were controlled. For the present sample, level of education was more closely related to egalitarianism than any variable.

It has been widely assumed by both laymen and social scientists that favorable information about a particular group or idea may have the effect of changing attitudes toward that group or idea in a more approving direction.[12] Such an assumption, for example, is basic to action programs such as the Voice of America, Radio Free Europe, and the Watchtower Society. Information presented in a favorable or

[12] Otto Klineberg, "Creating Attitudes Conducive to International Understanding," in Christian O. Arndt and Samuel Everett, *Education for a World Society*, New York: Harper and Brothers, 1951, pp. 44–60.

Table 4. **PERCENTAGE OF JAMAICAN STUDENTS WHO WERE EGALITARIAN, BY SELECTED SOCIAL CHARACTERISTICS**

Characteristic	*Per Cent Egalitarian*	
Level of Education		
Fifth Form	46.0%	(1,347)
Sixth Form	59.1	(635)
University	76.3	(215)
Sex		
Male	53.7	(1,087)
Female	51.8	(1,110)
Age		
14–16 years old	47.7	(809)
17–18 years old	51.8	(958)
19 years old & older	69.4	(330)
Residence		
Urban	55.2	(1,067)
Rural	50.7	(991)
Religion		
Protestant	54.1	(1,437)
Roman Catholic	50.2	(526)
Other	52.1	(121)
Father's Occupation		
High	54.5	(398)
Medium	52.8	(1,127)
Low	52.5	(472)
Father's Education		
None or Elementary	54.2	(982)
Teacher Training	58.9	(185)
Secondary	48.7	(704)
University	60.7	(135)
Color		
Black	61.6	(146)
Colored	53.1	(1,647)
White	42.5	(113)
Oriental	50.8	(185)
All Students	52.8	(2,197)*

*Numbers in some categories do not add up to the total because of non-response on certain questions.

even neutral manner results in greater tolerance. Conversely, statements containing unfavorable images and information may cause a change in attitude in a negative or unfavorable direction. Thus, education in terms of favorable images is promoted by many persons as a means of increasing toleration and understanding among men.[13]

[13] See for example The President's Commission on National Goals, *Goals for Americans*, New York: Prentice-Hall, Inc., 1960, p. 6, and Charles F. Marden and Gladys Meyer, *Minorities in American Society*, New York: American Book Company, 1962, pp. 472–473.

The philosophy of the liberal arts education, so basic to American education, assumes, among other things, that a broad education involving information about a variety of subjects and people will aid in the social adjustment of the individual in a complex world and in the solving of numerous world problems that owe their existence to lack of understanding among men.

The purpose of liberal education is usually viewed as the teaching of *general* knowledge on a broad scale in a neutral manner, in order to enable the individual to think individualistically and creatively, without the fetters of the prevailing prejudices and preconceptions of his society.[14]

Recent empirical studies have also demonstrated the importance of education in breaking down prejudices and traditional stereotypes. In a review of literature regarding prejudice, Harding and his associates conclude that the most consistent finding of numerous research studies is that education and prejudice are negatively but highly correlated.[15] Christie states that increased education leads to increased sophistication, which results in a more critical examination of popular stereotypes and attitudes, less fear of the unknown, and less distrust of out-group members.[16]

The practice of free inquiry, skepticism, the use of reason, toleration, and the acquisition of knowledge are fostered by the educational system in Jamaica, as well as by those in other Western nations. Increasingly, the same is true in non-Western nations where Western ways are being adopted. This enlightened education, as a result of the genuine knowledge it imparts, tends to result in a broadened view of mankind and greater toleration of other peoples and other ideas. Modern education

[14] See for example Theodore Meyer Greene, "Liberal Education Reconsidered," in Joe Park, ed., *The Philosophy of Education*, New York: The Macmillan Company, 1958, pp. 203–206.

[15] John Harding, et al., "Prejudice and Ethnic Relations," in Gardner Lindzey, ed., *Handbook of Social Psychology*, Cambridge, Massachusetts: Addison-Wesley Publishing Company, 1954, Volume II, p. 1039. See also A. M. Rose, *Studies in the Reduction of Prejudice*, Second Edition, Chicago: American Council of Race Relations, 1948; Gordon W. Allport, *The Nature of Prejudice*, Garden City, New York: Doubleday and Company, Inc., 1954, pp. 404–407; B. Samuelson, "Does Education Diminish Prejudice," *The Journal of Social Issues*, 1 (August, 1945), pp. 11–13; Cyril A. Rogers and C. Frantz, *Racial Themes in Southern Rhodesia*, New Haven: Yale University Press, 1962.

[16] Richard Christie, "Authoritarianism Re-examined," in Richard Christie and Marie Jahoda, eds., *Studies in the Scope and Method of "The Authoritarian Personality,"* Glencoe, Illnois: The Free Press, 1954, pp. 169–176. See also Herbert H. Hyman and Paul B. Sheatsley, "'The Authoritarian Personality' — A Methodological Critique," in Christie and Jahoda, *ibid.*, pp. 91–96; Bruno Bettleheim and Morris Janowitz, *Dynamics of Prejudice*, New York: Harper and Brothers, 1950, pp. 49–50.

leads to greater egalitarianism and tolerance.[17] This conclusion is generally supported by the accumulated research findings linking education to a reduction of prejudice and is consistent with the data on Jamaican students reported here linking education to egalitarianism.

The particular content of *values* and *attitudes,* as contrasted to sheer knowledge, presented to students by the school system is, of course, important as well in determining their attitudes. Jamaican schools tended to follow the broad ideological orientations of other Western schools which derive from the Enlightenment. Specifically, the values of the Rights of Man, rationality, toleration and liberalism were fostered by the school system. The content of these values is compatible with the values of economic and social equality, and adds support to these latter values. Egalitarianism, nationalism, and liberalism derive much of their intellectual, as well as emotional, support from the values of the Enlightenment, as Moskos has shown in detail in Chapter Three of this volume.

With specific reference to the content of the socialization process in Jamaican schools, the following statements may be made:[18]

First, the educational policy of the government favored equal opportunity for all children. The government emphasized equality publicly in its statements on education.

Second, Jamaican educational leaders were found by Bell in his 1958 study to be highly egalitarian, and it is probable that this attitude was shared by most other educators, both teachers and administrators. Since teachers were favorable toward equality, students were likely to be socialized to these values, either directly or indirectly. Students increased in their favorability toward equality as they progressed through the school system and became progressively socialized to the values of their teachers.

Third, efforts to "West-Indianize" the curriculum have undoubtedly

---

[17] C. Arnold Anderson, "The Impact of the Educational System on Technological Change and Modernization," in Bert F. Hoselitz and Wilbert E. Moore, eds., *Industrialization and Society,* UNESCO-Mouton, 1963, pp. 259–278. See also W. Arthur Lewis, *The Theory of Economic Growth,* London: Allen and Unwin, 1955, and Edward Shils, *Political Development in the New States,* Gravenhage: Mouton, 1962; Wendell Bell, "Equality and Attitudes of Elites in Jamaica," *op. cit.;* Bell, *Jamaican Leaders: Political Attitudes in a New Nation, op. cit.;* T. W. Adorno, Else Frendel-Brunswik, Daniel J. Levinson, R. Nevitt Sanford, *The Authoritarian Personality,* New York: Harper and Brothers, 1950, pp. 280–288; Seymour M. Lipset, "American Intellectuals: Their Politics and Status," *Political Man: The Social Bases of Politics,* Garden City, New York: Doubleday and Company, Inc., 1960, pp. 310–343; Stefan Nowak, "Egalitarian Attitudes of Warsaw Students," *American Sociological Review,* 25 (April, 1960), pp. 219–231. (This last article reports some data that contradict the stated conclusion.)

[18] See Duke, "Equalitarianism Among Emergent Elites in a New Nation," *op. cit.,* pp. 90–134.

resulted in more emphasis being placed on egalitarianism. New textbooks and other teaching materials, for example, stressing the role of the nationalist movements, and the values underlying them — especially equality — have already been introduced into some of the schools.

Thus, it appears as if both the sheer knowledge imparted during the educational process and the values and ideas upheld in the classroom by texts and teachers had a similar effect of increasing favorable attitudes toward economic and social equality as Jamaican students progressed through the school system.

Sex. Males were slightly more egalitarian than females, but the difference of only two percentage points is not significant. Both were about equally favorable to social and economic equality.

Age. Older Jamaican students were found to be more highly egalitarian than younger students. Over 69 per cent of those 19 years of age and older were egalitarian, whereas only about 48 per cent of those 14 to 16 years old were egalitarian.

Obviously, age is highly correlated with the level of education attained by the individual who is currently in school, although this is probably less true in Jamaica than in the United States because of the lower frequency of "social promotion" in Jamaica.

When level of education was controlled, no significant differences were found among age levels. Differences were still marked between different levels of education. Thus it is concluded that the correlation between age and egalitarianism is spurious for the age group under study here. Level of education appears to be the important determinant of egalitarianism, and age is largely a correlate of level of education for young persons still in school.

Urban-rural residence. Students who grew up in urban areas were more favorable to equality than those from rural areas. The difference was only 4.5 per cent, but with such a large sample, this difference requires recognition. From a practical point of view, urban or rural residence does not seem to be important in predicting whether a person will be egalitarian or inegalitarian.

Religion. Religion likewise was not an important determinant of egalitarianism. Protestant students were most egalitarian (54.1%), Roman Catholics were least egalitarian (50.2%), and those classified as "other" — generally Moslems, Hindus, and those who said they identified with no religious organization — were intermediate (52.1%). These small differences are not considered significant, especially when compared to the larger differences for level of education and other variables.

Father's occupation. The final three variables to be discussed are all measures of social status. As stated earlier, it has long been assumed that high status groups are unfavorable to equality, as a means of protecting their own perquisites, while low status groups are highly egalitarian as a means of raising their status.

Father's occupation is consistently recognized in the United States as a good indicator of social status. The same is probably true for Jamaica, but in Jamaica, father's occupation is not as closely related to the individual's overall standing in the community. The stratification system is undergoing relatively rapid changes, and other variables such as a person's own achievements are more important in Jamaica than in many other countries. Thus, while father's occupation is not unimportant, one should recognize that any single indicator is not a completely accurate measure of social status.

When father's occupation was used as the measure of social status, persons of high status were not significantly different from persons of low status in their attitudes toward equality. In fact, high status students were slightly more egalitarian than low status students. Unfortunately, this measure confounds at least two different variables: on the one hand higher education which is correlated positively with egalitarianism and on the other entrenched economic interest which is negatively correlated with egalitarianism.

Father's education. Differences were found when father's education was crosstabulated with egalitarianism. Students whose fathers had a university education were most egalitarian (60.7%). Those whose fathers had received a Teacher Training education (generally not the equivalent of a secondary education) were next most egalitarian (58.9%). Next came those who had received only a primary education or none at all (54.2%). Those whose fathers had received a secondary education were much less egalitarian (48.7%). These findings again stress the importance of education in producing persons favorable to equality. Families in which education was an important factor in the family's life (especially those with a university or teacher training education) were likely to produce egalitarian children.

The relationship between father's education and egalitarianism is "U" shaped. Those highest and lowest on the measure were egalitarian, while those who were intermediate were inegalitarian. This, of course, is consistent with the findings of Moskos and Bell in Chapter Six. It may reflect the operation of several explanatory variables: *status deprivation* leads to egalitarianism among students whose father's education is ranked as low; *maintenance of established wealth and position* leads to inegalitarianism among the intermediately ranked fathers reflecting the traditional educational patterns of many of the wealthy elite; and *enlightenment* of knowledge leads to egalitarianism of the most highly educated fathers, thus providing support for favorable attitudes toward equality.

Color. Students were asked to rate themselves as to their color, a rough approximation of the individual's race. The great majority of the students rated themselves as colored. This differed markedly from the color composition of the total population, where approximately 77 per cent of Jamaicans were listed as black by the Census Bureau.

Black students were markedly more egalitarian than colored[19] students, who in turn were markedly more egalitarian than white students. Orientals were intermediate in their attitudes, approximately at the level of colored students. Thus color does seem to be highly correlated with egalitarianism, and the group with the lowest status (blacks) were much more egalitarian than the group with the highest status (whites).

Jamaica has much less discrimination than does the United States today on the basis of race. However, some discrimination and prejudice still remains, and white people are often favored (often unconsciously) in many aspects of life.

ATTITUDINAL VARIABLES AND EGALITARIANISM

In every society there is a trend toward consistency in the values and attitudes present in the society. These values and attitudes are generally organized into a system, with each one elaborating on the other and influencing the other in a variety of ways. This trend toward consistency is never perfect, but the greater the inconsistency, the greater the conflict in the society.

In a causal sense, it is hard to determine whether some attitudes are causes and others are effects. Longitudinal studies of the development of attitudes, probably involving the collection of numerous extensive case histories such as those given by Ivar Oxaal in Chapter Two, are needed to supplement investigations of possible causal connections such as the one reported here. In the analysis to follow concerning the importance of certain attitudinal variables for egalitarianism, the mutual dependence of such variables is recognized.

Students were asked to give their opinions on a variety of political and economic issues. Many of these were highly specific. In the present report, only those attitudes are selected for analysis which seem to be relatively general, and which probably apply in a variety of areas.[20] Table 5 reports the percentage of Jamaican students who were egalitarian, as classified by their attitudes on selected general questions.

Conservatism-liberalism. Small differences were found among

[19] Students were asked to rate themselves as being "dark colored," "medium colored," or "light colored." No significant differences in egalitarianism were found between these groups.

[20] A separate report of the specific attitudes of Jamaican students on these social, economic and political questions is being prepared.

Table 5. **PERCENTAGE OF JAMAICAN STUDENTS WHO WERE EGALITARIAN, BY SELECTED ATTITUDES**

Attitudinal Variables	*Per Cent Egalitarian*	
Conservative-Liberal		
Conservative	51.1%	(419)
Liberal	54.9	(1,334)
Socialist	50.2	(247)
Status Concern		
Aretists (Low)	56.4	(1,371)
Agonists (High)	47.1	(715)
Discontent		
Discontented	65.4	(735)
Contented	46.4	(1,304)
Political Efficacy		
High	52.2	(999)
Low	54.3	(1,053)
All Students	52.8	(2,197)*

* Numbers in certain categories do not add up to the total because of non-response on certain questions.

students of different economic persuasions. Students who were economic liberals were most egalitarian (54.9%), while conservatives were less egalitarian (51.1%) and socialists were least egalitarian (50.2%). While the socialists preach an egalitarian ideology, the students who have accepted this philosophy did not themselves seem to be egalitarian. The great majority of students were liberal, with relatively few either conservative or socialist. The small differences with regard to egalitarianism lead us to conclude that economic conservatism-liberalism is not significantly related to egalitarianism for Jamaican students. This, of course, is at variance with the findings of Moskos and Bell for West Indian top leaders (Chapter Six). Perhaps the new generation of egalitarians are not committed to particular means of implementing their desires for an egalitarian society.

Status concern. Status concern as it was defined in the present study involves a relatively selfish personal interest regarding one's socio-economic position. Persons concerned with status desired to maximize their extrinsic rewards — their prestige, power, and economic position — at the expense of other values. Such persons were labeled as *agonists*. Those who were low on status concern were more interested in humanitarian service, creativity, self-expression, and concern with others. These persons were labeled *aretists*.[21]

[21] The terms "agonists" and "aretists" were derived from the Greek. They are more fully discussed in James T. Duke, "Equalitarianism Among Emergent Elites in a New Nation," *op. cit.*, pp. 75–82. See also Sir Richard W. Livingston, *Greek*

Aretists were found to be more egalitarian than agonists, although the difference is not large.

Persons who are primarily interested in extrinsic rewards, as the agonists in the current study, may view others primarily as competitors in the struggle for status and the rewards of status. In situations where one emphasizes the importance of status, the threat of loss of status or replacement by others is most likely present. Thus those to whom status is important probably tend to maximize the status differences which are perceived to be present in the society. A reduction of status differences would probably reduce the relative importance of the extrinsic rewards that are highly valued by such people. And since these respondents represent an elite group educationally, it would probably result in a lowering of their status in relation to others. The findings that agonists are less egalitarian than aretists is thus to be expected.

Conversely, aretists, because of their stress on the importance of activities rather than rewards, felt less frustration in the stratification system and little threat from others lower than themselves. But the chief explanation of the correlation between aretism and egalitarianism is to be found in the congeniality of the two values. Aretists, those students concerned with self-realization and helping others, are more favorable than the agonists to the creation of a social structure in Jamaica that would be more egalitarian than that which now exists. For them, the morality of equality is supplemented by the opportunities for greater self-development among a wider range of the Jamaican population than is now possible. Whether or not enlightened self-interest may be found behind this view can't be told from these data, but it is clear that narrow self-interest, such as that exhibited by the agonists, tends comparatively to make inegalitarians.

Discontent. Jamaican students were rated as contented or discontented according to the attitudes regarding the organization of the stratification system in Jamaica and the opportunities available for the achievement of success. Students replied either that they were "satisfied" or "dissatisfied" with such conditions in Jamaica. Those who were dissatisfied — or discontented — were much more egalitarian (65.4%) than those who were contented (46.4%). Discontent is more closely related to egalitarianism than any other variable examined in the present study except education and color.

Ideals and Modern Life, Cambridge: Harvard University Press, 1935, pp. 69–72; B. Jowett, translator and editor, *The Dialogues of Plato,* New York: Random House, 1937, Volume I; Troy Wilson Organ, *An Index to Aristotle,* Princeton: Princeton University Press, 1949, pp. 172–173; Aristotle, *Ethica Nicomachea* in W. D. Ross, translator, *The Works of Aristotle,* Oxford: Clarendon Press, 1925; and Aristotle, *On Virtues and Vices,* translated by H. Rackham, Cambridge: Harvard University Press, 1952, pp. 484–503.

The new ideas and ways of doing things brought by the imperial powers into their colonies had their greatest impact in the urban areas and there among the better educated colonials — colonials who had often been educated in the metropolitan center of the imperial power itself. The "revolution of rising expectations" came first within this segment of the population, and filtered down from them to the urban lower classes and to the rural population.[22] The better-educated group accepted what to them were new values and new consumer tastes appropriate to more industrialized nations. Discontent inevitably resulted when their own nation was deprived of the opportunity to provide for these new desires by the politically-dependent colonial nexus. This discontent was an important part of the syndrome of attitudes that included egalitarianism, and through it desires for political independence.

James S. Coleman has expressed it for Africa as follows:

> Susceptibility to psychological grievance is most acute among the more acculturated Africans. Social and economic discrimination and the stigma of inferiority and backwardness have precipitated a passionate quest for equality and modernity.[23]

Citizens of underdeveloped nations have "passionately" sought equality of prestige and the right of self-determination, a form of political equality. Egalitarianism, growing out of discontent, has thus led to nationalism.[24] Among others, Moskos (Chapter Three) has documented the role of egalitarian ideals in the drive toward political independence. But little data have yet been systematically brought to bear on the role of discontent in producing egalitarian attitudes under the political, economic, and social conditions of colonialism, although such discontent has been widely assumed to play a role.

The data presented herein demonstrate that discontent is closely related to egalitarianism. Whether discontent produces egalitarianism, or whether the opposite is true, cannot be determined from the present data. Probably they both develop together in mutual dependence, one feeding the other and vice versa. Further study of the social condi-

---

[22] See for example Eugene Staley, *The Future of Underdeveloped Countries*, New York: Harper and Brothers, 1954, especially p. 20.

[23] James S. Coleman, "Nationalism in Tropical Africa," *American Political Science Review*, 48 (June, 1954), pp. 42–43. See also Daniel Lerner, *The Passing of Traditional Society: Modernizing the Middle East*, Glencoe, Illinois: The Free Press, 1958, pp. 223–231 and 275–287; Elaine Catherine Hagopian, *Morocco: A Case Study in the Structural Basis of Social Integration*, unpublished Ph.D. dissertation, Boston University Graduate School, 1962.

[24] Barbara Ward, *The Rich Nations and the Poor Nations*, New York: W. W. Norton and Company, 1962, especially Chapter One and pp. 55–56.

tions and cultural values which tend to produce discontent should aid us in the understanding of why egalitarian attitudes develop.

Political efficacy. Students were asked how much of a personal voice they believed they would have in the political decisions of their nation. Students who had high political efficacy — who believed they would be able to have a significant influence on their government — were slightly less egalitarian than those with low efficacy. The difference was so small, however, that for practical purposes political efficacy does not seem to be related to or be predictive of egalitarianism.

MULTIVARIATE ANALYSIS

Four variables have been found to be significantly and consistently related to egalitarianism: (1) level of education, (2) color, (3) status concern, and (4) discontent. It remains, then, to examine the interaction of these variables, and their joint effect on egalitarianism.

For parsimony in presentation of data, the relationships between variables will not be presented in tabular form, but will be described and then discussed. After examining the relationship between each pair of the above four variables, the following statements about relationships can be made:

1. Level of education and color were not significantly correlated. There was a slight tendency for Sixth Form students to be lighter in color than either Fifth Form or university students, but the tendency was not marked.

2. Level of education and status concern were not significantly related.

3. Level of education and discontent were positively related. University students were much more discontented than Sixth Form students, who were in turn more discontented than Fifth Form students.

4. Color and status concern were positively related, with whites more concerned with status and blacks more aretistic.

5. Color and discontent were negatively related, with blacks more discontented than whites, with coloreds intermediate.

6. Status concern and discontent were not significantly related to each other.

The next step is to look at the joint effects of two variables upon egalitarianism. However, further analysis of the joint effect of color and other variables is unreliable. The distribution of students on the color variable was unfortunate as far as multivariate analysis is concerned. The great majority of students were in the colored category, with few either black, white, or oriental. It was not felt that it would be valid to include the latter variables in the same category, which would have resulted in a "colored vs. other" classification. The numbers of black, white and oriental students were not sufficient to allow multivariate comparisons. Thus, while color has been demonstrated to be significantly related to egalitarianism, it has had to be excluded in this portion of the analysis. Future studies may be able to more adequately examine the relationship between color and egalitarianism with other important variables controlled.

The distributions of the other three variables, level of education, status concern, and discontent, were more balanced. An examination of the joint effects of two variables upon egalitarianism results in the following findings:

1. Both level of education and status concern were independently related to egalitarianism when the other was controlled. The two taken together were highly predictive of egalitarianism. University students who were aretists were highly egalitarian (79%), while Fifth Form students who were agonists had a lower percentage who were egalitarian (42%). Level of education was more closely related to egalitarianism than was status concern.

2. Both level of education and discontent were markedly and independently related to egalitarianism when the other was controlled. Taken together, the two variables were highly predictive of egalitarianism. Discontented university students had a high percentage who were egalitarian (82%), while only 42% of contented Fifth Form students were egalitarian. Although discontent increased with level of education, the two independently were related to egalitarianism. However, level of education was more closely related to egalitarianism than was discontent.

3. Status concern and discontent were both independently related to egalitarianism when the other was controlled. Jointly, 69 per cent of discontented aretists were egalitarian while 41 per cent of contented agonists were egalitarian. Discontent was more highly related to egalitarianism than was status concern.

In conclusion, when two variables were examined together as to their relationship to egalitarianism, the greatest percentage differences were found with level of education, next with discontent, and the smallest differences were found with status concern.

Finally, the joint effect of all three variables upon egalitarianism was examined. The results are shown in Table 6.

When aretists were compared to agonists, with discontent and level of education controlled, aretists in every case were more egalitarian than agonists. When discontented students were compared to contented students on their level of egalitarianism, with aretism and level

**Table 6. PERCENTAGES OF JAMAICAN STUDENTS WHO WERE
EGALITARIANS BY LEVEL OF EDUCATION, ARETISM,
AND DISCONTENT**

| Aretism and Discontent | Percentages Who Were Egalitarian | | | | | |
| | Fifth Form | | Sixth Form | | University | |
	Per Cent	Num-ber	Per Cent	Num-ber	Per Cent	Num-ber
Aretists						
Discontented	61	(225)	71	(172)	85	(79)
Contented	44	(541)	57	(247)	71	(55)
Agonists						
Discontented	53	(131)	62	(81)	74	(39)
Contented	38	(327)	46	(96)	63	(19)

of education controlled, discontented students were more egalitarian
than contented students in every case. Finally, when students at different levels of education were compared, with aretism and discontent
held constant, university students in every case were more egalitarian
than sixth form students, and sixth form students were more egalitarian
than fifth form students. Each variable was independently related to
egalitarianism with the other two variables controlled.

In assessing the relative importance of the three variables in the
determination of egalitarianism, the size of the differences shown in
Table 6 was used. Greatest differences were observed between fifth
form and university students. These differences ranged between 21
and 27 points, averaging approximately 24 points. Differences between
contented and discontented students ranged between 11 and 17 points,
and averaged over 14 points. Differences between aretists and agonists
ranged from 6 to 11 points, and averaged 9 points. As a rough measure of the relative importance of these three variables, the differences
show that level of education was a more important determinant of
egalitarianism than either aretism or discontent, and that discontent
was a somewhat more important determinant of egalitarianism than
aretism.

Taken jointly, the three variables were highly related to egalitarianism. Among contented agonists in the Fifth form 38 per cent
were egalitarian; in comparison, among university students classified
as discontented aretists, 85 per cent were egalitarian, a difference of 47
percentage points. A fairly large amount of variation in attitudes
toward equality can be explained with these three variables; however,
not all of the determinants of egalitarianism have been isolated. The
consistency and magnitude of the differences noted demonstrate that
the three variables located in this study are major ones, and used jointly,

are highly predictive of egalitarianism. Any future explanation of variation in egalitarian attitudes should certainly take them into account.

SUMMARY

This study has shown that the level of egalitarianism differs markedly from one group to another, and that changes in egalitarianism over time are probable in both groups and individuals. Thus, egalitarianism, like many other attitudes, is subject to manipulation through social engineering. The distribution and strength of the attitude can change as other social changes take place. Within limits it is subject to planned change — just as the actual distribution of equality is in the society itself. Policies and programs which result in social, political, or economic changes can have a great influence on the attitudes toward equality of the citizens of any nation. But this too is part of a reciprocal process. Attitudes toward equality have an effect on the policies and programs that are suggested, are thought to be politically feasible, and are implemented within a society. Policy decisions on a large number of questions in the areas of economic development, education, agricultural schemes, taxation, and political representation are influenced by the presence or absence of egalitarianism in a substantial proportion of the population, especially among the elites.

The data given in this report lead to mild optimism concerning the future of Jamaica — that is concerning a future that contains more economic and social equality achieved without large-scale violence and bloodshed. Jamaican students generally were more favorable to the spread of equality than opposed to it, and this may augur well for a more egalitarian future. Such students will be entering education and government — change-leading agencies in Jamaica as in most new nations — and they will have opportunities to see their egalitarian attitudes translated into social action. Their influence on Jamaica's images of the future and social and economic policies in Jamaica designed to achieve that future will be much greater than their proportion in the total population, since they are in most cases destined for elite status in Jamaican society.

But the optimism on this score should be no more enthusiastic than is suggested by "mild," because some of the Jamaican students — even some at the university level — were not egalitarian in their attitudes. Although they were a minority, their inegalitarian attitudes should not be discounted in a society in which massive efforts must be made toward creating a more egalitarian new society in the immediate future if the current promises being made to the Jamaican people are to be adequately fulfilled.

Another consideration that sheds a ray of hope is the fact that egalitarianism increases with education. With the considerable efforts to expand educational opportunities in Jamaica, a higher proportion of the future population will receive an education, and a higher percentage should obtain a secondary and university education. An increasing proportion of Jamaican youth should therefore be egalitarian. But these efforts must be more sizeable than they have been to make these increases fast enough and large enough to produce any large-scale alterations in the face of a rapidly increasing school-age population. Keeping pace with sheer population growth alone necessitates rapid enlargement of the educational system. To stand still means to slip back.

Egalitarianism will probably increase in Jamaica in the future, but how fast is problematic. As these students take their place among the leaders and citizens of Jamaica, their attitudes will have increasing weight on public policies. Relaxation of the restrictiveness of the stratification system can result, with accompanying increases in the equality of opportunity and social mobility. The gap that has so long separated the lower classes from the upper classes in Jamaica can be narrowed, and increasingly the benefits of economic development and political democracy can be extended to all classes. Increased communication among the several classes can therefore be hoped for, and it should result in greater integration of the total society and more participation on the part of lower-class people.

The transition from a colonial, relatively stagnant society to a more modern, independent and progressing nation is seldom accomplished without disruption and discontent. But the discontent, as these findings suggest, may lead to a greater commitment to equality. And commitments to an egalitarian image of the future can lead to policies which reduce the distinctions and divisiveness within the new nation. The question remains whether the discontent will lead to violence and conflict before the results of egalitarian policies are felt. If the discontent is kept within limits, and if policies such as increased education are effectively instituted to expand equality of opportunity in Jamaica on a massive scale, then Jamaica should move peacefully through the democratic revolution. A new, more egalitarian era may be at hand.

CHAPTER **8** Race, Class, and Power
in Barbados*

RAYMOND W. MACK

RACE AND THE BOUNDARIES OF GROUPS

"You know Graham Leslie — the man at the bar with the redheaded girl? I met him night before last at a dinner party. Tell me: is he Negro?"

I realized that the question I was raising was a sticky one in many countries in the world today, but I was gambling that the quiet black man seated across the table from me would honor my good intentions instead of being offended by my blunt approach. We had spent three hours together over several rum punches and a lunch of flying fish, breadfruit, and mangoes. I was impressed with his intelligence and his insight into the subtle meanings of the vestigially colonial culture of his island home. He seemed glad enough of an outsider to talk with and therefore willing to tolerate my peculiar scholarly interests.

In reply to my question, he shook his head. "No, Graham's not Negro. His mother was, but he'd pass-as-white."

In Barbados, the existence of this hyphenated phrase is evidence of a sophistication as yet foreign to the United States: the admission that a man known to have a Negro ancestor can achieve the social status of a white person. We shall return to Barbados as an illustrative case; but first, let us look at the general theoretical question of the boundaries of human groups.

* * *

Would you want your daughter to marry a Negro? If a man abandons the Judaism of his forefathers and becomes a convert to

* Expanded version of a paper read at the meetings of the American Sociological Association, Los Angeles, 1963. I should like to express my thanks to the Program of Comparative Politics of Northwestern University, which financed part of my field work in Barbados, and to the Social Science Research Council. The paper was written during my tenure as a Faculty Research Fellow of the Council.

Roman Catholicism, is he still a Jew? What about English-speaking Jamaicans, born in the West Indies, descendants of African slaves: are they English? Jamaican? West Indian? African?

Every one of these questions (and many other similar ones) poses an issue about which many people care deeply. The first is considered by many white people the most telling stroke in a discussion of voting rights in Alabama, housing in Detroit, or immigration to England. The judiciary of Israel has had to address the question of who is a Jew in the same year that the Parliament of Great Britain has debated the status of Jamaicans.

These are questions of the boundaries of groups, questions of central concern to sociologists. When is race relevant to the boundaries of groups? Under what circumstances is it irrelevant? People are willing to lay down their lives for their group. But which group? During World War II, Italian-American soldiers fought Italian soldiers in Italy. In Italy, too, Japanese-American soldiers killed and were killed by white Christian enemies of their white Christian fellow Americans, at the same time that relatives of those Japanese-Americans were imprisoned in the United States because of their race. An American Indian (who at least escapes the onus of being a recent immigrant) was honored as a war hero and then refused burial in his hometown cemetery because he was not white.

Obviously, race is often at the center of group identification. When are racial characteristics used to establish and maintain the boundaries of human groups? Why are they not always used? Since our goal in sociological theory is to explain as much of the behavior of human groups as possible in the most parsimonious terms, we want to start at the most general level. The first question, then, is: what creates and maintains the boundaries of any group, regardless of whether or not race comes into play? If we can answer this question, we can then turn our attention to why race is sometimes, but only sometimes, relevant, and under what circumstances race is brought to bear in bounding a group.

What will account for the existence of a delimited group with its policies of inclusiveness and exclusiveness? What creates and maintains group boundaries? Sanctions do: social rewards and social punishments. People want to affiliate themselves with those groups in which membership promises them rewards: business associations which will increase their profits, unions which will increase their wages, parties which will promote their platforms, the denomination which seems to have the inside track to salvation, clubs in which they will find friends, congeniality groups in which they may find love, colleges which will educate them, fraternities which will help them get jobs, families which will improve their power, neighborhoods which will convey prestige.

Just as people seek rewarding associations, so do they avoid punishing ones.[1] They decline the invitation to the dull tea, the square congeniality group, the ineffectual commerce association, the low prestige country club. A man may date, but not marry, the girl from the wrong side of the tracks; he may study, but reject, the erroneous theology. In the same way, he will try to protect the prestige of his reward system by keeping the wrong people out. Indeed, excluding them is itself a reward. My wife claims to have been vice-president, at the age of five, of a three-person organization which had as its stated purpose: "To keep Bob Kingsley out." Neighborhoods band together to exclude those who would lower property values; sororities blackball candidates with foreign names; colleges discriminate against applicants with low CEB scores; churches excommunicate heretics; debutantes who marry inappropriate spouses are dropped from the Social Register.

Rejection in turn creates walls of defense. Discrimination creates a reaction to itself. Institutionalized exclusion spawns a culture of anti-discrimination. For example, the formation of Jewish clubs which exclude Christians is a function of the same process whereby minorities retaliate against rejection by inventing epithets for the dominant population. If a man must bear hearing himself referred to as a "spade" or "coon" or "nigger," he can at least enjoy the luxury of jeering about "ghosts" and "ofays."

Thus are group boundaries born and guarded. Men seek rewards, avoid punishments, and band together for both purposes.

When, then, is race relevant in creating and maintaining group boundaries? Race becomes socially meaningful when the social organization associates racial status with another status or structural characteristic which is sanction-conveying. Race becomes socially meaningful when biologically inherited characteristics are correlated or tend to match up with social characteristics which are considered especially desirable, such as a lot of education, or especially undesirable, such as low incomes. When a condition which is rewarding or punishing, such as social class with its concomitant life chances, is highly correlated with race, then race is a convenient shorthand for specifying the boundaries of groups enjoying or suffering that condition.

---

[1] As always in dealing with analyses of voluntaristic action, we must remember that the objective fact is the sociologist's, but that one of his objective facts is the actor's definition of the situation. The sociologist may watch an individual join the wrong fraternity and still recognize that his motives were pure — he believed it to be the right one. Or we may note that he seeks what we would objectively define as punishment rather than reward, but that is because punishment is rewarding to him. He is a datum for our colleague across the hall in the Department of Psychology; his perverse behavior does not undermine our theory.

RACE IN EMERGING SOCIETIES

The emergence of new nations — twenty-two in Africa alone since 1950 — gives new significance to the old question of who is a Negro when and where. For over three hundred years, the white portion of the world's population has dominated the colored portion, politically and economically. Suddenly, largely since World War II, the rules of the game have been altered. The political and economic maze has been restructured. The performers in the rat race have had to redefine roles and learn new paths of social organization. Farmers in Kenya, civil servants in Nigeria, shopkeepers in Indonesia, camel drivers in Pakistan, scholars at the University of the West Indies — all have felt the impact of rapid political change. In most such cases, a colored majority, historically disenfranchised under colonialism, finds itself in charge of the political machinery, or at least, for a change, governed by a non-Caucasoid oligarchy. What does this mean for the involvement of whites in the economic order? In some cases, independence may foment a black nationalism which expropriates the property of native-born whites suddenly defined as foreigners. On the other hand, it may result in a colored government dedicated to representing the interests of a propertied class which remains largely white.

White people have provided a three-centuries-old tradition of exploiting race as a critical variable in defining the boundaries of groups. Colored people have learned, literally at the feet of white people, that race can be used as an excuse for political dominance, economic power, educational opportunity, and differential access to life chances. As Sherif says: "The most elaborate 'race' superiority doctrines are products of already existing organizations of superiority-inferiority relationships and exploitations. The superiority doctrines have been the deliberate or unconscious standardizations of the powerful and prosperous groups at the top and not the ideas of the frustrated and deprived majority at the bottom."[2]

Is it possible, then, that a black proletariat suddenly granted political autonomy could resist the temptation to define privilege in racial terms? I think so — if some integrating process, crucial to the social order, cuts across racial lines instead of emphasizing racial differences.

We know, of course, that the emphasis of racial differences need not be a cultural tradition; both Hawaii and Brazil serve as examples. In Hawaii, the earliest contacts between whites and non-whites introduced neither master-slave relationships nor the hierarchy of foreign exploiter and colonial native. On the contrary, race relations were characterized

---

[2] Muzafer Sherif, *An Outline of Social Psychology*, New York: Harper & Brothers, 1948, p. 343.

by cordiality and relative social equality. For example, the king of
Hawaii, to express his pleasure and gratitude to some of the white men
who had served as his advisors, honored them by granting them permission to marry ladies of the royal court. Since, for many white
Hawaiian families, it was a sign of honor, recognition, and achievement
to have intermarried with a non-white group, it became meaningless in
Hawaii to employ race as a definer of group boundary lines. This
established a tradition of ignoring race as a factor in social status in
Hawaii; the consequences of this tradition are still evident today.[3]

The history of Brazil, too, demonstrates that circumstances different
from those of the slavery or colonial patterns of the United States,
Africa, and much of Asia can minimize the significance of race as a
boundary mechanism. The Portuguese, who colonized Brazil, had a
long history of contact with the Moors. This background included an
extensive period of Moorish supremacy and a considerable amount of
acculturation. The early Portuguese migration to Brazil consisted typically of unattached males — and unattached males with less race prejudice than they would have learned had they been Northern Europeans.
Slavery was abolished without the emotional scars which a war of
emancipation left in the United States, and the freeing of slaves was a
custom aided by backing from the Church. The status of freedmen
was clearly defined and protected legally. Therefore, it was possible to
evolve an ideology which approved the blending of diverse racial
stocks in "Brazilians."

> Today one finds at Bahia a freely competitive order in which indi-
> viduals compete for position largely on the basis of personal merit and
> favorable family circumstances. Individual competence tends to over-
> balance ethnic origin as a determinant of social status.
>
> However, the darker portion of the population . . . have had to con-
> tend with the serious handicap that their parents or grandparents or
> other immediate ancestors began on the bottom as propertyless slaves of
> the white ruling class and now bear constantly with them, by reason of
> color and other physical characteristics, indelible badges of this slave
> ancestry, ineradicable symbols of low status. It is not surprising, there-
> fore, to find that the relatively unmixed blacks are still concentrated in
> the low-pay, low-status employments and that they gradually disappear
> as one ascends the occupational scale, until in the upper levels they are
> seldom to be found . . .
>
> But it is just these few individuals who indicate most clearly the
> actual racial situation in Bahia. The Negroes began at the bottom. The
> acceptance, then, of an occasional black, a few dark mulattoes as well
> as numerous light mixed-bloods into the upper circles points con-

[3] Otto Klineberg, *Tensions Affecting International Understanding,* New York:
Social Science Research Council, 1950, p. 192.

clusively to the fact that if a person has ability and general competence, the handicap of color can be, and is constantly being, overcome.[4]

But in most of the underdeveloped areas now emerging as new nations, race has been socially defined as an important part of a colonial pattern of culture, and the utility of physical differences as boundary mechanisms is reinforced by economic and educational inequalities highly correlated with race. The possibility of minimizing the meaning of race, then, rests upon the existence of some process in the social order in which highly rewarding or very punishing consequences cut across racial lines. For example, cricket may be as important to the West Indies as baseball and football have been to the United States in weakening the acceptability of race as an acknowledged boundary criterion. The New York Giants' distinguished Mississippi alumnus, Charlie Conerley, finds Roosevelt Grier an acceptable teammate because Conerley would rather keep his health than his regional prejudices – and thousands of fans apparently share his conclusions. Similarly, when a white Barbadian speaks of "our cricket team," he means a predominantly Negro West Indian team, not a bunch of white foreigners.

One obvious example of the establishment of group boundaries is the structuring of groups around occupational specialities. Each situs, or family of related occupations, builds up a set of norms peculiar to it. These occupational subcultures insulate their participants from the members of another situs. Doctors and nurses have values not shared by railroaders or truck drivers; the occupational norms of the longshoreman are not those of the laboratory worker.

Societies with elaborate occupational differentiation, therefore, while bound together by a common culture, are at the same time fragmented by occupational subcultures. People who share an occupational history develop norms, enforce an ingroup ideology, and come to serve as a reference group for each other. We see this at its extreme when physicists from the Soviet Union and from the United States have more to talk about with each other than either group has with the farmers from their own country.

Craft knowledge, then, creates group boundaries. Any specialized learning is quasi-magic; it gives one power over others who do not have the information. Thus, from the earliest days of a priesthood and laity until very recently, a basic differentiating variable in most class systems has been literacy. But race comes to bear in such a system only if physical attributes are correlated with style of life and life chances. If

[4] Donald Pierson, *Negroes in Brazil*, Chicago: University of Chicago Press, 1942, pp. 177, 204.

race is associated with the opportunity for apprenticeship or entry into an occupation, or if race helps or hinders one's performance, then occupational groups may become racial castes. But if race is neither an aid nor a block to access or success, it remains irrelevant to the process of bounding the occupational group.

Race is used to demarcate an out-group when it is rewarding to use it. But if the process of stratification results in the flaunting of enough exceptions to racial stereotypes, then race is no longer a useful synonym for class. Hence the Barbadian withering of racial boundaries epitomized in the category "pass-as-white."

INTELLECTUAL STRATEGY AND RESEARCH TACTICS

My involvement with Barbados grew out of my interest in social organization and stratification. As a student of class structure, I have found myself drawn increasingly during the past decade into research on and analyses of the role of race in the social structure of the United States. One can hardly pretend to any significant comprehension of the American stratification system without addressing the peculiar definition of race in the United States, where institutionalized color-caste flaws the democratic ideal.

Having studied and written about race relations in the United States, I thought that I could broaden my perspective and might deepen my insight into the American situation by observing the meaning of race in another society. Reading about Caribbean societies led me to the conclusion that Barbados had experienced enough historical parallels to the American situation to make comparison meaningful, and was sufficiently different to make contrast enlightening.

Like the American South, Barbados had imported slaves from Africa and built a plantation system on fields worked by Negroes and owned and operated by Anglo-Saxons. Like American Negroes, Barbadian Negroes saw a century elapse between formal emancipation and significant participation in political power. Unlike American Negroes, Barbadian Negroes are a mathematical majority. Although social definitions of who is a Negro differ somewhat between the two societies, the American distribution of ninety per cent white and ten per cent Negro is roughly reversed in Barbados.

During the two years between my first look at Barbados and the writing of this manuscript, I was able to spend only about six months living in Barbados. If one is going to try, as I did, to achieve some understanding in such a brief period of how a total society is structured, then he must seize every available tool to help accomplish the mission. My work, therefore, cannot be described solely as library research, nor as participant observation, nor as an interview study. I was shamelessly opportunistic in data gathering.

I read seventeenth-century history, eighteenth-century political science, twentieth-century travel guides, and both daily newspapers in Barbados, the *News* and the *Advocate*. I studied census bulletins, government economic reports, civil lists, and gossip columns. I was a participant-observer at dinner parties, at picnics, on the beach, in bars and restaurants, at dances, and at cricket matches and horse races. I attended House of Assembly meetings and Town Council welfare hearings. I interviewed cane cutters, planters, taxi drivers, refinery owners, cooks, insurance brokers, maids, automobile salesmen, housewives, newspapermen, storekeepers, waiters, real estate speculators, government ministers, schoolteachers, clergymen, hotel owners, airplane employees, leisured expatriates, students, radio announcers, civil servants, one shoeshine boy, and the American Vice-Consul. My interviewees included white Barbadians from the "Big Six" families of the island's power structure, Negro Oxford graduates who have achieved enough political power to make the "Big Six" nervous, mulattoes whom an observer accustomed to the rules in the United States would call "Negro," but who are pass-as-white, old-family whites chronically in debt after the fashion of South Carolina "genteel poverty," working-class Negroes, and poor whites viewed with contempt by everyone else regardless of race, color, or creed. My conclusions are based upon data from no specifiable sample of the universe of Barbadians, but if total immersion is the way to salvation, I have tried to demonstrate good faith.

Since my goal was to learn about race and class and their interrelationship, my strategy led me to start at the bottom of the class structure. The tactic of avoiding early contact with members of the power structure was based on the assumption that I could present scholarly credentials later in the game which would explain lower-class associations to upper-class people, but if I became identified early with the occupants of seats of power, it would be extremely difficult later to achieve rapport with workers dependent upon the moguls or with middle-class people resentful of their exclusion from the inner circle.

So I talked first with taxi drivers, bus conductors, waiters, the yard man next door, and gradually became involved in a network of informants: the baby sitter expressed an opinion, the baby sitter's boyfriend disagreed, the baby sitter's boyfriend suggested that I meet and talk with his friend who worked on the docks, and so on. I used to work as a dance band musician before retiring into social science; this provided useful entree into the night world of the island. Many of the musicians working in hotels and night clubs had listened to records and become greatly interested in jazz, and I was able to play with them and talk with them after working hours. My pre-school children spent hours on the beach, and were good enough to introduce me to the parents of their friends, who spanned the color spectrum and the power pyramid.

Gradually, my network of middle-class acquaintances widened. My landlord introduced me to the extension officer of the University of the West Indies. He in turn introduced me to a school principal, a newspaper columnist, and a government officer. The newsman took me to a welfare hearing; the school principal introduced me to a police officer.

I learned to capitalize on the Barbadian's enthusiasm for his island, using it as a probing open-ended question. When new acquaintances asked what I was doing there, I answered truthfully that it was a delightful place for my wife and children to vacation, and that I was writing a book on race relations and social class in the United States. Almost invariably, a Barbadian would respond to this information with the observation that "If you're interested in race relations and social class, you ought to study Barbados." However the Barbadian phrased this sentiment, I replied with questions. Barbados is pretty similar to the United States, isn't it? Yes, I write about social class and race — why? What's unusual about Barbados? Yes, politics has a good deal to do with race relations in the United States; does it here, too?

Such an informal approach to a design for data-gathering has its obvious disadvantages. But I came to the task of analysis and writing thinking that the shuttling from library to observation to interview and back to library had not only equipped me with reliability checks, but had given me insights I might have missed with a more limited armamentarium.

THE SETTING

Barbados is the easternmost of the Lesser Antilles and the largest island, since the departure of Jamaica and Trinidad, in what used to be the British West Indies Federation. It has the approximately triangular shape of a pork chop; its greatest length is 21 miles and it is 14 miles across at its greatest width, with a total land area of 166 square miles. There are a few hills, but the highest point, near the center of the island, is only 1,100 feet above sea level, and most of the terrain is flat or gently rolling.

Barbados lies almost outside the hurricane belt; it has experienced only two severe hurricanes within the past century. But as in other trade-wind islands, the breeze is a constant part of the environment. The average wind velocity is 11.2 miles per hour, and velocities of less than 3 miles per hour are extremely rare. There are no great variations in temperature: the annual mean Fahrenheit reading is 75° on the windward side of the island, 79° on the leeward side. Temperatures range from a low of 61° to a high of 91°. The average annual rainfall varies from 40 to 80 inches.

Bridgetown, the chief port and capital city, and Speightstown, on the northwest coast, have populations of 18,650 and 2,600, respectively. But the population density in the suburbs of these urban parishes ranges from 10,000 to 20,000 per square mile. In the 166 square miles of Barbados, the 1960 census counted 232,100 people, a density of 1,400 persons. The population density of Barbados is nearly twice that of Rhode Island, the most densely populated state in the United States. The entire island is as densely settled as the suburbs of London, a statistic the more astonishing when one realizes that 83 per cent of the island is devoted to farmland. A capsule description of the paradox of such population density in an agricultural economy is the saying that "Barbados is a city where sugar grows in the suburbs."

Of the 106,470 acres of land in Barbados, approximately 83,000 are arable. Nearly 85 per cent of this farmland is in estates of 100 or more acres. Agriculture in Barbados is not highly diversified; sugar cane is the principal cash crop, and the sugar industry dominates the economy. Some 46,000 acres are planted in sugar cane: about 10,000 acres of sugar cane are distributed among 30,000-odd peasant holdings, while the remaining 36,000 are owned by 260 sugar estates.[5] The 1960 crop yielded 153,668 long tons of sugar, of which 11,775 tons were consumed locally and the rest exported. Almost 90 per cent of Barbadian exports are destined for the United Kingdom and the Commonwealth. The extent to which Barbados can be characterized as a one-crop economy is evident from its export figures. Domestic commodity exports in 1960 totalled 35 million dollars;[6] of this, 26.8 million was sugar, 3.2 million was molasses, and 2.4 million was rum: 93 per cent of the total domestic commodity exports were sugar and sugar products. This is well over one-fourth of the total 1960 gross national

---

[5] Detailed statistical tables on land use, percentage of farmland in mature sugar cane, percentage of land in cane reaped, average tons of cane cut per acre, and so on, appear in David Lowenthal, "The Population of Barbados," *Social and Economic Studies*, 6 (December, 1957), pp. 455–501. Most of the data in this paragraph are from quarterly publications of the Barbados Statistical Service: the Statement of Imports and Exports, the Overseas Trade Report, and the Digest of Statistics. Also useful to the social scientist are the monthly reports of the Department of Agriculture and the annual reports of the Department of Labour and of the Barbados Development Board.

[6] All figures in this section are in West Indian dollars. One West Indian dollar equals about sixty U.S. cents; one U.S. dollar equals about $1.67 in West Indian currency.

product of 120 million dollars. The Labor Department's estimate of the distribution of labor during March 1960, when employment was at its peak, emphasizes the dominance of the sugar industry (see Table 1).

Table 1. DISTRIBUTION OF EMPLOYED WORKERS IN BARBADIAN
LABOR FORCE, MARCH 1960*

Industry	Number of Full-Time Employees	Per Cent of Total
Sugar Estates	19,445	27.7
Sugar Factories	2,646	3.7
Hotel, Guest Houses, Clubs	210	0.3
Retail Clerks	719	1.0
Manufacturing	517	0.7
Repairing	298	0.4
Minor Industries	2,047	2.9
Construction	1,128	1.6
Domestics in Private Homes	15,000	21.3
Agricultural Workers in U.S.A.	1,274	1.8
Other Trades and Professions	26,726	38.2
TOTAL	70,010	100.0

(percentages do not total 100 because of rounding)

* Computed from Barbados Department of Labour, Special Report, 1961.

Even leaving aside the extent to which workers in repairing, construction, or domestic service, for example, may derive their incomes through the sugar industry, sugar estates and factories alone employ nearly one-third of the labor force.

Any comment on the labor force should note that estimates of the number of people unemployed during most of the year run as high as 30,000. As in most underdeveloped areas, unemployment and underemployment is endemic. Both have been aggravated, at least temporarily, by progress: at a cost of 28 million dollars, the government has built a deep-water harbor which permits direct bulk loading of sugar. What it also does, of course, is throw out of work all the men who used to put sugar in bags at the sugar factories, load the bags onto trucks, unload the bags at the wharves and place them in small boats called "lighters," row the boats out to the ships waiting in deep water, and transfer the bags of sugar from lighters to cargo ships.

Another facet of the story is that, since the deep water harbor opened in 1961, large cruise ships which used to bypass Barbados find it easier to stop there, thus contributing to the island's second most important industry: tourism. In 1960, in addition to the 35,535 tourists who visited Barbados, 24,172 cruise ship passengers visited the island for less than a day. The Barbados Development Board estimates that, at the present rate of expansion, the tourist industry may provide as much income for Barbados as sugar by 1965.

But the deep-water harbor is only a first tentative step toward industrialization, and no other important moves seem imminent. Sugar cane is reaped by hand. It is planted in depressions approximately three feet in diameter, called "cane holes." A mechanical reaper would cut the cane above ground level, leaving a considerable part of the stalk still in the hole. The Sugar Association contends that mechanical reaping would be uneconomical. At the moment, it is not industrialization but rapid political change that seems to provide the catalyst for restructuring the racial and social fabric of Barbados.

A BRIEF ETHNIC AND POLITICAL HISTORY OF BARBADOS[7]

During my first visit to Barbados, I was given a succinct synopsis of its racial and cultural history by a Negro taxi driver. Since we had disposed of the weather, which, while relatively invariable, is lovely enough to merit a daily tribute, I sought to continue the conversation by remarking that I found in Barbados no evidence of the Indian, French, Spanish, East Indian, Dutch, and other influences which one associates with other Caribbean islands. My black informant replied in clipped British accents: "Oh, no! We've always been English, you know."

And so they have. Early histories suggest that the bearded fig trees led Spanish or Portuguese mariners who first visited the island about 1600 to call it "Los Barbados." Archeological evidence — weapons and

[7] My most important sources for this section were Morley Ayearst, *The British West Indies: The Search for Self-Government*, London: George Allen & Unwin, Ltd., 1960; Alan Burns, *History of the British West Indies*, London: George Allen & Unwin, Ltd., 1954; G. E. Cumper, "Employment in Barbados," *Social and Economic Studies*, 8 (June, 1959), pp. 105–178; Great Britain Colonial Office, *The Colonial Office List*, 1958, London: H. M. Stationery Office, 1958; Great Britain Colonial Office, *Annual Report on Barbados, 1956–1957*, London: H. M. Stationery Office, 1959; J. H. Parry and P. M. Sherlock, *A Short History of the West Indies*, London: Macmillan & Co., 1957; and Ronald V. Sires, "Government in the British West Indies: An Historical Outline," *Social and Economic Studies*, 6 (June, 1957), pp. 109–132. Also useful are E. H. Carter, G. W. Digby, and R. N. Murray, *History of the West Indian People — Book IV*, London: Thomas Nelson and Sons, 1953; Annette Baker Fox, *Freedom and Welfare in the Caribbean*, New York: Harcourt, Brace & Co., 1949; Richard Ligon, "A True and Exact History of the Island of Barbados, 1647–1650," *Caribbean Affairs*, 1957 (abridged); Frank Wesley Pitman, *The Development of the British West Indies: 1700–1793*, New Haven: Yale University Press, 1917; John Poyer, *The History of Barbados*, London: J. Mawman, 1808; Agnes M. Whitson and Lucy F. Horsfall, *Britain and the West Indies*, London: Longmans, Green & Co., 1948; and Hume Wrong, *Government of the West Indies*, Oxford: Clarendon Press, 1923.

sea shell implements — indicate the presence of Caribs or Arawaks as late as the sixteenth century. But the English, when they came, found neither Iberian nor Indian. Various reports place the first British contact with Barbados from 1605 to 1625. At any rate, the first English settlers — 80 of them — came to the island in 1627; by the end of 1628 there were 1,850 persons there. The early social structure was one of small freeholders who raised tobacco with the help of indentured servants and a few slaves. Thirteen years after it was settled, the island had become divided into 11,000 small holdings, most of them poor because they were unable to compete successfully with the tobacco grown in the North American colonies.

Then, in 1640, the introduction of sugar cane to Barbados sparked a social and economic revolution which set the pattern of life on the island for almost two centuries. The cultivation of sugar necessitated large plots of land and a much larger labor force. As tobacco prices fell, small landholders were forced out, the tobacco acreage was converted to sugar, and Barbados became a land of estates. Many of the small proprietors emigrated to the French islands or the mainland, or joined the cadre of settlers of Jamaica. There had been 11,000 holdings in 1640; by 1665 the number of proprietors was reduced to slightly more than 700.

Faced with the enormous need for labor, the planters resorted to purchasing slaves from the Dutch. Thus, the Negro population began to increase as the white population was decreasing through emigration. Historians' estimates vary widely, but the white population seems to have reached an all-time high of between 23,000 and 40,000 in the period between 1640 and 1655. Since then, whites have declined slowly and steadily in number to their present population of less than 10,000. As a proportion of the total population, the white decline was swift and drastic. The ratio of Negroes to whites in Barbados was about 1 to 35 in 1629, 1 to 1 by 1658, 2 to 1 a decade later,[8] 4 to 1 a century later, and by now whites constitute only about 5 per cent of the population.

The original English settlers of Barbados came as a company under proprietary letters patent from the King's Court, and Barbados has been under English law ever since. Representative government dates

---

[8] Estimates of the Negro–white population ratio for the period between 1665 and 1685 range from 2 to 1 to 10 to 1. On the basis of what we know about rapid social change and the visibility of a minority population, I incline to favor the conservative estimates. Consider, for example, the implications of the data in William M. Kephart, "Negro Visibility," *American Sociological Review*, 19 (1954), pp. 462–467, reprinted in Kimball Young and Raymond W. Mack, *Principles of Sociology: A Reader in Theory and Research*, Second Edition, New York: American Book Co., 1962, pp. 161–165.

from the Royal Charter granted by the Crown in 1627 and confirmed by Parliament in 1652. An elected legislative body, the House of Assembly, was established in 1639.

In 1807, an act of Parliament made it illegal for any British subject to trade in slaves. This worked no hardship on Barbadian planters, since the rate of natural increase among the slaves assured an adequate labor force. Suspicions of a continuing illicit trade in slaves spawned a Bill in Parliament in 1815 requiring the registration of slaves in all the colonies. This Registry Bill is credited with inspiring the slave uprising which took place in Barbados in 1816; the Bill supposedly led the slaves to believe that emancipation was imminent.

Parliament in 1831 abolished all civil and military distinctions between free British subjects regardless of color. This, with the Reform Bill of 1832, prepared the ground for the abolition of slavery in 1833. On August 1, 1834, the Abolition of Slavery Act, passed by Parliament a year earlier, became effective throughout the Empire.

In many British colonies, including Barbados, the social structure was altered little by emancipation; true freedom is more realistically dated from the abolition of the apprenticeship system in 1838. The apprenticeships were intended to provide a transitional status for the ex-slaves, who would gradually emerge as an independent peasantry. Actually, since they were in an open labor market where there was virtually no free land available, most ex-slaves were forced by economic necessity to remain as wage-earning laborers on the estates. During this post-emancipation period, therefore, Barbados did not experience the labor shortage suffered by some of the other West Indian islands, and hence did not draw the waves of indentured servants and East Indian immigrants who poured into neighboring islands ("We've always been English, you know").

Indeed, not immigration but emigration has for years been a basic fact of the social and economic life of Barbados. Immediately after emancipation, fear of a labor shortage led the House of Assembly to try to restrict emigration. But with the fall of sugar prices, a long period of drought, and the ensuing economic crisis, the government began, early in the 1860's, to foster emigration as a definite economic policy. Conservative estimates place emigration during the next 60 years at over 100,000 (see Table 2). No systematic records of migration were kept prior to 1903; some estimates place the emigration total between 1861 and 1921 as high as 150,000. The importance of emigration as an instrument of social policy is obvious when these figures are compared with the census report of a total Barbadian population in 1921 of 156,774.

There have been only two periods in recent history when im-

Table 2.   NET EMIGRATION FROM BARBADOS, 1861-1921*

Period	Male	Female	Total	Percentage Migrating to Neighboring Colonies
1861–1871	7,500	2,600	10,100	90
1871–1881	7,600	3,400	11,000	85
1881–1891	6,700	1,600	8,300	85
1891–1911	33,500	16,200	49,700	35**
1911–1921	13,700	10,700	24,400	30**
TOTAL	69,000	34,500	103,500	

* Adapted from data presented on pp. 275–276 in G. W. Roberts, "Emigration from Barbados," *Social and Economic Studies*, 4 (September, 1955), pp. 245–288.
** The reason for the sharp drop in the percentage emigrating to neighboring colonies between 1891 and 1921 is that the bulk of those leaving during this period went to work on the Panama Canal. After the Canal was completed, many of the workers went to the United States.

migration to Barbados has exceeded emigration from it: from 1923 through 1933, when Barbadians who had worked in Panama were being repatriated, and from 1947 through 1949, when people returned from war work and from the Armed Forces. During the 1950's, emigration again exceeded immigration, with thousands of workers moving to the United Kingdom.

Since the emigrants have been predominantly young males, their departure has resulted in a skewed age distribution and a low sex ratio: in 1956 there were only 4 men to 5 women in the 15–64 age group.

Despite the dwindling for three centuries of the white population, both in numbers and as a proportion of the total population, Barbados remained in 1940 a plantocracy, governed politically, economically, and socially by whites. Executive power was in the hands of an Executive Committee consisting of the Governor, the Colonial Secretary, and the Attorney General (all ex-officio and all appointed by the Crown), plus such other persons as the Governor chose to appoint. The nine Superior Courts are presided over by the Chief Justice, who is also a Crown appointee. The legislature was, and is, bicameral, consisting of a Legislative Council appointed by the Crown and of the House of Assembly, composed of 24 members: two members from each of the eleven parishes and two from the city of Bridgetown. Before 1940, a candidate would often be elected in his constituency without opposition. Given the severely restricted suffrage, the mass of the population took little interest in politics.

But a young colored barrister, Grantley Adams, was elected to the House of Assembly in 1934 and gained celebrity when he defended Clement Payne, the leader of the 1937 riots. Then Hope Stevens, a Barbadian returned from the United States, founded the Progressive League in 1938, and in 1939 Adams became its president. The League stood for moderate socialism, social welfare and an extension of the franchise. It attracted a high proportion of the few qualified black and colored voters, and when it ran its first slate, in 1940, elected five of its six candidates. Thus began the marked change in the Barbadian power structure, which would see political power used to bring about alterations in the boundaries of groups.

RACE AND CLASS: THE STRATIFICATION STRUCTURE OF BARBADOS

Another colored Barbadian, Hugh Springer, returned from Oxford, was instrumental in the founding of the Barbados Workers' Union in October 1941; Adams became its first president. The Progressive League became the Barbados Labour Party. Adams and his supporters achieved two crucial political successes: he was appointed to the Executive Committee, and a bill was passed reducing property require-ments for voting by almost one-half and extending the franchise to women. The bulk of the black population was still excluded from the polls, for even with the reduced property requirement, voters were still required to have an annual income of £30 or more, and most cane-field workers earned about £25 per annum. Nonetheless, the voting reform bill spelled the end of automatic white political dominance, as can be seen from Table 3, for it increased the electorate from about 6,000 to nearly 30,000.

Table 3.   **POPULATION OF BARBADOS BY RACE, 1946***

White	9,839
Black	148,923
East Indian	100
Syrian & Asiatic, not shown elsewhere	7
Chinese	29
Mixed or Colored	33,828
Not specified	74
TOTAL	192,800

* Great Britain Colonial Office, *Digest of Colonial Statistics*, No. 36 (January–March, 1958), London: H. M. Stationery Office, 1958, p. 67.

With this expansion of the non-white electorate, Adams, as president of both the Barbados Labour Party and the Barbados Workers' Union, was able to dominate the political scene, picking his candidates and throwing the power of the union behind them. In 1944, the B.L.P. increased its House representation to eight, and Springer joined Adams on the Executive Committee. By forming a coalition with another socialist group, the National Congress Party, which had also won eight seats, the B.L.P. gained a two-to-one majority over the conservative Electors' Association.

Now that the whites could no longer politically validate their economic and social dominance, subsequent changes came swiftly. In September, 1949, the House of Assembly requested the establishment of a full ministerial system. The next year, property qualifications for membership in the House were abolished, the life of the House was extended to three years, and — most important from the point of view of changing the significance of racial status in the social structure — universal adult suffrage was introduced. In the December, 1951 elections, the B.L.P. won 16 seats in a House of 24. Five salaried ministerial posts were established and, on February 1, 1954, Grantley Adams became the first Premier of Barbados.

The correlation between race and class was starkly evident during the debate in the Legislative Council on the eve of the introduction of the ministerial system. Legislative Councillors have been chosen generally on the basis of the representation of private economic interests — notably sugar, of course. The Crown-appointed Legislative Council has been almost exclusively white in membership; in 1954, only two Councillors were colored. At the same time only three members of the elected House of Assembly were white, and one of those was a maverick, a left-wing member of the B.L.P The Councillors attacked the proposed ministerial system "mainly upon the cost involved, with about half of the Labour Party's elected members now due to receive ministerial salaries. Die-hard conservative members in the Legislative Council asserted that universal suffrage had been granted prematurely and predicted grimly the financial collapse of the government, the breakdown of popular government and an eventual dictatorship."[9] The Honourable Ronald G. Mapp, one of the new ministers, retaliated in the House of Assembly: "A lot of people are disappointed that Barbados isn't like BG. . . . They want to see ministerial status collapse. . . . They want to say that the coloured boys cannot run anything. The Malans do not want to see the Nkrumahs come up by their side."[10]

Mapp's remarks reflect accurately the traditionally rigid stratification structure of Barbados. The criteria of class differentiation have been chromatic and economic, with considerable congruity between racial and occupational status. The importance of money and skin color are, if anything, magnified by the absence of other differentiation among the population on other characteristics which might serve as

[9] Ayearst, *op. cit.*, p. 93.
[10] *Ibid.*

criteria of class status in a less homogeneous society. In Barbados, for example, unlike Jamaica, literacy is virtually universal: as long ago as 1946, the percentage of illiteracy in the population over 10 years of age was only 7.3, the lowest in the British Caribbean. Similarly, religion hardly counts as a class indicator where there is an Established Church of such influence, and despite the fact that the religious attitudes of the populace seem fundamentally evangelical, the Anglican Church claims two-thirds of the population as members. Basically, then, neither religious nor educational status has, in the past, been sufficient to override economic and racial status, and property position and race have been highly correlated. The island has been accustomed to a social structure composed of a white upper class of plantation and sugar factory owners, appointed high government officials, and top professionals; a colored middle class of lower professionals, shop-keepers, middle range government employees, and clerical and kindred workers; and a black lower class of craftsmen, peasant farmers, cane-field hands, and other laborers.

Here, then, was a population in which, as recently as the Census of 1946, occupations classified as professional, public service, clerical, trade, and finance accounted together for about one-eighth of the labor force. Over 85 per cent of the labor force consisted of poor or landless peasants and laborers. Average weekly household income was about ten U.S. dollars a week. In this social structure, race was so closely associated with class position that they could usually be used as synonyms. There were a few poor whites; there were some educated, relatively prosperous Negroes. But in general, black meant that one was a peasant or laborer, while white could be taken to refer to both the color and the collar.

Barbados has long had the reputation among West Indians of being the most prejudice-ridden island in the British West Indies. Yet in only a few years, racial boundaries have lost much of their significance to Barbadians.

Fermor summarizes his impressions of the Barbadian way of life, gained during a visit to the island in the late 1940's, as follows: "Looking backwards we could almost see, suspended with the most delicate equipoise above the little flat island, the ghostly shapes of those twin orbs of the Empire, the cricket ball and the blackball."[11]

Yet, less than 15 years later, the widely institutionalized discrimination which offended Fermor has all but disappeared. During a total of over six months which I spent on the island in three separate visits during 1961 and 1962, I interviewed, observed, and investigated various

[11] Patrick Leigh Fermor, *The Traveller's Tree*, London: John Murray, Ltd., 1950, p. 108.

areas of discrimination reported by Fermor: in restaurants, bars, government meetings, business discussions, and social gatherings in private homes. The world he observed has changed, and in a remarkably short time.

SOCIAL CHANGE AND INSTABILITIES IN STATUS

Barbadians are notorious among West Indians for their local pride, ethnocentrism, and insularity. I have long ago lost count of the number of times I have been assured that Barbados is a better place to live than Trinidad, or than St. Lucia, or than Jamaica, and many Barbadians simply state that there is no other place anywhere as nice to live as Barbados. Some of the people who told me of the virtues of Barbados as contrasted with less desirable lands were adults who had never been to "the other side of the island" — 14 miles away. In such a tight little island society, we might expect to find well-defined status groups, relatively few status aggregates of ambiguous rank in the class hierarchy, and a minimum number of status dilemmas and contradictions.

And so it was until the seizure of political power by non-whites. To understand the rapidity and extent of change in the past 20 years, one must remember its racial and demographic context. As in Jamaica,[12] the gradual dwindling of the white population coupled with the growth of a sizable mulatto population helped to define the relevance of race to the boundaries of status groups. The lack of an adequate supply of whites to staff the middle-class positions, and the presence of a mulatto population over three times as numerous as the white segment, afforded the colored population the opportunity to differentiate themselves from the blacks.

Hence, when the whites lost absolute political power, an educated, ambitious elite of non-whites stood ready to exploit their opportunities.

Furthermore, despite recognized social differences between colored and black Barbadians, the political ideology of the new leadership tended to ignore these distinctions; the principal notice taken of race was a sentiment not of contempt for the blacks at the bottom of the hierarchy, but of resentment toward the whites above who had long blocked the road to mobility.

The whites, who had run the society politically, economically, and socially, no longer exercise political dominance. Once this is true, it is no longer rewarding — indeed, it could be severely punishing — for them to try to maintain their social dominance through institutionalized segregation. The only way in which the whites can

12 See Leonard Broom, "The Social Structure of Jamaica," *American Sociological Review*, 19 (1954), pp. 115–125, reprinted in Young and Mack, *op. cit.*, pp. 165–173.

protect their economic power is to accommodate to black political power, which means the weakening of social distinctions associated with race.

Universal suffrage has resulted in a black Premier, a Negro cabinet, and a House of Assembly where only two of 24 legislators are white. But more important, racial distinctions have been blurred by an increasingly open stratification system. Where there are some poor, uneducated whites and an increasing number of powerful, educated Negroes, the old automatic interpretation of skin color becomes untrustworthy. The status of mulattoes becomes increasingly ambiguous, and race is used less as a group boundary line. If the formerly all-white club is to boast the Premier among its members, it cannot remain an all-white club. (This is not a hypothetical illustration; the Premier's invitation to membership broke the color barrier of one of the last white clubs in Barbados in 1961.)

Barbados, of course, is not a unique case. Emily Hahn's report of the coming of independence in Tanganyika provides another illustration of how swiftly and drastically change occurs where political power can be translated into increased social acceptance.

> The sight of Africans and Europeans dining together amicably at the Twiga [Hotel] pointed up for me the contrast between Dar es Salaam today and the city I vaguely remembered from the thirties. It was a smug little place then — as socially ingrown a community as I have ever seen. In those days, its hotels were, of course, segregated, and any European out shopping would have been haughtily incredulous if it had been suggested to him that he wait his turn while an African was being served. Now Europeans wait their turn quite pleasantly, and Africans go where they like, if they can afford it. . . .
>
> British girls in Dar were working placidly away as secretaries for new, African bosses, though I have no doubt that up to very recent times they had felt this to be the one thing they would never, never do. Africans were to be seen dancing in public with the wives of British dignitaries. And at a beach that stretches its spreading shallows just north of the city anyone who wanted to go swimming — African, Asian, or European — was free to do so.[13]

What has occurred in Barbados is the emergence of status aggregates which cut across racial boundaries, although they are aggregates of persons similar in income, education, occupation, religion, and amount of social power. One such aggregate might include a white Canadian investor and a university-educated Negro cabinet minister. Neither was an integral part of the old status structure, but, as Stone and

[13] Emily Hahn, "Changeover in Tanganyika," *The New Yorker*, XXXIX (April 27, 1963), pp. 110, *et passim*. Quoted material from p. 124.

Form point out,[14] their presence is vital to explain the mechanisms of change. For, because of the similarities in life style of the members, these status aggregates are gradually becoming status groups. As they do so, the emerging class structure obliterates the old meaning of race.

In these circumstances, people of an ambiguous class status are placed according to color, while people of ambiguous racial ancestry are placed according to class status. That is, a small store proprietor who has ten years of education and a slightly above average income is white if he looks white and black if he looks black. But a person who in the United States would be called light mulatto is white in Barbados if he is an educated, prosperous, business or professional man, but black if he is a poor laborer.

In Bridgetown, a shoe-shine man of ambiguous racial ancestry uses as his opening conversational gambit the observation that he is in business for himself because he "wouldn't work for any of those niggers" — a fairly bald attempt to reap social rewards and avoid punishments by drawing boundaries around the privileged group so that he is included. The existence of the hyphenated phrase "pass-as-white" indicates an awareness among Barbadians that class position can override genetic history.

The extent to which group boundaries can be socially defined in the process of seeking rewards through association is illustrated by a Barbadian brother and sister, one of whom has run for public office as a Negro, while the other is a member of an exclusively white club! Their mother was mulatto; their father white. Both the brother and sister have relatively Caucasoid features. One has chosen to be white. The other prefers to be colored for the political advantages this offers in a predominantly colored society. People are aware of their background, and respond to them on the basis of the choices they have made. Obviously, an "exclusively white" club in Barbados is working on a different set of social definitions than it would in the United States. But they are social definitions, and clear examples of bounding groups to maximize social rewards.

In Barbados, race is used less as a group boundary line than it used to be because it is less meaningful as it fails to correlate with other criteria of class status. A peasant or laborer can still sponsor a social hop (a juke box dance in a hired hall with drinks and a modest admission charge) with confidence that all his guests will be black, but a businessman can no longer extend invitations for cocktails to the

---

[14] Gregory P. Stone and William H. Form, "Instabilities in Status: The Problem of Hierarchy in the Community Study of Status Arrangements," *American Sociological Review*, 18 (1953), pp. 149–162, reprinted in Young and Mack, *op. cit.*, pp. 136–145.

ten most influential Barbadians and have a party that is all white. A meeting of the Town Council of Bridgetown, or of school principals, or of Barbadian writers, or of the Barbados Flying Club — any such gathering based upon shared education or mutual interests will be an interracial affair. A well-educated pass-as-white girl may prefer the attentions of an educated mulatto suitor to those of a poor white man — and furthermore, she is considerably more likely to have met socially a mulatto or Negro of a class status comparable to hers than a white man who is beneath her in the stratification system. A pass-as-white girl's dating a Negro man is, of course, less startling in Barbados than it would be in the United States; as a white Barbadian man said to me: "No sensible person whose family has been here for over two hundred years would claim that he's all white — for sure."

SUMMARY

We have addressed here one of what Bell and Oxaal in Chapter One have called "the big decisions of nationhood": What kind of social structure should the new nation have? Leaders of new nations do not usually take the answer to this question as pre-ordained or historically determined; they talk as if there were a possibility of man making himself. I heard Prime Minister Barrow address the white businessmen of the Barbados Hoteliers Association in 1962; speaker and audience seemed caught up in an image of the future calculated to force a change in the realities of racial discrimination in Barbados. "We," said Barrow, "are all Barbadians, and we must learn to trust one another and to work together to achieve the best society for us all." The two proprietors I was sitting with had come to the meeting filled with suspicion and hostility; they left reassuring one another, "I think he's right"; "I think we can do it."

The self-conscious decision to try to create a certain kind of social structure will itself, of course, have enormous impact on Bell and Oxaal's other big decisions of nationhood such as: What should the new nation's global alignments be? What form of government should the new nation have? What role should the government play in the affairs of the society? What should the new nation's cultural traditions be? What should the national character of the people be?

But most critically, this paper has addressed the question which Bell and Oxaal believe is fundamental to each of the big decisions of nationhood:[15] How have new national decision makers decided on a par-

---

[15] See Wendell Bell and Ivar Oxaal, *Decisions of Nationhood: Political and Social Development in the British Caribbean,* Denver, Colo.: Social Science Foundation, University of Denver Press, 1964.

ticular version of the nation's social reality?" Beliefs about reality affect images of the future and the policies formulated to make such images reality, and nowhere more drastically than where race is defined as coterminous with class, and where perceived racial differences are used to reinforce group boundaries.

In Barbados, we have seen how class differences can create and maintain group boundaries. When the division of a population according to race is almost the same as the division according to property or income or some other important criterion of social power, race is highly relevant to the boundaries of groups.

The recent history of Barbados also suggests that, when class boundaries shift rapidly, the boundaries of races also become fluid. The acquisition of political power by non-whites allowed them to use that power for rocking the rest of the social system.

But this diminishing of the importance of racial distinctions in Barbados was able to occur because there were many non-whites eager and able to fill statuses previously held by whites. Too, the insularity and intimacy of the society made it difficult to pretend that these ambitious, educated, powerful Negroes were not there. In the United States, on the other hand, it is possible for many white people to have little or no contact with Negroes except as their social inferiors: bellboys, bootblacks, cleaning women, janitors, parking lot attendants, steel mill laborers, and field hands. Ambitious, educated, wealthy, powerful Negroes live and prosper in America, but the United States is not a small island like Barbados, and most white Americans can remain conveniently unaware of the existence of Negroes whom they might have to reckon with as their intellectual or economic equals.

Where an efficient segregation system minimizes one's exposure to members of a minority who do not conform to the stereotype of what they should be like, a culture of discrimination can flourish. Since many white Americans deal most of the time with Negroes who conform to their stereotype of Negroes — that is, Negroes who are poor and ignorant and subservient — it is easy for white Americans to think of the term Negro as a synonym for poor, ignorant, and subservient. If one is as isolated from the mainstream of society as many whites are in the American southern states, this culture of discrimination can become a norm in itself, further isolating them from "outsiders" who do not share their belief in Negro inferiority, or do not share it with the same intensity and conviction. When discrimination is basic to the culture, when it is part of a people's "way of life," it is easy for them to think of it as a natural, even an inborn, trait. Thus people may justify racial discrimination as a consequence of the "natural human aversion" to differentness, rather than the learned behavior which it is.

When psychologists want, for experimental purposes, to turn a normal little white rat into a neurotic one (and some psychologists do), they change the rules of everyday life on him. They teach the rat that, if he finds his way through a maze and trips a lever with his paw, he will be rewarded with a piece of cheese. Then they block one of the passages he has learned to expect, changing the path of the maze. When the rat takes what used to be the correct turn to reach the lever and the cheese, he bumps into a wall. Suppose the little chap has sufficient emotional strength to sustain this frustration and learn the path of the new maze. When he finally arrives at the lever and presses it with his paw, the psychologists have fixed it so that, instead of his cheese, he gets an electric shock. Even a well-balanced, secure little rat from a happy home environment will take only so much of this before he goes all to pieces. An abrupt change in the rules he has learned to live with puts a strain on one's emotional balance, whether one is a rat or a man. A sudden alteration in the path of the maze causes the cheese to seem hard to get at or even unattainable, and the rat will become irritable and perhaps quit trying. A sudden alteration by a new dean in the promotion policy of a university causes salary increases to seem hard to come by, and the psychologist may also become surly or even quit trying. When the rules are changed, the game of life seems difficult or incomprehensible. Ambiguity and uncertainty about what is expected may lead either rats or people to abandon their goals. Instead of using their energy to achieve what used to be ends which were well understood, they are likely either to withdraw or lash out at the environment, using up their resources in random aggression and expressing their hostility toward an unfair world. Ambiguous and uncertain situations may be risky, but they also can create the conditions under which new and better goals can be set, new values and behavior patterns learned.

New political and economic situations are unsettling, but they may for that very reason be destructive of traditional patterns of racial prejudices and discrimination. It becomes increasingly obvious that the caste system of India will not be able to withstand the assault of urbanization and industrialization. Despite the tenacity of cultural norms, it is difficult to maintain patterns of prejudice and discrimination against a group as it loses its identifying sociological characteristics — and especially difficult if the group loses its physical stigmata.

The new nations offer fertile breeding grounds for political upheaval, economic chaos, social unrest, and the exacerbation of racism.

But where stratification is an integrating process cutting across racial lines, they also offer fertile breeding grounds for revolutions in attitudes of racial prejudice and in the practice of racial discrimination as concomitants of revolution in the political and economic structure. In Barbados, the latter process seems to have begun and the emergence of a new society along more egalitarian and socially inclusive lines seems likely.

CHAPTER 9 Management and Workers Face an Independent Antigua

ANDREW P. PHILLIPS

To maintain a nation-state as an "on-going enterprise" certain functional requisites must be met. According to Bell and Oxaal, these requisites may be identified by asking the question: what must men do and become – or think they must do and become – in order to establish and maintain the type of organization called a nation-state?[1] The answer to this question, say Bell and Oxaal, involves ten big decisions of nationhood. One of these has to do with the shaping of a national character. Presumably, in order to preserve itself as a territorial unit and interact with other nation-states with some degree of distinctive identity, the nation-state must orient its citizens in certain directions.

The question is: in what direction should the citizenry be oriented? In the more abstract terms of social science theory: what should the national character of the people be? This chapter addresses itself to that question.

Of course, the leadership of an emergent nation does not usually phrase the question in the abstract terms of social science. Leaders are usually practical men, and they ask the question in practical terms. From this standpoint the leadership seems to reason something like this: "Here we are, an independent nation; well, anyway, independence or at least full internal self-government will come in a few years, so we are practically independent. If we are going to survive as an indepent or semi-independent nation, our people are going to have to put their shoulders to the wheel. Is there any area where people are falling down on the job? If so, we have got to encourage them to do better."

[1] Wendell Bell and Ivar Oxaal, *Decisions of Nationhood: Political and Social Development in the British Caribbean*, Denver, Colo.: Social Science Foundation, University of Denver Press, 1964. Also see Chapter One in this volume.

From the practical standpoint of leadership, the encouragement of people to "do better" really constitutes a social problem that must be solved to make independence work. Underpinning this practical reasoning are at least three assumptions: a) there is some sort of connection between new demands or responsibilities that come with independence and the particular orientation of the citizenry; b) the leadership in general thinks it knows how citizens should be oriented; and c) leaders believe citizens should be encouraged in this orientation.

Of course, it is impossible to orient people in a given direction without at the same time molding their character, if only in some general way. Hence, in solving their practical social problem leaders are really making decisions about what they think the national character should be.

At least, this is the way things seemed to happen on the small island of Antigua, lying about five hundred miles southeast of Puerto Rico in the Eastern Caribbean.

CHOICE OF RESEARCH SITE

At first glance Antigua might seem an unlikely place to conduct research. Covering an area of only 108 square miles, the island is roughly twenty miles long, varies from about ten to fifteen miles in width, and in 1962 boasted a population of about 55,000. Certainly, in terms of size Antigua seems unimportant; but its social structure proved most interesting.

During the last century the island was a wealthy sugar-producing British colony. Its class structure was polarized between the white plantocracy on the one hand and Negro slaves on the other. After the Emancipation of 1834,[2] the slaves were freed but polarization remained. Subject to extreme drought, the island's climate does not favor small-scale farming; consequently, no sizeable class of independent peasants emerged. After Emancipation the ex-slave was merely transformed into an agricultural wage-laborer for the white plantation owner.

In 1939 wage-laborers organized the Antigua Trades and Labour Union which, by 1962, had succeeded in organizing about ninety per cent of the island's 19,000 laborers. After World War II the British Colonial Office considerably extended voting rights to include universal suffrage, and gradually introduced the principle of elected internal self-government. Responding to these political changes, the union organized the Labour Party in 1945. None of its candidates has ever lost an election. By 1962 the Party had captured

[2] Antigua emancipated its slaves without an apprenticeship period in 1834. This was four years before the general emancipation in the British Empire.

all ten elected seats in the island's legislature; the president of the union had become Antigua's first Chief Minister. In short, the Labour Party was in complete command of the process that would lead Antigua to independence or to near independence in association with the United Kingdom as now appears likely. At the time I collected my data in Antigua it was widely believed that Antigua would become fully independent politically as part of a federation of the eight small Eastern Caribbean islands.

Here, then, we have an island diminutive in size, small in population, polarized in class structure, with the political leadership solely concentrated in the hands of one group. The smallness of size and simplicity of social structure allowed social problems to be seen in bold relief; moreover, given these conditions, the processes underlying the problems could be more easily identified. If decisions about nationhood were going to pose social problems, then Antigua seemed a good laboratory for studying them in detail.

SPECIFICATION OF THE RESEARCH PROBLEM

Poll of Antiguan community leaders. Before going to Antigua, I had already decided to do research on "national character," so I arrived on the island with a pre-existing research interest. By the term "national character" I mean nothing mystical; I define the aspect of national character I wanted to study as the sum-total of responsibilities that leaders *think* citizens should accept in order to make the emergent nation-state a going concern. Specifically, I wanted to know two things: a) what kinds of responsibilities did leaders think citizens should accept?; b) which responsibilities did leaders think citizens were shirking?

To answer these questions I conducted an opinion poll among Antiguan community leaders during February and March, 1962. To qualify as a "leader" for this poll a person had either to:

1) occupy formally the top executive position in a voluntary or statutory organization such that he was entitled to formulate development policy or advise on such policy; or
2) be an elected or appointed member of the Legislative Council.

In February letters were sent to the following fifty-five community leaders with a request for a personal interview:

1) Seventeen political leaders consisting of the ten elected members of the Legislative Council; the two Nominated Members; the two Official Members (representing the Crown); and three executive officers of opposition political parties.

2) Seventeen educational leaders, including twelve headmasters or headmistresses of the island's secondary schools (I concentrated only on secondary schools because at the time the island was having problems in extending secondary education); four civil service executive officers in the field of education; and the local representative of the adult education program of the University of the West Indies.

3) Twenty-one economic leaders, including eight civil service officers in the field of economic development; nine executive officers of private business organizations; and four executive officers of trade unions.

Note that leaders fall into the three areas of politics, education, and economics. These three areas of leadership were selected on the basis of a content analysis I had made of Antiguan newspapers dating from 1 January 1960 to 31 December 1961. This analysis indicated Antiguans were most concerned with political, educational, and economic issues; consequently, only leaders from these three areas were selected for interview.

Forty-seven (85 per cent) of the fifty-five leaders agreed to answer the following four questions:

1) What is the most important social problem confronting Antigua at the present time?

2) What is the most important social responsibility that people will have to accept in order to make an independent Antigua a going concern?

3) What is the most important difficulty in getting people to accept that responsibility?

4) Among what section of the population does this difficulty seem to loom largest?

Major findings. Only four leaders (9 per cent) felt the island's political problems were of paramount importance. All four spoke of initial difficulties stemming from the changeover from Crown Colony to responsible, internal self-government. All felt these problems would resolve themselves in time. The remaining forty-three leaders (91 per cent) felt economic and educational problems were more important. Of these, only six (14 per cent) felt the island's political, educational, and economic development had not gone far enough to expect much from the citizenry. The other thirty-seven (86 per cent) believed enough improvement had been made so that the ordinary citizen could be expected to pull his share of the load. Of these thirty-seven, seventy per cent felt the Antiguan citizenry deficient in exercising

An old sugar mill in Barbados. *Photo by W. E. Alleyne.*

In the cane fields of Trinidad. *Photo by Paul Rupp Associates.*

Cane moving from carrier to mill. *Courtesy of the Jamaica Sugar Manufacturers Association.*

Machines and workers in a West Indian sugar factory. *Courtesy of Jamaica Industrial Development Corporation.*

Known as "higglers," these Jamaican women travel from country parts to markets throughout the island each week

A wattle and daub house and occupants in Antigua. *Photo by Walker's Art Studio.*

A neighborhood in West Kingston, Jamaica. *Photo by John W. Evans.*

West Kingston, Jamaica. *Photo by John W. Evans.*

West Kingston, Jamaica. *Photo by Amador Packer.*

West Kingston, Jamaica. Photo by Amador Packer.

Cricket being played at Sabina Park in Kingston, Jamaica. *Courtesy of the Jamaica Tourist Board.*

One of cricket's legendary three-somes: Barbadians Frank Worrell (from left), Everton Weeks, and Clyde Walcott.

their economic responsibilities (Table 1). Although economic conditions had improved, workers allegedly were not willing to take a responsible attitude toward work; nor were they willing to train their children to do so. Some supposedly wasted their increased earnings on frivolous purchases. A minority of thirty per cent argued that the educated middle class, small though it was, should exercise a more

Table 1. OPINIONS ABOUT THE LACK OF RESPONSIBILITY VOICED BY THIRTY-SEVEN ANTIGUAN COMMUNITY LEADERS WHO SAID CONDITIONS FOR GENERATING CITIZEN RESPONSIBILITY WERE PRESENT

Opinion	*No. of Cases*		*Per Cent*
Economic conditions are present but responsibility is absent		(26)	70
1) Economic conditions have improved but responsibility toward work has not	(17)		46
2) Economic conditions have improved but parental responsibility has deteriorated	(8)		21
3) Economic conditions have improved but monetary responsibility has not	(1)		3
Educational conditions are present but responsibility is absent		(11)	30
1) Educational conditions have improved but there has been no corresponding willingness by the educated to assume responsibilities of leadership	(5)		14
2) Educational conditions have improved but there has been no corresponding willingness to readjust social values	(6)		16
Totals		(37)	100

responsible leadership position in the community. In general, educated middle-class people were accused of clinging to anti-egalitarian social values at variance with the social philosophy of the Labour Party.

In short, leaders felt that both wage-laborers and the middle class posed problems; but of the two, wage-laborers posed the greater problem because they held an irresponsible attitude toward work. In addition, thirteen leaders cited worker irresponsibility as a problem subsidiary to the main one they mentioned. When these opinions were added to those who singled this out as the main problem, a total of thirty leaders out of forty-seven (64 per cent) saw the lack of a responsible attitude toward work as an obstacle to Antigua's future development. So far as leaders were concerned, Antigua's "national character" seemed deficient in its work commitment.

Meaning of poor work performance. Table 2 shows what these thirty leaders meant by worker irresponsibility. Fifty-three per cent accused the worker of cheating with his time and labor. Typical responses under this category included such remarks as: the laborer "shirked his work," "sat down on the job," "stood up and argued," "tried to do as little as he could," "talked while he was supposed to be working," and "would only work when supervised." Upon withdrawal of supervision, the worker sat down or stood up again, whatever the case may be.

Table 2. CLASSIFICATION OF TYPES OF POOR WORK PERFORMANCE AS SEEN BY THIRTY ANTIGUAN COMMUNITY LEADERS IN PRELIMINARY OPINION POLL

Type of Poor Work Performance	*Number of Times Mentioned*			
	By Those Who See Work as Main Problem	*By Those Who See Work as Subsidiary Problem*	*Total No. of Times Mentioned*	*Total Per Cent*
Cheated with time and labor	11	5	16	53
Displayed lack of job interest	4	6	10	33
Lacked initiative for improving self	2	0	2	7
Displayed arrogance and inconsideration	0	2	2	7
Totals	17	13	30	100

Thirty-three per cent felt the worker displayed a lack of job interest. The laborer, so they believed, felt that "society owed him a living"; hence, he "had no pride in his work," but "just got through the job as quickly as he could whether it was well done or not." Supposedly, he lacked "a sense of duty or conscientiousness," "had no push for the business," and "did what he was told and nothing more."

Two leaders saw workers as unwilling to accept the responsibilities of promotion. It was asserted, for example, that young people in general desired better paying positions, yet few seemed willing to take the extra time needed to acquire skills requisite for promotion. Another two respondents thought clerical personnel with secondary education displayed arrogance and inconsideration toward the public. Supposedly, they manifested "feelings of superiority."

Sections of labor force displaying poor work attitudes. The majority of leaders singled out non-agricultural manual wage-laborers for the brunt of criticism. In Antigua the term "non-agricultural laborer" referred to anyone who did not specifically engage in agricultural field work. Examples include domestic servants, sugar factory workers, employees on construction projects with the Government Public Works Department, and employees in the burgeoning tourist industry. Among laborers in these occupations, those between the ages of 18 and 39 were thought to have the most irresponsible attitude toward work. No leaders specifically found fault with older, upper-class business executives or civil service department heads; nevertheless a minority believed poor work attitudes to be generally distributed throughout the entire labor force from the top to the bottom.

Readers might be surprised that leaders should focus their criticism upon *non-agricultural* manual workers, especially since Antigua has had a predominantly agricultural economy. A moment's reflection, however, will show the leaders' concern to be logical. Agriculture has traditionally been unable to absorb large portions of the labor force; consequently, the economy has suffered from a high degree of under-employment and unemployment. Creation of so-called "secondary industry" to absorb these excess laborers has been defined as the solution to this problem. As a result, economic development has come to mean the opening up of non-agricultural employment opportunities. Leaders thus defined worker performance in the non-agricultural sphere of the economy as crucial to the success of the Government's economic development program.

It might be argued that these findings primarily tapped conservative political sentiment; perhaps they did not truly reflect the opinions of the liberal Labour Government. There seem no grounds for this objection: apparently these findings cut across political orientation. Indeed, the Labour Party itself has on more than one occasion alluded to the problem of worker responsibility. Consider the following sentiments appearing in the official organ of the Antigua Trades and Labour Union, the *Workers' Voice*, on September 28, 1962:

An undisciplined and disorganized labour force in this day and age can foul the machinery for economic progress and retard its growth.

Industrial development without adequate and disciplined labour can only be imaginative and not real.

A country progresses substantially on the basis of the number of manhours gained. The hallmark of prosperity is production at the highest level. Manhours lost from slackening on the job, absenteeism, irresponsible strikes not sanctioned by the union all tend to reduce production and are a deterrent to prosperity . . . .

In this respect we can do a little simple economic study. If it can take a man one hour to do a piece of work and instead he did it in two hours, the man has utilized a whole hour of his time that could be used to do something else and it increases the cost of the job because of the longer time put on it. That is waste. If 100 persons did the same thing that would be 100 hours wasted and the productivity of the island would be reduced as a result.

If Antigua is to stand on its feet economically and the island is to become viable, we cannot entertain waste . . . .

As if to drive home the point, the Twenty-Third Annual Conference of the union in September 1962 severely reprimanded laborers in the Public Works Department. A resolution charged them with "not doing a full day's work for a full day's pay" and demanded the Minister of Public Works request "every foreman-of-works to give a full report of the workers every week. 'You have got to be responsible,' " said the Chief Minister who was also president of the union.[3]

LEADERS EXPLAIN POOR WORKMANSHIP

Leaders' explanations. Leaders who argued that Antigua's national character was deficient in its commitment toward work often volunteered explanations to account for this phenomenon. Others were asked a series of informal, open-ended questions to see whether they had any opinions on the subject. Out of these answers five general explanations emerged. Workers were unwilling "to give a fair day's work for a fair day's pay" because: 1) they imitated improper role models such as non-laboring tourists; 2) they had a low level of subsistence needs, hence they had nothing to work for; 3) they were overimpressed with the material benefits won by the union and were resting on their laurels; 4) they had no vocational interest in their jobs and worked simply to make money; and 5) they still saw themselves as "exploited" and withheld part of their labor out of resentment.

Each one of these explanations actually constituted a hypothesis that purportedly explained low work commitment. To test these hypotheses in some sort of scientific fashion we would need to do three things: a) find a group of non-agricultural workers to interview; b) divide

[3] The *Workers' Voice*, September 28, 1962.

this group into "good" and "poor" workers on the basis of some criteria; and c) compare the two groups in terms of the five characteristics enumerated above. If any of these hypotheses were valid, the "bad" characteristic should be present among "poor" workers and absent among "good" workers.

Choice of interview group. Non-agricultural workers were primarily concentrated in three areas of the Antiguan economy: the Government Public Works Department, the tourist industry, and the sugar factory. Our time schedule forced us to choose only one of three, so we chose the sugar factory. There were several advantages in doing so: it was the largest employer of labor on the island (about 750 workers); its management proved very much interested in the overall plan of research and was most willing to cooperate; and the factory itself was a highly mechanized operation requiring a work-force well disciplined to the work-roles of manufacturing activity. If economic development meant the opening up of industrial work-roles, the factory labor force comprised something of a "prototype" of the kinds of workers Antigua would need in the future.

Management's criteria of good workmanship. Out of a total of 751 employees in 1962, 453 were manually employed either in actual milling operations, the machine shop, or the factory yard. Most of these were either unskilled or semi-skilled; skilled laborers were found only in the machine shop.

Because the factory did not operate on a piece-rate system, it had devised no objective method for evaluating the individual productivity of its manual laborers. To surmount this difficulty the Chief Overseer (General Foreman) was asked to rate the performance of all 453 manual workers as "good," "average," or "poor." The purpose of the three ratings was to encourage the Chief Overseer to differentiate clearly workers whom he considered "good" or "poor" from those he thought merely "average." We planned later to eliminate the "average" group from consideration and interview only the two extremes. The Chief Overseer was not told of this beforehand because we did not want his ratings biased by this information.

The Chief Overseer made his evaluations on the basis of his own personal observation of worker performance. In the case of workers with whom he might not be personally acquainted, he usually deferred to the evaluation of shift overseers (foremen) who might have more direct knowledge. He said he used three criteria to make the ratings: pride of workmanship; exercise of personal self-discipline; and the exercise of initiative. With these criteria in mind he produced a list of 29 "good" and 37 "poor" workers. The remaining 387 he considered "average."

It is of course possible that certain subjective biases may have entered into the Chief Overseer's ratings. To estimate the extent to which this might be so, we asked three "check" questions in later interviews with factory workers.

Before talking to workers at the factory, we conducted a series of preliminary interviews among laborers in a village near our residence. Through these interviews we discovered that workers themselves tended to classify their fellow-workers into two groups: those who worked for "fame" or "the name" and those who worked for "the money." In general, workers motivated by money tended to deprecate those working for "fame." They felt toward them much the same way as the American worker feels toward the so-called "rate-buster."[4] "Fame" was a foul epithet used by these workers to depict a laborer who allegedly placed pride of workmanship above his wage earnings. Such laborers, they suspected, were "company men" out to win favors from management. On the other hand, workers motivated by "fame" tended to have little use for those who worked primarily for the money. They accused the latter of showing no interest in their work and of cheating with their time and labor. If management's first criterion (pride of workmanship) were in fact operating, "good" workers should have been working for fame. Poor workers would be working for the money. Our findings upheld this argument: a high degree of association existed between the managerial rating and the workers' own system of classification (see Table 3).

Table 3. ATTITUDES TOWARD WORKING FOR FAME AND MONEY AMONG GOOD AND POOR WORKERS (N = 60).

Attitude	Good Workers (Per Cent)	Poor Workers (Per Cent)
Worked for money	21	71
Worked for fame	72	19
Worked for neither	7	10
Totals	100	100
Number of cases	(29)	(31)

Chi Square = 16.7, p< .001.

Management's second criterion (the exercise of personal self-discipline) proved much more difficult to validate. The Chief Overseer

[4] Melville Dalton, "The Industrial 'Rate-Buster': A Characterization," *Applied Anthropology* (now *Human Organization*), 7 (Winter, 1948), pp. 15–18. Out of 300 men in the factory studied by Dalton, only nine (3 per cent) were classified as "rate busters." By comparison the Chief Overseer was far more generous in his evaluations. Out of 453 workers, he classified twenty-nine (6 per cent) as "good."

suggested that the display of family responsibility might serve as a good index of self-discipline. Presumably he believed that family responsibilities might put pressure on the worker to behave more responsibly toward his work. If this were so, "good" workers would more likely be married men; "poor" workers would be single. Our findings did not bear out the Chief Overseer's contention. Table 4 does show a slightly higher proportion of good workers to be married; but the maritial status of good and poor workers did not markedly differ. Perhaps it should be pointed out that West Indian marital status is not always clear-cut, at least to an American. Many West Indians enjoy a common-law relationship but do not define themselves as "married" because no legal or religious ceremony has been performed. Others may consider themselves "married" despite this fact. The interviewer tried to do the best he could; but he sometimes found it difficult to probe deeply into the workers' marital relationships. Consequently, the categories in Table 4 may not accurately reflect the true nature of things. To the extent that they are accurate, they indicate the Chief Overseer had no systematic bias toward rating married men as good workers.

Table 4. MARITAL STATUS OF GOOD AND POOR WORKERS (N = 60).

Marital Status	Good Workers (Per Cent)	Poor Workers (Per Cent)
Married (civil or common law)	59	52
Single	38	45
Other (separated or widower)	3	3
Totals	100	100
Number of cases	(29)	(31)
Chi Square = 0.1, p < .80.		

To test management's third criterion (exercise of initiative) workers were simply asked whether they liked to exercise initiative or do exactly as they were told. According to the Chief Overseer, good workers should fall into the first category, poor workers into the second. Table 5 shows this was pretty much the case.

The evidence above seemed sufficient to accept the managerial criteria as a fairly valid basis for worker classification.

Forty-five-minute interviews were begun with the sixty-six workers on the Chief Overseer's list during June and July 1962. To ensure privacy management provided us with a separate office in an engineering shed in back of the millhouse. Despite this seclusion, six workers rated as "poor" were either unavailable or unwilling to cooperate.

Table 5. ATTITUDES TOWARD EXERCISING INITIATIVE AMONG GOOD AND POOR WORKERS (N = 60).

Attitude	Good Workers (Per Cent)	Poor Workers (Per Cent)
Liked to exercise initiative	86	32
Did not like to exercise initiative	10	68
No answer	4	0
Totals	100	100
Number of cases	(29)	(31)

Chi Square = 17.5, p < .001.

Test of hypothesis #1: improper models of economic behavior. The one leader who suggested this hypothesis thought many workers modelled their work attitudes after wealthy tourists who had no visible means of employment. Supposedly the worker took the tourist as his "ideal." If the tourist spent his time in idleness and fun, the worker should do the same.

To test this hypothesis workers were asked about the standard of life they were aiming for when they first entered the labor force. If they named a style of life lived by people outside Antigua, we asked: "How did you find out about that kind of life?" and "What did you like about that standard of life?" Additional probe questions were directed at getting workers to name specific examples of people who lived the kind of life to which they aspired. If the leader's hypothesis was correct, a large proportion of poor workers should have cited tourists as their examples. Results are in Table 6.

Not one worker mentioned either tourists or foreigners as examples of people living the style of life he desired. On the contrary, most Antiguan workers appeared realistic. The majority of both good and poor workers (66 and 55 per cent respectively) aspired only to the "ordinary" West Indian lower middle-class level typified by the successful skilled worker or shopkeeper. Only three per cent of the poor workers aspired to a level above the ordinary. Even more interesting, 42 per cent of the poor workers were *unable* to articulate clearly the style of life they desired. Most of them simply said they wanted to "better their conditions in life" in some general way. When these responses were added to those who aspired to the "ordinary" level, 97 per cent of the poor workers originally strove for a standard of life that would make them at least "ordinary." The same was true for 86 per cent of the good workers. There seems almost no empirical support for our first hypothesis.

Table 6.   STYLE OF LIFE TO WHICH ANTIGUA SUGAR FACTORY WORKERS ASPIRED (N = 60).

Style of Life	Good Workers (Per Cent)	Poor Workers (Per Cent)
Upper-class white	0	3
West Indian politician's standard	4	0
Professional level (including engineers)	10	0
"Ordinary" West Indian lower middle-class	66	55
Unspecified	20	42
Totals	100	100
Number of Cases	(29)	(31)

Test of hypothesis #2: low level of aspiration. Two leaders believed Antiguan workers did not have enough to strive for: the workers' level of subsistence had traditionally been so low that it could be very easily met. Once it had been achieved, the worker withdrew his zest to labor.

The results obtained from testing our first hypothesis do indicate that workers in general did not strive for an abnormally high standard of living. As we probed deeper, however, we discovered almost as many subsistence levels as there were workers. For example, if the worker had no house, he wanted a "wooden tenement," as a movable wooden cottage on rented land was called. If he already had a tenement, he wanted electricity. Having that, he wanted piped water and either a bathroom or a kitchen (many laborers did their cooking outside behind the house on a coal-pot, African style). If he had all those things, he then wanted a concrete block house on his own land. If he had no transportation, he wanted a bicycle and then a motor bike and perhaps, later on, a second-hand car. In sum, what the worker wanted depended upon what he already had; and the more he had, the more he seemed to want. There was no difference between good and poor workers in this respect; hence hypothesis #2 did not appear to have much support.

Nevertheless, we decided to pursue the matter a little further. We attempted to classify the present-day goals of the laborer to discover whether good and poor workers differed in the *type* of goal toward which they were oriented. Workers were asked to enumerate all the things they were striving for and rate them in order of importance. Goals ranked as first in importance are listed in Table 7. The desire for house and land was considered a strictly subsistence goal. Others we arbitrarily termed non-subsistence. Seventy-seven per cent of the poor workers were striving for house and land compared to only forty-eight per cent of the good workers. In contrast, 52 per cent of the good workers but only 23 per cent of the poor were oriented toward non-subsistence goals. This difference was not statistically significant but it came close.

Table 7. PRESENT-DAY LIFE-GOALS OF ANTIGUA SUGAR FACTORY WORKERS (N = 60).

Life-Goals	Good Workers (Per Cent)	Poor Workers (Per Cent)
Subsistence	48	77
House and land	48	77
Non-subsistence	52	23
Vocational (self-employment)	21	13
Vocational (change of employment while remaining wage-earner)	10	0
Furthering of education of self or children	10	10
Ownership of vehicle (bicycle, motor bike, or second-hand automobile)	7	0
Money	4	0
Totals	100	100
Number of cases	(29)	(31)

Chi Square = 3.5, p < .10.

At the same time these data did not really answer the most important question: did these non-subsistence goals cause good workmanship or was it the other way around? Good workmanship might bring higher wages and allow the worker to satisfy his major subsistence goals. These might then decline in importance as the worker fixed his sights on other things.

Test of hypothesis #3: overconfidence with labor union gains. The possibility exists that poor workers might believe their subsistence goals could be very easily met given the improved working conditions in modern Antigua. Three leaders argued that many workers had been overly impressed with the material gains the union had achieved since 1939. Not only the worker's job security but also his political power had been most definitely enhanced when the Labour Party was able to form the Government. The right to strike had been recognized, employers' rights to dismiss peremptorily had been circumscribed, wages had risen, and a workers' housing program implemented. Under these conditions, said the leaders, the will-to-work had declined as workers were relaxing on the job.

To test this hypothesis workers were asked: "Are there any things standing in the way of achieving your goals here in Antigua?" If, indeed, the "ordinary" level of subsistence were easily within reach because the Antiguan frame of reference was limited and the union provided job security, the majority of poor workers should have seen no obstacles to their goals.

Results obtained in Table 8 failed to confirm this hypothesis. Only one poor worker and two good workers saw no obstacles. Low wages comprised the greatest obstacle for 90 per cent of the good workers and 87 per cent of the poor. There seemed little evidence for assuming that workers had become so overawed with union successes they felt catapulted into utopia. These findings also throw some light on our second hypothesis which said that workers' aspirations were so low they had nothing to strive for. So far as the workers were concerned, wages were too low to achieve even the ordinary level of subsistence to which they aspired.

Table 8.   OBSTACLES STANDING IN THE WAY OF GOAL ACHIEVEMENT PERCEIVED BY ANTIGUA SUGAR FACTORY WORKERS (N = 60).

Perception of Obstacle	*Good Workers (Per Cent)*	*Poor Workers (Per Cent)*
No obstacles perceived	7	3
Low wages	90	87
Lack of regular employment	3	7
Poor management policy of factory	0	3
Totals	100	100
Number of Cases	(29)	(31)

Test of hypothesis #4: lack of vocational orientation. Twelve leaders suggested that poor work performance could be explained by the fact that many workers were not vocationally oriented. Because of the lack of proper vocational training in school and because of widespread unemployment, many workers supposedly seized any job available and then became rapidly dissatisfied. Presumably vocationally oriented workers a) would try to select jobs consistent with their vocational likes; b) would be more likely hired when competing with others with no clear-cut occupational preferences; and c) would find greater job satisfaction when they were actually employed at their chosen work.

I tested this hypothesis by examining whether at the time of entrance into the labor force good workers had been more vocationally oriented than poor. All were asked: "When you first started to work, what were you aiming at in life? What did you want to make you feel happy in life so that life would really be worth living?" Several probe questions were directed at finding out whether the worker had a definite occupation in mind. Workers who named a specific occupation were classified as vocationally oriented. Others, who replied they were bent on "general uplift" or something similar, were considered oriented toward general improvement. If hypothesis #3 were valid, poor workers should have been overwhelmingly concentrated in the latter category.

Table 9 reveals a tendency in the predicted direction, although the difference between good and poor worker responses does not quite achieve statistical significance. About twice as many good workers (45 per cent) said they held vocational goals when they started out to work as did poor workers (23 per cent). In contrast, over three-fourths of the poor workers had primarily set their sights on general improvement compared to only 55 per cent of the good workers. Note, however, that the majority of *both* groups said they were non-vocationally oriented when they first entered the labor force.

Table 9.   LIFE-GOALS OF ANTIGUA SUGAR FACTORY WORKERS AT TIME OF ENTRANCE INTO LABOR FORCE (N = 60).

Life-Goal	Good Workers (Per Cent)	Poor Workers (Per Cent)
Vocational	45	23
General improvement	55	77
Totals	100	100
Number of Cases	(29)	(31)
Chi Square = 2.4, p < .20.		

It should be emphasized that in answering the interview question, some workers had to recall how they felt perhaps twenty years before. Recall questions of this nature are not always too accurate; consequently, Table 9 may not present an altogether valid picture of reality. To the extent that it is accurate, it lends some credence to the leaders' hypothesis.

Test of hypothesis #5: feelings of exploitation. Twelve leaders vouchsafed the opinion that laborers had withdrawn their commitment to work because they felt exploited. To get at this underlying resentment we asked workers if they thought management were "robbing" them. At first glance such a question sounds emotionally charged; but, on the average, workers had only a fourth or fifth grade education and did not understand the meaning of the word "exploitation." From probe questions we discovered they interpreted exploitation to mean robbery in the sense that wages were felt to be inconsistent with actual output. Despite the emotional connotation, we stuck to the word the workers understood and which they themselves used in conversation. In keeping with the leaders' hypothesis, a larger proportion of poor workers should have felt robbed.

Table 10 provides evidence consistent with this premise: 87 per cent of the poor workers felt robbed compared to only 48 per cent of those rated good. This difference in response was statistically significant. In fact, this was the only hypothesis that produced a statistically significant difference in worker response. Clearly, of all five hypoth-

Table 10. FEELINGS OF BEING ROBBED BY THE COMPANY AMONG ANTIGUA SUGAR FACTORY WORKERS (N = 60).

Feeling	Good Workers (Per Cent)	Poor Workers (Per Cent)
Company was robbing workers	48	87
Company was not robbing workers	42	7
Don't know	10	6
Totals	100	100
Number of Cases	(29)	(31)

Chi Square = 9.2, p $<$ .01.

eses, this was the only one most definitely supported by the data. This finding was even more interesting when compared with the results in Table 8 which showed an almost equal proportion of good and poor workers complaining of low wages (90 and 87 per cent respectively). Although the majority of all workers felt wages were too low, *it was primarily the poor workers who made charges of outright robbery.*

AN ALTERNATIVE HYPOTHESIS: THE PERCEPTION OF OPPORTUNITY

The question is: why did poor workers feel so exploited? What was operating here to produce this difference in orientation? In answer to this question we propose an alternative hypothesis not advanced by any Antiguan leader: *work commitment is dependent upon the worker's perception of opportunity. The will-to-work is heightened when the worker perceives opportunities to obtain his own personal goals through his work performance. Conversely, when the worker perceives no opportunity to achieve his personal goals through his labor, his will-to-work declines.*

I arrived at this hypothesis by asking workers a series of thirty-four questions concerning: a) the five hypotheses previously discussed; b) their work history from the time they entered the labor force up to the time of interview; c) their attitudes toward company policy; and d) their background characteristics such as age, religious preference, etc. Management ratings of good and poor were then cross-tabulated with the items covered by these thirty-four questions. In this way we were able to isolate a set of ten variables significantly differentiating good from poor workers. As a second step, we cross-tabulated these ten variables with one another in an effort to discover the underlying process that connected them all together and explained good workmanship. Although the above hypothesis is *post factum* in nature and needs to be subjected to further test, it does provide a tentative explanation that accounts for all ten variables differentiating good from poor workers.[5]

Variables differentiating good from poor workers. As can be seen from Table 11, poor workers tended to attend church less than every Sunday and originally had difficulty finding employment before coming to the factory. At first they liked working there, although they had experienced few promotions and earned less than $20.00 (BWI) per week. They also evinced a significant inclination to complain about the way they were treated, the promotion policy of the company, being pushed around, and being robbed. They felt promotions were based upon favoritism rather than ability.

In contrast, good workers were prone to attend church every Sunday, had little original difficulty finding employment, yet at first disliked the factory. A larger proportion of them had been promoted, earned $20.00 (BWI) or more per week, and had fewer complaints about company policy.

Church attendance. Cross-tabulations with the other nine variables indicated that regular church attendance was significantly associated with a feeling of original dislike for factory work and with a factory record of eleven years or more. It was further discovered that a significantly larger proportion of those who had worked at the

---

[5] A copy of the workers' interview guide together with a more extended discussion of these cross-tabulations may be found in the author's unpublished doctoral dissertation, "The Development of a Modern Labor Force in Antigua," University of California, Los Angeles, 1964.

Table 11.   **TEN FACTS FOUND ASSOCIATED WITH POOR WORKERS**

Fact	Chi Square	Level of Significance
Irregular church attendance	6.6	< .01
Difficulty in originally finding employment	11.3	< .001
Originally liked working at factory	12.4	< .001
Had not been promoted	13.2	< .001
Earned less than $20.00 (BWI) weekly	7.2	< .01
Disliked treatment	10.0	< .005
Felt pushed around	19.2	< .001
Disliked promotion policy	17.1	< .001
Felt robbed by company	9.2	< .01
Felt company did not promote on ability	8.0	< .01

factory this length of time were married, over 39 years of age, had been promoted, and had experienced little original difficulty in finding work.

These findings suggest that regular church attendance may have been part of a general pattern of stability that set in among workers in their early middle-age after at least a decade of factory work. This pattern of stability will stand out more clearly after we have considered some of the other variables. Religious beliefs, at least as measured by church attendance, apparently had little or no effect upon workers' attitudes toward company policy.

Previous difficulty finding employment. This variable was significantly concentrated among workers who: a) had worked at the factory ten years or less; b) originally liked factory work; c) had not been vocationally oriented; d) earned less than $20.00 (BWI) per week; e) disliked the way they were treated by management; and f) felt pushed around.

The association between difficulty in finding employment and an original liking for factory work seems hardly surprising. It was to be expected that, under conditions of high structural underemployment, the worker would have been extremely pleased to find a job.

The lack of vocational orientation might also help explain why the worker originally experienced difficulty finding work.

Traditionally when jobs have been scarce, strong job competition has existed. In years past unemployment has reached as high as fifty per cent of the labor force during the out-of-crop season, so one may well imagine an extremely high degree of job competition. Those keenly interested in certain lines of work probably had a greater likelihood of being hired than those whose only interest was in taking any kind of job to tide them over. After employment, those with a decided vocational interest might also be more likely candidates for promotion. This line of reasoning would explain why workers who had difficulty finding employment were also confined to the lower wage-brackets and had more complaints about company policy. It also suggests that the absence of a vocational orientation may affect *both* one's chances for obtaining a job as well as one's chances for increased earnings after employment.

Through further cross-tabulations we discovered that vocationally oriented workers in general had been reared by both parents and had received seven or more years of formal education.

Bi-parental rearing tended to be an exception to the rule in Antigua. A high rate of illegitimacy has existed, and children have been reared primarily by their mothers.[6] It may be that homes with two parents were economically better off and thus better able to send their sons to school for a longer period. Then, too, the presence of a father may itself have had an independent effect upon shaping vocational interest. Perhaps children in such homes became more aware of possible vocations through talking with their fathers. At the very least, they had the occupation of their father to emulate. Moreover, fathers may have laid more stress upon choosing a vocation and given more vocational guidance than mothers. If a mother were unmarried, she may have placed more emphasis upon the son's entering the labor force as soon as possible by taking any job he could get to help defray family expenses.

Additional cross-tabulations disclosed that those with seven or more years of schooling not only were more vocationally oriented, but also made significantly fewer complaints about being treated poorly by management. Complaints about treatment and about being pushed

---

[6] In 1946, for example, census figures listed 45.2 per cent of all Antiguan mothers as unmarried, while 70.1 per cent of all births that year were illegitimate. See George Cumper, *Social Structure of the British Caribbean*, Kingston, Jamaica: Extra-Mural Department, University College of the West Indies, n. d., Part II, pp. 8, 11. Part of the problem of illegitimacy probably stems from the vestiges of slavery combined with depressed economic conditions that did not foster marital stability.

around tended to crystallize among workers with less than seven years of formal schooling.

In sum, the one-parent home, less than seven years of schooling, and lack of vocational interest seemed to have had some effect upon one's chances for finding employment. While at first a worker from such a background seemed happy to have found a job at the factory, he probably found it difficult to compete with better educated, more vocationally oriented workers for higher paying positions. Consequently, he rapidly became disillusioned and began to complain about the way he was treated.

Original feelings about factory work. In addition to experiencing difficulty finding employment and being confined to the lower wage-brackets, workers who originally liked factory work attended church irregularly. Their lack of church attendance might tie in with their generally poor economic situation. I received the distinct impression that most Antiguans liked to "dress up" when they appeared at public gatherings, such as church services. For example, one worker told me of receiving a wedding invitation six months in advance so the guests would be able to save up enough money to buy a new suit of clothes. A low income would impose limitations upon one's wardrobe, and this fact might have contributed to the lack of church attendance.

An original dislike for factory work was significantly associated with higher earnings. This finding seems rather peculiar and needs to be examined closely. First, it should be noted that, under conditions of high structural underemployment, a worker might be reluctant to give up his job even though he were discontented and had been previously able to find work. Certainly, the act of quitting involved a risk, and it might not pay to try one's luck. Second, those who had previously experienced little difficulty finding work tended to be better educated and more vocationally oriented. An initial feeling of disappointment may have ensued when these workers compared what they wanted with what the factory actually had to offer. In actuality, the factory had only limited promotion opportunities. It might take fifteen or twenty years to work up to the position of foreman. Although the factory had an apprenticeship program for the training of skilled workers, only a limited number of opportunities were open.

To surmount their original disappointment, these workers may have kept a sharp lookout for advancement opportunities. When they found them, they may have gone "all out" to win advancement by working in a way that management considered "good." Management was not bound by union contract to promote on seniority but favored ability as the sole basis for promotion; hence, these workers would have had a greater probability of reaching the higher wage-brackets. As a result, their original discontent was probably dissipated gradually as new opportunities for higher earnings presented themselves during their factory work career.

In short, I am positing a rapid attitudinal shift for poor workers and a gradual attitudinal shift for good workers. My reasoning stems from the following logic. We noted previously that consumer wants tended to rise as purchasing power increased and former wants were satisfied. If a) the worker started out with fairly well-defined goals but felt dissatisfied with opportunities for achieving his goals at the factory; and if b) to overcome his initial disappointment, he kept alert to promotion opportunities; and if c) he engaged in the kind of work behavior management considered "good," and won advancement; then d) the resulting pay increase might have the effect of inducing him to pitch his goals still higher. Therefore, the dissipation of discontent would proceed only at a slow rate.

If, however, a) the worker had not clearly formulated his goals before coming to the factory, b) his aspiration level would rise only *after* factory employment because c) his starting wage would represent an increase in earning power when compared to that previously the case under conditions of unemployment. This type of worker would be resting on his laurels precisely at the time when others were attempting to better their chances for advancement. Consequently, his feeling toward factory work would most likely move rapidly from satisfaction to dissatisfaction when he found it difficult to compete with better educated or more vocationally oriented workers who had formulated their goals long before he had.

Table 12 presents the results of an attempt to test this notion. The original feelings of good and poor workers toward factory work were compared with their feelings at the time of interview. Twenty-five poor workers originally liked the factory. Sixteen of the twenty-five (64 per cent) later moved to a position of dislike. Seventeen good workers originally disliked the factory, out of which eight (47 per cent) changed their feeling to one of liking. A higher rate of attitudinal change occurred among poor workers who moved from like to dislike than among good workers moving from dislike to like. While hardly conclusive, these findings support the general line of argument.

Weekly earnings and promotions. Weekly earnings in excess of $20.00 (BWI) were associated with a past record of promotions, which was to be expected. Promotion itself was concentrated among married workers and among those who had been at the factory more than ten years. These findings suggest that it took about ten years to

Table 12.   COMPARISON OF ORIGINAL AND LATER FEELINGS TOWARD FACTORY WORK AMONG GOOD AND POOR WORKERS (N = 60).

Attitude	Good Workers	Poor Workers
Originally liked working at factory and still do	4	9
Originally liked working at factory but later disliked it	6	16
Originally disliked working at factory and still do	9	3
Originally disliked working at factory but later liked it	8	1
No opinion	2	2
Totals	29	31

achieve weekly earnings in excess of $20.00. In this financial bracket the worker probably felt economically secure enough to marry.

Age. Perhaps a few words should be said about age because many leaders argued that low labor commitment was concentrated in the age group from 18 to 39. This would mean that, in general, the post-war generation was less work-committed than the prewar. In Antigua significant changes occurred in the employment situation in 1941 when an American military base was constructed and wages increased. Presumably, with this increase in wages workers began to relax on the job. A worker 39 years of age in 1962 would have been eighteen years old in 1941; hence, all those 39 years old and younger should have been influenced by economic changes since that date. If the two generations of laborers differed in their work attitudes, poor workers should have been younger, and complaints about company policy should have been centralized in this group. No such pattern could be detected. No significant differences in either backgrounds or attitudes could be found between prewar and postwar generations.

Attitudes toward company policy. So far we have analyzed only factors in the worker's background and his promotion and wage history. It is interesting that of all the background factors mentioned, only two were significantly associated with attitudes toward company policy. Those with less than seven years of formal education disliked the way management treated them; so did those who had difficulty finding employment who also complained of being pushed around. Attitudes toward company policy bore no significant relationship either to the worker's promotion record or his weekly earnings.

Table 13. **MATRIX OF CORRELATIONS FOR ATTITUDES TOWARD COMPANY POLICY**

Characteristic	Disliked Treatment	Felt Pushed Around	Felt Robbed	Disliked Promotion Policy	Felt Management Did Not Promote on Ability	Difficulty in Finding Work	Less Than Seven Years of Schooling
Disliked treatment	—	.76	.47	.30	.22	.30	.26
Felt pushed around	.76	—	.51	.27	.23	.29	.17
Felt robbed	.47	.51	—	.32	.31	.18	.06
Disliked promotion policy	.30	.27	.32	—	.74	.14	.04
Felt management did not promote on ability	.22	.23	.31	.74	—	.02	.02
Difficulty in finding work	.30	.29	.18	.14	.02	—	.22
Less than seven years of schooling	.26	.17	.06	.04	.02	.22	—

To get a better picture of the relationships between the five attitudes toward company policy, fourfold correlation coefficients (ϕ) were computed. They are listed in Table 13.

The association between complaints about treatment and being pushed around was exceptionally strong ($\phi = .76$). In fact, to many workers poor treatment consisted primarily in being pushed around. Dislike of treatment was less strongly linked to feelings of robbery ($\phi = .47$), while the association with complaints about promotion policy was weaker still ($\phi = .30$).

The relationship between feelings of being pushed around and being robbed was also rather noticeable ($\phi = .51$). Again, the correlation with complaints about promotion policy was much weaker ($\phi = .27$).

The strong links between complaints about treatment and being pushed around and between the latter and feelings of robbery suggest that these three attitudes hang together in a cluster. Complaints about promotion policy and charges that the company did not promote on the basis of ability also were closely interwoven ($\phi = .74$) and formed a second cluster of attitudes.

The relationship between these two clusters was not at all clear. All the phi-coefficients linking the two had about the same strength (.27 through .32). This condition did not permit the tracing out of any distinct line of connection. Only the first cluster showed a definite relationship to background factors. The second cluster was not so related and apparently stemmed from something else. These two clusters quite possibly represented different types of discontent that had emerged from different causes.

It is conceivable that those who had difficulty finding employment may have fallen into undisciplined work habits while they were unemployed. Their limited formal education and lack of vocational orientation were also drawbacks in formulating a disciplined attitude toward work. Despite their original liking for the factory, this group might have easily become dissatisfied with well-routinized factory work discipline. As a result, they might have at first felt somewhat poorly treated and pushed around. This type of discontent would have essentially centered around initial problems of adjustment to factory work procedures.

Complaints about robbery and promotion policy might have arisen only later in the factory work career in response to the frustration of individual worker goals. Previous analysis indicated that those who had difficulty finding work tended to have a lower level of aspiration; but it has been argued that this level "rose" or became more articulate after employment when a steady income allowed for more definite planning. Once goals had become more specific, the "psychological position" of these workers would have been essentially the same as those who had originally arrived at the factory with clear-cut goals in mind. Thus, at this point, *despite the workers' previous pre-factory background*, their responses to the factory work situation would tend to become similar: both would tend to appraise that situation in terms of the opportunities available for achieving their individual goals. If they perceived obstacles to goal achievement, their discontent might have initially been expressed in generalized charges of robbery. Wanting to get ahead, but seeing no opportunity for doing so, they might have felt the company was "robbing" them of their chances for advancement. As this discontent grew, it might later have become crystallized around dissatisfaction with promotion policy.

This interpretation was consistent with the previous data that showed how aspiration level interacted with the work situation. It also took into account the fact that complaints about robbery were significantly associated with complaints about promotion policy but not with actual wages earned. The interrelationship between these two complaints suggests that charges of robbery were more saliently linked to a perception of limitation upon *future* earnings than to dissatisfaction with *actual* earnings. Lastly, it provided an explanation of why complaints about treatment and being pushed around were significantly related to pre-factory backgrounds, but complaints about robbery, promotion policy, and promotion criteria were not. The former arose from initial adjustment to work routines made somewhat difficult by backgrounds of unemployment. The latter emerged from a dynamic interaction between worker aspirations and factory possibilities for their achievement.

Formation of the hypothesis and further evidence. Two bits of evidence suggest the hypothesis that work commitment varies with the perception of opportunity. First, workers' feelings of like or dislike for factory work seemed to fluctuate with their assessment of opportunities for increasing their earnings. Similarly, complaints about promotion policy seemed to increase as workers perceived decreasing opportunities for advancement.

To determine whether or not workers actually behaved in the manner predicted by the hypothesis, we sub-divided them into three groups: those who worked for fame and were willing to exercise initiative; those who did neither; and those who were willing to do one or the other but not both. We then tabulated the reasons workers gave for working as they did.

According to our hypothesis, those willing to do both should have included in their reasons an expectation of increased wage-earnings; in other words, they should have had a positive perception of opportunity. Conversely, those who worked for neither should have felt that no wage-increase would result from their efforts. That would constitute a negative perception of opportunity. In-between cases who were willing to do one or the other but not both should believe that "maybe" some wage increase would be forthcoming. They should have a "moderate" perception of opportunity.

Reasons given by the workers to explain their attitudes are set forth in Table 14. All laborers willing to work for fame and to exercise initiative perceived good chances for increasing their wages through regular promotion, the obtaining of work on the maintenance crews during the out-of-crop season, or through individual merit raises. Some

Table 14.   **REASONS GIVEN BY WORKERS TO EXPLAIN THEIR WORK ATTITUDES (N = 60).**

Reason	Willing to Work for Fame and Exercise Initiative (Per Cent)	Willing to Do Either But Not Both (Per Cent)	Not Willing To Do Either (Per Cent)	
Good chance for obtaining wage increase	100	0	0	
a) Might obtain promotion	45	0	0	
b) Might obtain regular work during out-of-crop season	15	0	0	
c) Might obtain recommendation to another firm	30	0	0	
d) Might obtain individual raise	10	0	0	
Some chance for obtaining wage increase	0	100	0	0
No chance for obtaining wage increase	0	0	100	
Totals	100	100	100	
Number of cases	(20)	(21)	(19)	

even saw their work performance at the factory as the basis for a good recommendation to another firm. Laborers with mixed attitudes toward work were all oriented toward promotion, but they saw their actual chances as being somewhat ambiguous ("maybe," "might," "it all depends," "could be in a few years"). Workers perceiving no chance at all for increased earnings had almost completely withdrawn their commitment to work.

Table 15 shows that laborers' work attitudes were rather closely associated with managerial ratings. The majority of good workers were willing to work for fame and exercise initiative. The majority of poor workers were willing to do neither. A large proportion of both good and poor workers had mixed attitudes. Good workers in this category tended to be either in the beginning stages of their work career when they disliked the factory or in the later stages, when having reached the highest pay-brackets open to them, they could expect no further wage increases. Poor workers in the same category tended to have worked at the factory from five to ten years. Presumably, during the first four years these workers had come to dislike factory employment very much. Between the fifth and tenth years, however, some of them believed they had been around long enough for promotion, and this belief encouraged them. They felt that perhaps if they worked harder and exercised some initiative, they might make the grade.

Table 15.   ATTITUDES TOWARD WORKING FOR FAME AND EXERCISING INITIATIVE AMONG GOOD AND POOR WORKERS (N = 60).

Rating of Workers	Willing to Work for Fame and Exercise Initiative (Number)	Willing to Do Either But Not Both (Number)	Not Willing To Do Either (Number)
Good	18	10	1
Poor	2	11	18
Totals	20	21	19

The data allowed me to make one last and final test of my hypothesis by applying it to worker complaints about company policy. These should have been inversely related to the perception of opportunity; thus, as the perception of opportunity decreased, complaints about policy should have increased. Data presented in Table 16 were generally consistent with this prediction. Those who perceived the greatest number of opportunities had the least number of complaints. Criticisms steadily mounted as workers perceived decreasing opportunities.

It is interesting to note that good workers with a perception of some opportunity still had fewer complaints about policy than did poor workers with the same perception. Complaints by good workers in this category seemed to represent a progressive disillusionment following either high vocational hopes at the beginning of the work career or a record of promotions up to a foremanship after which no additional promotion was possible. Poor workers in this category originally

Table 16. PERCENTAGE OF COMPLAINTS ABOUT COMPANY POLICY MADE BY WORKERS WITH VARYING PERCEPTIONS OF OPPORTUNITY (N = 60.)

	Good Opportunity (N = 20) Per Cent	Some Opportunity		No Opportunity (N = 19) Per Cent
Complaint		Good Workers (N = 10) Per Cent	Poor Workers (N = 11) Per Cent	
Attitude toward management's treatment of worker				
Liked the way they were treated	80	80	45	26
Disliked treatment	20	20	55	74
Attitude toward being pushed around				
Felt pushed around	20	30	73	95
Did not feel pushed around	80	70	27	5
Attitude toward being robbed by the company				
Felt robbed	40	60	82	95
Did not feel robbed	60	40	18	5
Attitude toward promotion policy				
Liked policy	80	80	27	16
Disliked policy	20	20	73	84
Perception of promotion criteria				
Management promoted on ability	80	50	36	16
Management did not promote on ability	20	50	64	84

may have perceived no opportunity for advancement. After about five or ten years they may have muted their criticism of company policy somewhat after believing themselves eligible for promotion. The toning down of their complaints might represent a progressively increasing optimism following an earlier disillusionment.

SUMMARY

To maintain a nation-state certain functional requisites have to be met, and such requisites have implications for the formation of a national character. For purposes of analysis I defined the aspects of national character that I wanted to study as the sum-total of responsibilities that leaders *think* citizens must accept in order to make the nation-state a going concern. Using this frame of reference as the analytical take-off point, I asked forty-seven Antiguan leaders to name a social responsibility where they thought citizens were falling down on the job. The majority believed the citizenry delinquent in their attitudes toward work. From the standpoint of the theoretical orientation underlying the decisions of nationhood, this meant the Antiguan national character was lacking in satisfactory work commitment. Leaders felt this lack of responsibility to be especially concentrated among non-agricultural manual laborers between the ages of eighteen to thirty-nine. They volunteered five hypotheses to explain why this problem had arisen.

These hypotheses were tested on twenty-nine sugar factory workers rated "good" and thirty-one rated "poor" by the factory management. Only one hypothesis seemed valid: poor workers felt more "exploited" than did good workers. I then addressed the question: why did poor workers feel more "exploited"? To find an answer I cross-tabulated all thirty-four items on the interview guide. By doing this I discovered that, in addition to feeling exploited, poor workers could be differentiated from good by nine other items. By cross-tabulating all ten items I came up with the tentative hypothesis that labor commitment varies with the perception of opportunity.

Next, this hypothesis was tested with data gleaned from interviews with the workers. It was found that workers with a high work commitment tended to have a positive perception of opportunity; those with a low commitment had a negative perception; those with a mixed commitment had only a moderate perception. Cross-tabulating these perceptions with complaints about company policy resulted in the discovery that as the perception of opportunity decreased, complaints about policy increased. The data available were generally consistent with the hypothesis, but quite obviously a more adequate test needs to be made. The hypothesis was formulated only after data had already been collected; consequently, there was not enough information at our disposal to provide rigorous testing.

It might be interesting to speculate why Antiguan leaders were not generally able to come up with more adequate hypotheses to explain the lack of work commitment. Perhaps a clue to leadership thinking may be found by looking at the content of their five hypotheses. A common theme ran through them all: in general, economic development was being held up because workers wouldn't work properly. In short, workers were lazy and their laziness was holding up progress. After all, what businessman would want to invest capital on an island with a lazy work-force? Certainly that would be a poor investment.

The data did not lend support to this line of reasoning. Instead, they suggested that the lack of opportunity posed the central issue. The problem seemed not so much that the worker wouldn't work; rather, he saw little to work for. Presumably, had he seen his work as leading to some desired personal goal, he might have been more committed to performing his task. It is true that lazy workers waste the limited capital resources that have already been invested; but perhaps this laziness stems from the very fact that capital investment has been too limited. Perhaps even greater investment could unleash worker motivation. Investments in new enterprises could provide workers with greater opportunities for bettering their condition; and with greater opportunity the laborer might work harder. Perhaps it is not only indolence that retards progress but also progress that retards indolence.

Viewing the problem in this light, I am tempted to say that the Antiguan leadership may have fallen victim to an easy explanation. The political leadership in particular was charged with attracting capital for new investment. By and large they had performed their job well; they had been extremely successful in building up tourism as a secondary industry to help offset the fact that sugar was dying. Under present competitive conditions operating on the world market, the sugar factory may not be able to continue operation for many more years.

But the attraction of capital has proven a very difficult business: the political leadership must plead with the Colonial Office for financial grants for various undertakings; it must make foreign private investment attractive while at the same time laying down conditions to protect Antiguan sovereignty. Simultaneously, the Antiguan population has been constantly increasing, so the labor force grows larger and larger. Just to stay in the same economic position the political leadership must attract new investments that will create job opportunities proportional to the population increase. But Antigua has begun its economic advance with traditionally high levels of structural underemployment and unemployment. If economic progress is to take place, Antigua cannot remain in the same economic position: the rate at which job opportunities are created must *exceed* the rate of population increase.

To sum it all up: the political leadership in 1962 was experiencing a tremendous difficulty just in running as fast as it could to stay in exactly the same place. Through tremendous effort, they had even managed to get just a little bit ahead of the game, and unemployment had been reduced. Nevertheless, leaders faced the future possibility of seeing the sugar industry deteriorate in the face of increasing population. They faced the awesome task of creating job opportunities that would not only absorb population increases but also offset the decline in sugar. Given these tremendous pressures, one might argue that leaders would be tempted to "pass the buck" to the workers: "If only workers weren't so lazy, the island could attract more capital." There must have been times when the Antiguan leadership has been tempted to think in this manner. Hopefully, they will avoid such temptations and continue to concentrate their efforts upon increasing the opportunities available to Antiguan workers.

CHAPTER 10 Images of Jamaica's Future*

JAMES A. MAU

Despite the fact that notions of "progress" are clearly out of vogue as scientific characterizations of change and development, the idea of progress should not be ignored by social scientists as a popular guiding and motivating ideology. The belief in progress as a popular ideology is relatively modern, stemming from the Enlightenment era of the European intellectual tradition. Since its emergence in the first years of the seventeenth century, the idea of progress has been variously accepted as a credo, developed as philosophy, scorned as foolish or naïve, and rejected as bourgeois nonsense. Whether accepted or rejected, the idea of progress in its changing conceptions has been a dominant theme in modern intellectual history. As embodied in utopian images of the future, it has influenced social philosophy and science, socialism and sociology. Until recently, the historic impact of the idea of progress on man's images of the future has been restricted to a small proportion of the world's people. Its influence has been limited to the European and North American continents while the mass of Asians, Africans, and Latin Americans have been clinging to the present or looking with hope to the golden ages of the past. Today this is no longer true. Peoples throughout the world are turning to the future with awareness, and the presently growing importance of these people to the future of the world in part lies in their images of the future, in their belief – or disbelief – in progress.

The belief in progress in the island-nation of Jamaica during the

* The data reported in this chapter are drawn from a larger study reported in James A. Mau, "Social Change and Belief in Progress: A Study of Images of the Future in Jamaica," unpublished Ph.D. dissertation, University of California, Los Angeles, 1964. A more complete reporting of the detailed findings will soon be available in the author's forthcoming book in this series, *Social Change and Images of the Future: A Study of the Pursuit of Progress in Jamaica*. For another report from this study, see Mau, "The Threatening Masses: Myth or Reality?" in F. M. Andic and T. G. Mathews (eds.), *The Caribbean in Transition: Papers on Social, Political, and Economic Development*, Rio Piedras, Puerto Rico: Institute of Caribbean Studies, University of Puerto Rico, pp. 258–270.

final stages of its transition to political independence constitutes the core subject of this chapter. The idea of progress was one of the themes of the democratic revolution which began in Jamaica in the late 1930's. In the last twenty-five years, Jamaica has begun its political development, and has experienced rapid economic change and considerable technological advance. This paper explores the impact of these and related changes on the images of the future of their nation held by Jamaicans in the months preceding the achievement of politically independent status within the British Commonwealth of nations.

In Jamaica, as in many of the developing countries, numerous aspects of social change have become the objects of history-making decisions. It has been argued that in the advanced nations of the Western World, economic and political development are no longer features of change that are consciously amenable to history-making.[1] In the developing countries today, this need not be the case; and in Jamaica it does not seem to be the case. Wendell Bell has written with reference to Jamaica:

> Conscious direction of the polity, economy, and society became the preoccupation of the new indigenous elite. What should be done? How should it be done? What should Jamaica's national goals be? How can they be best achieved? . . . the transfer of power from a colonial to an indigenous regime forcefully raises a large number of societal policies which become highly problematic, subject to change, and, most of all, potentially amenable to manipulation in accordance with the collective will of the citizens and the leaders of the new nation.[2]

Within this context of directed change, Bell reports findings which bear on Jamaica's decisions regarding the form of the political system, the nature of the social structure, the selection of global alignments, and the nature of Jamaica's social and cultural history.

In these societies in which features such as these are amenable to history-making by conscious decision, the images of the future held by the leadership, their attitudes toward change, and specifically their expectations regarding the nation's potential are critically important. Decision is based not only on knowledge and ideology, but on expectations. "In other words, a decision is an act, or a series of

---

[1] For example, see Robert L. Heilbroner, *The Future as History*, New York: Grove Press, 1961, especially pp. 181–184.

[2] Wendell Bell, *Jamaican Leaders: Political Attitudes in a New Nation*, Berkeley and Los Angeles: University of California Press, 1964, pp. 156–157; a more detailed discussion of such decisions may be found in Wendell Bell and Ivar Oxaal, *Decisions of Nationhood: Political and Social Development in the British Caribbean*, Denver, Colo.: Social Science Foundation, University of Denver Press, 1964.

acts, involving the simultaneous manipulation of facts, values, and above all, expectations."[3] Decision-making "turns in part upon a picture of significant changes in the emerging future."[4] Therein lies the importance of images of the future.

It is a central assumption of this chapter that man's thoughts about his existence in time — his history, what he is, what he might have been, and what he might possibly become — are of critical importance for his choices and decisions concerning what he ought to be. Man can see contradictions between his life and an ideal of something better. He can form an idea of a more desirable state of affairs and employ the means to achieve it.[5] The work of F. L. Polak offers the idea that the history of mankind can be written as the history of its images of the future; that without this capacity to envision a better possible future there can be no progress, and that man's images of the future by his purposeful intervention influence the unfolding of the actual future.[6]

In an extension of Oswald Spengler's thesis that cultures may be differentiated by the meanings that they give to time, Kluckhohn and Strodtbeck assert that a great deal can be predicted about the direction of change in a society if one knows the people's conceptions of past, present, and future.[7] To the extent that their proposition and our assumptions are tenable, we should attach even greater significance to knowing the views of the past and images of the future held by a society's leaders. This significance is further enhanced in situations in which those leaders are overtly concerned with planning change, concerned with a choice among goals, and concerned with the emerging future of their new nation.

Thus, the purpose of the research reported here was to analyze attitudes toward social, economic, and political changes that were taking place in Jamaica during the transition from colonial to politically independent status. Specifically, I offer a tentative interpretation of the variation in belief in progress expressed in personal interviews by

[3] Heinz Eulau, "H. D. Lasswell's Developmental Analysis," *The Western Political Quarterly*, XI (June, 1958), p. 230.

[4] Harold D. Lasswell, "Legal Education and Public Policy," in *The Analysis of Political Behavior*, New York: Oxford University Press, 1948, p. 30, as quoted in Eulau, *ibid.*

[5] Howard Selsam, *Ethics and Progress: New Values in a Revolutionary World*, New York: International Publishers, 1965, p. 12.

[6] F. L. Polak, *The Image of the Future*, 2 vols., New York: Oceana Publications, 1961.

[7] Florence Rockwood Kluckhohn and Fred L. Strodtbeck, *Variations in Value Orientations*, Evanston, Ill.: Row, Peterson and Co., 1961, pp. 4–14; see also Florence Rockwood Kluckhohn, "Dominant and Substitute Profiles of Cultural Orientations: Their Significance for the Analysis of Social Stratification," *Social Forces*, 28 (May, 1950), p. 380.

a group of Jamaican leaders. In the analysis to follow, these leaders' attitudes toward their island-nation's potential for progress are discussed and explained.

THE RESEARCH FOCUS

The data reported here were collected in Jamaica between August 7, 1961, and September 21, 1962, a period significantly marked by three important political events in the history of the island. Growing anti-federation sentiment culminated in a referendum on September 19, 1961, which resulted in Jamaica's withdrawal from the fledgling West Indian federal union and the eventual collapse of the Federation. In the light of the referendum results, general elections were called to determine which political party would form the first government of the new nation, and these elections, on April 10, 1962, brought victory to the Jamaica Labour Party (JLP). Finally, political independence was granted on August 6, 1962, when the island-nation of Jamaica became a Dominion in the British Commonwealth. These events comprise the "environment" in which this study was conducted. It is hard to imagine a single year filled with more changes of such importance to the people of Jamaica than 1961–1962. One could hardly have wished for a more opportune time to study attitudes toward the trend of change, past and future, than when the people of Jamaica were so conscious of change, so frequently thinking about its meaning, and so willing to talk about Jamaica's future. For, as independence approached, the Jamaican citizenry was preoccupied with speculations about the island's potential, its problems, and the likelihood of making independence a success.

Prior to the formal data collection for this study, numerous preliminary interviews were conducted with a variety of persons including Cabinet-level politicians and elected parochial officials, top civil servants and minor governmental employees, welfare administrators and welfare field workers, and a bishop and several slum-based clergymen. These preliminary interviews were instrumental in the delineation of an issue or focused set of significant obstacles facing independent Jamaica. They revealed that among the numerous nationally significant problems during this period of rapid change, one issue that was uppermost as a source of concern and controversy among those contacted centered around the burgeoning urban lower classes of West Kingston, and the significance of these people and their problems for the new nation.

A brief look at the analyses of the 1960 census reveals that while the population of the island increased by 30 per cent since the 1943 census, the population of the Kingston Metropolitan Area increased by 87 per cent. Even more striking was the increase of nearly 174 per cent since 1943 in the urban St. Andrew area.[8] A major part of the area broadly referred to as "West Kingston" falls within that district.

These changes in the distribution of the population reflect the continually increasing importance of Kingston as a commercial, administrative, and industrial center. Kingston has become the distribution center for the island because of the importance of imports and the increased consumption of imported goods in recent years. On the average since 1952, nearly 80 per cent of all cargo tonnage of imports have been discharged at Kingston.[9] This dominance of Kingston, coupled with the effects of the government Industrial Development Corporation and incentive legislation, has been influential in the pattern of industrial location and development. Maunder has noted that these factors have had their greatest effect upon the Kingston area which is the seat of light industry.[10] The result has been what Prime Minister Sir Alexander Bustamante bemoaned as the "daily flocking into Kingston seeking non-existent employment."[11] The western part of Kingston in particular became an urban reception center for growing numbers of migrants from the rural areas, and came to be viewed by many Jamaicans as a symbol of the shortcomings of a development program that was creating new problems as it attempted to overcome others.

Jamaica is quite typical of developing countries in the inability of its urban areas to absorb the increased numbers and the resulting concentrations of unemployed, in the vast numbers of substandard houses, and in the generally inferior services and facilities. The trend of internal migration has not slackened, nor have there been any effective attempts to deal with the more evident problems of the growing urban lower classes in their ghetto-like world. In Kingston, as in the other principal cities of the Caribbean and Latin America, and for that matter in the Philippines, Hong Kong, Turkey, Pakistan, and numerous other countries,[12] the results of the flood of migrants include an alarmingly increased density in old and deteriorating permanent buildings near the center of the city. It has resulted in the spread of

[8] *Economic Survey, Jamaica, 1961.*
[9] *Annual Abstract of Statistics, 1962,* No. 22, Kingston: Department of Statistics, 1964, p. 53.
[10] W. F. Maunder, *Employment in an Underdeveloped Area,* New Haven: Yale University Press, 1960, pp. 60–62.
[11] *Spotlight,* XXIV (March, 1963), p. 10.
[12] Charles Abrams, *Man's Struggle for Shelter in an Urbanizing World,* Cambridge, Mass.: The M.I.T. Press, 1964, p. 13.

a type of urban shelter built of refuse and scavenged material, whose inhabitants are known in Jamaica as squatters, and in Latin America as *rancheros, favelados,* and *conqueros.*[13] These hovels of board, canvas, cardboard, and tin sheets are generally illegally built on the edges of the city and intended as temporary shelter, but most often they are transformed into an almost permanent fixture, an everpresent temporary community protected from destruction by the social and economic pressures of rapid and continuing urban growth. These squatters constitute an estimated 12 to 15 per cent of the population of Kingston, and an equal or greater number of people are found in the more densely populated areas of deteriorating permanent buildings.

Jamaica's urban growth and the contrasts in Kingston have been attributed to both prosperity and destitution — to the growing middle classes riding the crest of economic advancement, and the mushrooming urban masses who had fled from the frustration of the rural areas. Ruth Glass has written:

> The top groups have climbed up to new suburbs. . . . Down Below, the dreadful shack dumps of West Kingston have become darker, denser, larger. . . . The sights, the smells, the sounds, even the forces of heat and rain, are those of a different world. Here there are flimsy miserable huts, thrown together, made of refuse — paper, cardboard, packing cases, bits of sticks, and parts of discarded motor-car bodies. . . . The Kingston jungles are exceptional both in the extent and the degree of abandonment they expose.[14]

The problems for the nation presented by Kingston's expanding slums and the difficulties faced by the growing urban masses have intruded more and more in the life of all Jamaicans. The significance of the urban masses has been more clearly realized as their conditions have worsened and as their protests could no longer go unheeded. These problems which emerged in preliminary interviews as some of the most significant problems for the future of the nation became the focusing issue of this research. This focus consolidated a social issue, a geographical area, and several social, economic, and political problems that linked it significantly with the development of the island as a whole. Thus, the focus on this issue-area served to delimit the universe of Jamaican leaders to be sampled, and served to provide the concrete areal and topical referents in the interviews.

---

[13] See Lloyd H. Rogler, "Slum Neighborhoods in Latin America," forthcoming. See also the discussion of housing and urban facilities in the chapter on urbanization in Latin America in the *Report on the World Social Situation*, New York: United Nations, 1957, chapter IX, pp. 183–188.
[14] Ruth Glass, "Ashes of Discontent: The Past as Present in Jamaica," *Monthly Review*, XIV (May, 1962), pp. 26–27.

BASIC DATA

The basic data of the study were collected in interviews completed with a sample of 54 persons drawn from a systematically defined universe of Jamaican leaders. These leaders included Members of Parliament, Cabinet Ministers, high-ranking civil servants, heads of major community organizations, elected local politicians, religious leaders, and several prominent barristers, solicitors, and businessmen. These leaders were selected from a universe of leaders defined by reputational or "power attribution" methods as persons who were influential in spheres of decision-making and the formulation and implementation of policy concerning West Kingston and its people. Specifically, the first three persons interviewed were chosen on the basis of their formal roles or institutional positions as persons likely to wield influence regarding the problems of West Kingston. Each of these persons was asked during the interview:

> Now, I'd like you to tell me the names of the people you think are most important in determining and carrying out policy in relation to the problems of West Kingston.

This procedure was followed throughout the interviewing with any person nominated three or more times being included in the universe of persons to be interviewed. By this method the total list of leaders grew to include 66 persons.[15] The 54 completed interviews included 90 per cent of the 50 top-ranked persons. Five persons could not be interviewed because they were temporarily off the island, and I was unable for various reasons to arrange appointments with the remaining seven leaders.

IMAGES OF JAMAICA'S FUTURE

Four questions were asked of the Jamaican leaders to discover their images of the future of the new nation. These questions were constructed so that the leaders were free to discuss any aspects of the future about which they were interested and to which they gave highest priority. With one exception, the questions were designed to elicit the leaders' visions of future developments, with the respondents themselves providing the terms in which they answered and choosing the aspects of the future they wished to stress.

In the order in which they were asked, these questions, presented in Table 1, proceeded from the general to the specific. The first question

[15] Two persons included in the universe of leaders were added on the basis of their formal institutional position. A complete discussion of the methodology of the larger study from which these data are drawn will soon be available in the author's forthcoming volume on images of Jamaica's future in this series.

Table 1. **PERCENTAGE DISTRIBUTION OF JAMAICAN LEADERS ACCORDING TO THEIR RESPONSES TO FOUR QUESTIONS ABOUT THE FUTURE**

1. "Generally, do you think the people of Jamaica will be better off, about the same, or worse off after independence (that is, in the future)?"

		Per Cent
Better off		61
About the same		4
Worse off		35
	Total	100
	Number of cases	(54)

2. "Do you think that independence itself will make any difference?"

Yes, for the better		38
No		48
Uncertain		6
Yes, for the worse		8
	Total	100
	Number of cases	(52)
	No answer	(2)

3. "With particular reference to that area [Western Kingston], do you expect any significant changes to take place after independence (that is, in the future)?"

Yes, for the better		44
No		40
Uncertain		2
Yes, for the worse		14
	Total	100
	Number of cases	(50)
	No answer	(4)

4. "A few people have told me that some form of civil disorder or violent outbreak is likely to arise out of West Kingston. Do you think it is likely?"

No, not likely at all		40
No, but possible		26
Uncertain		4
Yes, it is likely		30
	Total	100
	Number of cases	(50)
	No answer	(4)

referred to the future of the island-nation most broadly; the second dealt with the expected effects of political independence upon the nation; and the last two questions specifically asked about the respondents' images of the future of Western Kingston, whose 100,000 residents had become, as discussed earlier, the symbol of the most important social problems facing the newly independent country.

The leaders were prepared for the generality of these questions by the question which was asked just before those on images of the future. This preceding question queried them about the trends of change from 1938 to the present. The year 1938, more than any other, had marked the beginning of the development of modern political consciousness among the Jamaican people, and the events of that year started the drive which was to culminate in the achievement of independence. Having just evaluated these changes wrought upon the economy, polity, and society in the recent past, the leaders generally were prepared to project their thoughts into the new era marked by independence. In fact, several respondents anticipated the questions about the future.

On the first question about Jamaica's future progress, the leaders were quite optimistic in their views, with 61 per cent contemplating a favorable future, 4 per cent suggesting that things would be about the same, and 35 per cent saying that the Jamaican people would be worse off. Looking at the responses to the second question, one can see whether the changes resulting from independence provided the basis for the beliefs revealed in the replies to the first question. Forty-eight per cent of the leaders foresaw no effect of independence, while 8 per cent anticipated deleterious consequences. Thirty-eight per cent of the leaders thought independence was likely to give favorable impetus to Jamaica's development. Thus, among these leaders, favorable images of Jamaica's future were in the majority, but only part of this optimism was based on the advent of independence. That is, some leaders foresaw a favorable national future irrespective of the political transition to independence.

When asked about the future of West Kingston, the leaders' images of the future were less favorable than those for the island as a whole. Forty-four per cent of the leaders anticipated a more favorable future for the lower-class area, while 14 per cent predicted further deterioration. The next largest group of 40 per cent expected no changes in the area. Given the conditions in the West side of Kingston in 1961–62, I would argue that because there was so much room for improvement, the expectation of no change amounts to consigning the area and its people to everlasting deprivation. Recalling that these respondents are all in some sense community welfare leaders whose interest and responsibilities lie in some measure with the betterment of West Kingston, the reader may well conclude that the figure of 40 per cent expecting no change in the area is an unfortunate finding, particularly when thought of as a statement of futility. Further, designating this answer as unfavorable is consistent with Polak's definition of favorable images of the future as those ". . . which express the optimistic belief that the Other World is not only radically different but also an infinitely Better World."[16] The favorable image of the future characterized by an idealistic vision of progress in time yet non-existent is not to be found in expectations of things to remain as they are, particularly in West Kingston.

[16] Polak, *op. cit.,* p. 58.

The last question in Table 1 is somewhat different and more specific than the preceding questions. Is violent civil disorder thought to be likely? The relevance of this aspect of the future to this research and these leaders was underscored by the frequent discussions, both during formal interviews and in the preliminary research, of the likelihood of outbreaks of violence in West Kingston. Many anxious and worried comments about the possibility of violent disturbances were made by the leaders at some point in the interview prior to my question on the subject. Consciousness of these possibilities probably grew in part from a reputed attempt to incite Ras Tafari cultists to armed violence. The Ras Tafari brethren are a heterogeneous collection of Jamaicans who believe that Ras Tafari, the Emperor Hailé Selassié of Ethiopia, is the living God. Further, they believe that salvation for the black man can come only by means of repatriation to Africa. Early in the summer of 1960, Claudius V. Henry, a self-styled religious leader of the cult, recently returned from the United States, and several of his followers, were arrested for possession of an arsenal of firearms, gunpowder, and explosives. In addition to the confiscation of these weapons, the alleged discovery of documents linking the group with Cuban and American subversive backing resulted in charges of treason being brought against Henry and some of his followers. In June, 1960, another group was captured in the hills to the west of Kingston where two British soldiers and three Ras Tafari brethren had been killed earlier. These incidents and the courts of inquiry and trials which followed received widespread coverage in the island's mass media. The publicity given to these incidents and to the threat of extremists, the Ras Tafari brethren and Communists, rekindled old fears of many Jamaicans.[17] In the summer of 1962, these incidents of two years earlier were very often referred to by the Jamaican leaders interviewed.

When asked about the likelihood of violent disturbances in the future, 40 per cent of the leaders thought such occurrences were not likely at all, and many scoffed at the suggestion that such civil disorder was to be expected. But 56 per cent of the leaders said that such an incident was either likely or possible. One of the more frenetic politicians said:

> It's inescapable. I hear them talk. They don't care for man or God. And they're sure not going to care what they do to the man up top.

---

[17] The background of these incidents and the developments in the months following are discussed in detail in the Jamaican news magazines, *Newday*, IV (May, August, 1960), and *Spotlight*, XXI (June, July, August, 1960). See also the Jamaican newspaper, *The Daily Gleaner*, for that period. The incidents are also discussed in Katrin Norris, *Jamaica: The Search for an Identity*, London: Oxford University Press for the Institute of Race Relations, 1962, pp. 49–51.

I think some sort of civil disturbance is impossible to avoid, and right now . . . the security of the individual is at a low ebb. . . . Even the police walk in fear down here.

Another respondent, a clergyman working in West Kingston, said the pressure was building up in the area and the lid was likely to blow off.

None of these leaders indicated that they would favor violent civil disorder as a potential lever for progressive change. Expectations of such disorder were viewed as an unfavorable prediction while the belief that such occurrences were *not* likely was taken as a favorable prediction about the future.

AN INDEX OF BELIEF IN PROGRESS

Although the unity of content of the four questions concerning Jamaican leaders' images of the future has not been stressed, it has probably been evident to the reader that there is an essential similarity of these questions in their combination of both evaluative and temporal aspects regarding Jamaica's potential for dealing with some significant problems of national development. For purposes of analysis and discussion, these four questions are combined into a single Index of Belief in Progress that conveniently allows these data to be handled as a single score for each leader. This Index of Belief in Progress was tested for unidimensionality as a cumulative scale by means of Guttman scale analysis following the Cornell scaling technique.[18]

The results of the application of scale analysis to the Index of Belief in Progress are summarized in Table 2. A coefficient of reproducibility of .894 was achieved, which is taken as a satisfactory approximation to the criterion of .90 suggested by Guttman. This level of reproducibility shows considerable improvement in prediction over the coefficient of minimum marginal reproducibility of .545.[19] In no case are the marginal frequencies in the modal response categories sufficiently extreme to result in spuriously high reproducibility.

Two factors warrant at least some skepticism in accepting the unidimensionality of the universe of attitudes defined as attitudes toward progress. The first is the relatively small number of items in the index.

[18] This method of scale analysis is extensively discussed in the following: Louis Guttman, "A Basis for Scaling Quantitative Data," *American Sociological Review*, IX (April, 1944), 139–150; "The Cornell Technique for Scale and Intensity Analysis," *Educational and Psychological Measurements*, VII (Summer, 1947), 247–280; and Chapters II and III in S. A. Stouffer, *et al.*, *Measurement and Prediction*, Princeton, N.J., Princeton University Press, 1950, pp. 46–90.
[19] Allen Edwards, *Techniques of Attitude Scale Construction*, New York: Appleton-Century-Crofts, Inc., 1957, pp. 191–193.

Table 2.   SCALE CRITERIA RELATED TO THE INDEX OF BELIEF IN PROGRESS

Scale Criteria	(N = 54)
1. Coefficient of reproducibility	.894
2. Range of marginal frequencies	The extreme modal categories contain 48 to 46 per cent of the responses. The remainder fall within that range. This range is sufficient to provide a range of scores.
3. Minimum marginal reproducibility	.545
4. Number of items and response categories	There are four items all of which are dichotomies.
5. Pattern of error	There is one segment of non-random error containing 6 responses.
6. Error to non-error ratio	No answer category has more error than non-error.

Although Guttman has used as few as four to six statements, he also has suggested that a small sample of items from a non-scalable universe might yield low error when all response categories are dichotomies.[20] Secondly, examination of the scalogram reveals one segment of non-random error containing six responses. Although these errors constitute only two per cent of the total responses, they do suggest the possibility of an additional variable in the index. With these cautions in mind, the hypothesis of unidimensionality for the Index of Belief in Progress is tentatively accepted.

The percentage distribution of scale scores for the Jamaican leaders on the Index of Belief in Progress is shown in Table 3. This final distribution was arbitrarily dichotomized as close to the median as possible for purposes of later subgroup comparisons and analyses. Those leaders who gave favorable responses to at least two of the four items, and who received a scale score of two or more, were labeled as believing in progress. Those persons who scored zero or one, by giving unfavorable answers to at least three questions, were designated as persons who did not believe in progress. In this manner, 56 per cent of the Jamaican leaders were classified as believing in progress, and 44 per cent as not accepting this view. Although it would have been preferable to retain a larger number of categories, the small number of leaders interviewed required this dichotomous treatment.

In summary, as measured here, belief in progress is the affirmation that the nation's future will be better than the present; that the advent

[20] *Ibid.*, p. 177.

Table 3. PERCENTAGE DISTRIBUTION OF JAMAICAN LEADERS ACCORDING TO SCALE SCORES ON THE INDEX OF BELIEF IN PROGRESS

Scale Score	Jamaican Leaders (Per Cent)
4 (Highest)	16.7
3	22.2
2	16.7
1	16.7
0 (Lowest)	27.7
Total	100.0
Number of cases	(54)
As dichotomized:	
2–4 (Believes in progress)	56
0–1 (Does not believe in progress)	44
Total	100
Number of cases	(54)

of independence will have beneficial consequences; that the future of West Kingston and its people will also be better than the present; and finally, that there is not likely to be a violent outbreak of civil disorder in Western Kingston. This is the favorable extreme of the continuum. At the opposite end of the scale should be found those leaders who negate these beliefs, those who expect a doubtful future, see independence as an ineffective political change, and anticipate misfortune and violence for the people of West Kingston. Thus, the Index of Belief in Progress is based on the leaders' evaluations of the nature and direction of the social, economic, and political changes they foresee. Labeling these beliefs as "progressive" is no more than the equation of progress with betterment, and implies nothing *a priori* about the nature of betterment or progress. Rather, it is based upon the leaders' defining criteria of these evaluations.[21] In fact, the content of the view of progress held by the Jamaican leaders was essentially consistent with the idea of progress coming out of the rationalism of the Enlightenment. Edward Gibbon, said to be the greatest Enlightenment historian, conveyed this meaning of the idea of progress in his assertion that ". . . every age of the world has increased, and still increases, the real wealth, the happiness, the knowledge, and perhaps the virtue of the human race."[22]

[21] A more lengthy discussion of the content of the leaders' images of the future of the nation is presented in my forthcoming book in this series, *Social Change and Images of the Future*, Cambridge, Mass.: Schenkman, 1967.
[22] Edward Gibbon, *The Decline and Fall of the Roman Empire*, ch. xxxviii, quoted in Edward Hallett Carr, *What is History?*, New York: Alfred A. Knopf, 1962, p. 146.

SOCIAL CORRELATES OF BELIEF IN PROGRESS

In the introduction to this chapter, I said that the images of the future held by a nation's leaders, their attitudes toward change and toward their nation's potential, are critically important because of the numerous aspects of change that are amenable to conscious history-making decisions. Images of the future are the foundation of the decision-making process by which the future is shaped. Furthermore, the national significance of leaders' belief in progress is conditioned partially by the various social positions they hold and by their social characteristics. Thus, one should ask, "Who are the leaders who believe in progress in Jamaica?" "What are their social positions and characteristics?" Answers to these questions will also provide the necessary background to deal with the "Why?" of the variations in belief in progress.

Because the belief in progress may have been affected by the general elections of April, 1962, and the repudiation of the Peoples' National Party (PNP) government, we should begin by examining the relationship between the leaders' belief in progress and their political party preference. In this case it is desirable not only to determine the effect of party preference per se upon belief in progress, but also to delineate as far as possible, the effects of the election and the resulting change in government. For this reason, those leaders who preferred the PNP should be considered separately against all others, including those who preferred the JLP and those for whom there was no indication of party preference. Looking at the top of Table 4, it may be seen that the leaders who preferred the PNP were less likely to believe in progress than those with other political preferences. I have no doubt that a large part of this difference must be explained by reference to the outcome of the elections, which unquestionably crushed some of the idealism and confidence with which the PNP viewed the future of Jamaica. Those leaders who were not adherents of the PNP, and who had probably lost nothing, but rather gained by the election outcome, were considerably more likely to believe in progress than were PNP adherents.

The variations in belief in progress by the selected social characteristics summarized here are presented in detail in Table 4. In addition to political party preference, the clearest differences which emerge are by race–color, occupational rating,[23] and religious preference.

---

[23] The measure of occupational rating was adapted by Wendell Bell for use in Jamaica from W. Lloyd Warner, Marchia Meeker, and Kenneth Eells, *Social Class in America*, Chicago: Science Research Associates, Inc., 1949, pp. 140–141; and Carson McGuire, "Social Status, Peer Status, and Social Mobility," a mimeographed memorandum for research workers based upon procedures used in studies for the Committee on Human Development, University of Chicago, Chicago, Ill., 1948.

Table 4.   **PERCENTAGE OF JAMAICAN LEADERS WHO BELIEVE IN PROGRESS BY SELECTED SOCIAL CHARACTERISTICS**

Selected Characteristics	Percentage Who Believe In Progress	No. of Cases on Which the Per Cent is Based
Political Party Preference		
Jamaica Labour Party	69	(13)
Peoples' National Party	42	(26)
Other	67	(15)
Age		
50 and over	55	(20)
40–49	50	(22)
39 and under	67	(12)
Education		
University or college graduate	59	(17)
Some university or college	56	(9)
Secondary school or less	54	(28)
Race–Color		
White	50	(14)
Brown	79	(14)
Black	46	(26)
Occupational Rating		
1 (Highest)	68	(28)
2–4 (Lowest)	42	(26)
Religious Preference		
Anglican	80	(15)
Other Protestant	56	(16)
Roman Catholic	57	(7)
Jewish	—	(1)

Those who are brown in skin color, have a high occupational rating, and are members of the Anglican Church, were most likely to believe in progress. When political party preference is controlled, each of these groups remains highest on belief in progress. In addition, those leaders who were under 40 years of age were somewhat more likely to believe in progress than either of the older groups; however, this held true only for the adherents of the PNP. Age differences had little or no effect on belief in progress among leaders who preferred the JLP and those for whom party preference was undetermined. Moreover, among the university-educated leaders this relationship between age and belief in progress was reversed with the older leaders more likely to report a favorable future for the island than the younger respondents. Taken alone, educational attainment was only slightly related to belief in progress with the highest educated leaders being most likely to affirm Jamaica's potential for progress. This relationship with education was greatest for those leaders who preferred the PNP, but reversed in the cases of the leaders who were not adherents of the PNP.

Additional information about differences in belief in progress is presented in Table 5, where the percentage of leaders who believe in progress is shown by the type of leadership position they held.[24] By far, the group most strongly committed to belief in progress was the non-governmental community welfare leaders. More persons of this group, made up of religious leaders and leaders of voluntary welfare associations such as YMCA, YWCA, and youth clubs, were likely to believe in progress than was any other single category of leaders. The members of the clergy led this group, with 78 per cent believing in progress. This suggests, as we shall see below, that attitudes toward progress may be some function of broader ideological commitments.

Table 5. PERCENTAGE OF JAMAICAN LEADERS WHO BELIEVE IN PROGRESS BY TYPE OF LEADERSHIP POSITION

Type of Elite Position	Percentage Who Believe In Progress	No. of Cases on Which the Per Cent is Based
Politicians	57	(21)
Members of Parliament	69	(13)
KSAC Councillors	38	(8)
Government Officers	38	(16)
Civil Servants	40	(10)
Jamaican Social Welfare Commission	33	(6)
Non-Governmental Community Welfare Leaders	71	(17)
Clergy	78	(9)
Other	63	(8)

The elected politicians were next highest in belief in progress with 57 per cent. However, there was important variation within that category with only three of the eight leaders who were members of the elected Kingston-St. Andrew Corporation (KSAC), the municipal governing body, indicating expectations of progress. This is less surprising when it is noted that the local government of the Kingston Area was dominated by PNP members. Among the elected politicians at the national level, about two-thirds of the Members of Parliament

[24] The leaders holding more than one leadership position were classified by that position which was most relevant to their role in dealing with the urban classes and Western Kingston.

who were interviewed indicated a belief in progress. While two of these MP's were PNP representatives, the remainder were Government Members (JLP) including many Cabinet Ministers.

The members of the government service, including civil servants and the Jamaica Social Welfare Commission staff, were not strongly convinced of Jamaica's future potential for progress. The lowest figure found in Table 5 is that for the Welfare Commission officers. It is likely that this finding may also be explained partially by reference to the political party preference of the respondents, and the belief on the part of many welfare workers in the urban area that their community development programs would be limited or discontinued by the political workings of the new JLP regime whose major strength was in the rural parishes. On the whole, the data presented in Table 5 indicate that the Members of Parliament and the non-governmental leaders were most likely to believe in progress, while the locally elected KSAC councillors and the government officers were least likely to hold this positive outlook for the future of the nation.

Turning from this brief discussion of the social background factors and type of leadership positions correlated with belief in progress, we next examine further data that help answer the crucial question of why some of these leaders believe in progress and others do not. What differentiates those who hold sanguine expectations for their nation's future from those who anticipate decline and deterioration, increased violence and continued poverty?

EGALITARIANISM AND BELIEF IN PROGRESS

The idea of equality and the idea of progress have a logical similarity: both are what may be called normative ideas, or ideals. As suggested by Talcott Parsons, the referent of a normative idea may or may not already exist. If it does exist, the normative idea implies the obligation to protect or maintain its existence. If it does not exist, the normative implication is ". . . an obligation to attempt its realization at some future time."[25] Both the belief in equality and belief in progress are ideas with this normative or obligatory quality. Thus, each in this sense is an ideal.

The Age of Enlightenment, and particularly the French revolutionary movement in the second quarter of the nineteenth century, saw the close association of the ideals of equality and progress.[26] For

---

[25] Talcott Parsons, "The Role of Ideas in Social Action," in his *Essays in Sociological Theory* (rev. ed.), Glencoe, Ill.: The Free Press, 1954, p. 21.
[26] This discussion is based primarily on the work of Professor J. B. Bury, *The Idea of Progress*, New York: Dover Publications, Inc., 1955, pp. 182–183; pp. 212–213; and p. 319.

the most part the writings of Fontenelle and Voltaire made only small reference to the masses concerning progress, and saw the benefits of progress accruing to a privileged minority, but in the writings of Leroux, Condorcet, and Rousseau, the belief in progress was clearly associated with notions of social equality. For Rousseau and Condorcet, equality became the goal of social and political progress; for Leroux the approach to the egalitarian ideal became the measure of progress, and the goal would be achieved when man became synonymous with equal. This compatibility between belief in progress and the ideal of equality found in the history of modern thought underscores the relevance of egalitarianism to the focus of this research. Thus, we ask whether this association between the belief in progress and the ideal of equality after the Enlightenment tradition was to be found among the Jamaican leaders.

Social fragmentation, the existence of barriers to full and equal participation in society, is founded on the criteria of social worth which prevail in that society.[27] If worthiness is defined by characteristics which are ascribed rather than achieved, or if opportunities for achievements are differentially distributed according to an ascriptive system, incomplete social equality obtains. Basically, differential opportunities beget differential opportunities. Thus, social divisions based on inequity become both cause and consequence of the perpetuation of inequity. Although social differentiation need not imply inequality, the existence of a social hierarchy which restricts the internal inclusiveness of a society by the maintenance of ascriptive barriers to participation and achievement is inimical to the attainment of social equality. It is from this capsule of theory that a measure of egalitarianism was derived. Attitudes toward equality are here equated with attitudes toward the maintenance or reduction of status differences and ascriptive barriers which limit participation in the social process.

The Jamaican leaders were asked:

> Do you think it is advisable that any barriers to full interaction of people in Jamaica should be broken down, or are there some status differences which you feel should be maintained?

Those leaders who favored the reduction of such barriers to participation were categorized as egalitarian. Leaders who did not clearly favor the reduction of these limitations, or who gave equivocal answers, were classified as inegalitarian. Two respondents who said there were no barriers were also classified as inegalitarian, since informed judgments

[27] I am here using society in the sense which includes the polity and economy: this discussion is strongly influenced by the theory of Godfrey and Monica Wilson, *The Analysis of Social Change*, Cambridge: University Press, 1954.

agree that in fact there are.[28] By this measure of attitudes toward equality, 60 per cent of the Jamaican leaders were found to be egalitarian. The remainder were inegalitarian with two respondents excluded because there were insufficient data to classify them properly.

The percentage of Jamaican leaders who believed in progress is shown in Table 6 by their attitudes toward equality. Nearly two-thirds of those leaders who were egalitarian believed in progress, compared to 43 per cent of the inegalitarians. This relationship was found to be only slightly conditional upon age, education, race–color, occupational rating, or political party preference of the leaders.

Table 6.   PERCENTAGE OF JAMAICAN LEADERS WHO BELIEVE IN PROGRESS BY ATTITUDES TOWARD EQUALITY

Attitudes Toward Equality	*Percentage Who Believe In Progress*	*No. of Cases on Which the Per Cent is Based*
Egalitarian	65	(31)
Inegalitarian	43	(21)

On the whole, the relationship between the ideal of equality and belief in progress which is historically evident in the Enlightenment tradition of thought was borne out among these leaders in Jamaica. Although the association was not great, those leaders who indicated acceptance of the normative implications of the ideal of equality were also somewhat more likely to hold a vision of a more perfect future for their nation. Their image of a progressive future and their view of the Good Society tended to include a desired social structure capable of allowing and promoting opportunity for full popular participation on the basis of equality.

POWER AND PROGRESS

It is a basic thesis of this book that many aspects of modern nation-building have increasingly become the products of decisions rather than being left to fate or destiny, and that these decisions of nationhood are shaped importantly by the ideological commitments and images of the future of the nation held by the decision-makers. Writing about

[28] Obviously, this measure of attitudes toward social equality is similar to the measure of social inclusivism used by Moskos in Chapter Three of this volume and by Moskos and Bell in Chapter Six, but it is also related to their measure of equality of opportunity as the co-relationship between the two measures showed. For a methodological discussion of another measure of egalitarianism used in Jamaica in 1958 by Bell and later by Duke, see James A. Mau, Richard J. Hill, and Wendell Bell, "Scale Analyses of Status Perception and Status Attitude in Jamaica and the United States," *Pacific Sociological Review*, IV (Spring, 1961), pp. 33–40.

history as fate or decision, C. Wright Mills contended ". . . that 'men are free to make history' and that some men are now freer than others to do so, for such freedom requires access to the means of decision and of power by which history can now be made."[29] In accepting Mills' contention we must ask "What shall the nature of that history be?" Will the power of decision be directed toward good or ill, toward the golden ages past, toward the frustration of change, or will it be used to lead change and foster progress? It is precisely here that the role of ideas emerges importantly in the historical process. The impact of ideas upon the course of history increases as men better utilize their resources and increase their power to shape that history. Thus, in asking what the nature of that history shall be, we must simultaneously ask how power and ideology are linked.

Power linked with the ideals of the Enlightenment produced the historic founding of new national states, as Moskos made clear in Chapter Three. Here we ask how the relative power of these Jamaican leaders was associated with their commitment to the Enlightenment ideal of progress. Can we expect the power of these Jamaican leaders to be directed toward the achievement of future progress? Did greater access to the councils of decision contribute to the frequency of belief in progress among the leaders studied here?

In order to determine the relative power of each leader a two-factor index of power was constructed on the basis of responses to the question which asked each leader interviewed to nominate persons he thought to be important in determining and implementing policy in relation to the problems of West Kingston. The first factor in the Index of Power is a reputational influence score for each individual based on the number of nominations he received. The second factor is a score representing the accuracy and completeness of each leader's awareness of the influence of other leaders. Thus, the measure of relative power includes both the leaders' reputation for effective action, and their degree of integration into, or awareness of, the system of power relations relevant to the issue-area in question.[30] These two component scores were averaged and the resulting distribution of scores was dichotomized at the median interval. In this manner, 50 leaders were rated according to their relative power, with half being designated as most powerful and half as least powerful. There was not sufficient information to classify four leaders

29 C. Wright Mills, *The Causes of World War Three*, New York: Simon and Schuster, 1958, p. 14.
30 This use of the knowledge of the power of others is not unlike that of Foskett and Hohle in their community power research. See John M. Foskett and Raymond Hohle, "The Measurement of Influence in Community Affairs," Proceedings of the Pacific Sociological Society, *Research Studies of The State College of Washington*, XXV (June, 1957), pp. 148–154.

reliably. Again, it should be noted that this measure indicates only the relative power of the leaders, and is restricted to the issues concerning the people of West Kingston.

From the data presented in Table 7, it appears that the less powerful leaders were somewhat less confident than the most powerful leaders about Jamaica's potential in facing the obstacles presented by the future. Forty-six per cent of the less powerful leaders believed in progress compared to 63 per cent of those who were most powerful. This relationship remained with few modifications when the social characteristics of the leaders were controlled. This difference in belief in progress by the relative power of the leaders was found not to be spurious when age, race–color, occupational rating, and political party alignment of the leaders were each introduced. The relationship remained also among those leaders with some college or university training and among those with secondary education or less. However, it was found that among the university graduates the least powerful leaders were most likely to believe in progress. When this finding was examined in the light of the type of leadership position held by the leaders, it becomes apparent that the religious leaders are the "deviant" cases. They are typically highly educated and likely to believe in progress irrespective of their relatively low power ratings.

Table 7. PERCENTAGE OF JAMAICAN LEADERS WHO BELIEVE IN PROGRESS BY THE INDEX OF POWER

Index of Power	Percentage Who Believe In Progress	No. of Cases on Which the Per Cent is Based
Most powerful	63	(27)
Least powerful	46	(26)

Although the partial correlation by religious preference did not confirm the initial relationship between power and belief in progress, it is also true that this particular comparison is not reliable because of the clearly non-random distribution of those leaders for whom there was no information concerning religious preference. Nearly two-thirds of those whose religious preference was unknown had low scores on the Index of Power and were doubtful about the island's potential for progress. Finally, the relationship between power and belief in progress when compared by the type of leadership positions held by these leaders reversed only for the non-governmental community welfare leaders. The clergy discussed above comprised nearly half of this group. In general, there seem to be adequate grounds for accepting the association between power and belief in progress as not spurious.

The percentage difference, though not large, clearly reveals that relationship, and the pattern of relationships within subgroups is largely consistent.

KNOWLEDGE AND PROGRESS

Knowledge is a third element of critical importance to be combined with power and the ideals of equality and progress in the conscious determination of future history. Facts along with values and expectations are the basic components of the decision-making process by which the future is shaped.[31] Kenneth Boulding has stated that it is only by means of knowledge ". . . that we can hope to understand the social system sufficiently well to be able to control it and to be able to move into a positive image of the future through our own volition and policy."[32] The creation of future oriented policy and the feasibility of planning increases as our knowledge of the facts and conditions of society increases. Without knowledge, directed change and the planned future are impossible; with insufficient knowledge, ". . . we are merely slaves of necessity or victims of chance."[33]

Again, we may ask the important question which has been implicit throughout this discussion: Is progress in Jamaica likely? Very likely? Thus we turn to the more concrete questions concerning the Jamaican leaders studied here. Do they have the requisite knowledge concerning the nationally significant problems of West Kingston and the people there to be able to direct change and plan for the future effectively? Is their acceptance of the idea of progress informed by the facts necessary in the combination of elements in the decision-making process? What is the link between the relative knowledge of the leaders and the likelihood that they believe in progress?

The knowledge we are concerned with in this discussion, like the universe of leaders, was defined as knowledge about the urban lower classes and West Kingston. These leaders were all in some measure responsible for the betterment of the social and physical milieu of West Kingston. Consequently, we might expect them to be aware of the various shortcomings of the area which the residents desire to have corrected. However, Oscar Lewis has suggested that the elite in most developing countries do not usually have much knowledge of the poor or the subculture created by poverty.[34] Data reported here will allow us to see if this was true for Jamaica, and most importantly, to de-

[31] Eulau, *op. cit.*, p. 230.
[32] Kenneth Boulding, "The Relations of Economic, Political and Social Systems," *Social and Economic Studies*, XI (December, 1962), pp. 358–359.
[33] *Ibid.*, p. 359.
[34] Oscar Lewis, *Five Families*, New York: Basic Books, Inc. 1959, p. 2

termine whether the possession of knowledge about the people of West Kingston affected the likelihood that the leaders would believe in Jamaica's future potential.

The measure of the leaders' knowledgeability is based on the accuracy and completeness of their knowledge of the complaints and discontents of the lower-class people who reside in West Kingston. Both the leaders and a sample of lower-class respondents were asked to list the most important complaints and sources of discontent in West Kingston.[35] Each leader's list was scored according to the extent of agreement with the discontents reported by the lower-class people themselves. In the resulting distribution of leaders according to their level of knowledge, 63 per cent of the leaders were classified as most knowledgeable about the needs and problems of the people of West Kingston; the remaining 37 per cent were relatively less knowledgeable. Although this index does not purport to measure the leaders' knowledge of the problems of the urban lower classes in any absolute sense, it does provide an indication of their knowledge relative to one another.

The percentage of Jamaican leaders who believed in progress is shown in Table 8 by their level of knowledge about the discontents of the urban lower classes of West Kingston. It is clear that belief in progress is positively associated with higher knowledge. Sixty-two per cent of the leaders who were most knowledgeable were committed to the notion of future progress, compared to 45 per cent of those leaders who were low on the Index of Knowledge. This relationship between the leaders' knowledge and their belief in progress remained when political party preference, race-color, religious preference, and type of leadership position were introduced as controls. However, the strength of the original relationship was affected when specified by age, education, and occupational rating. There was no difference in the frequency of belief in progress by level of knowledge about West Kingston among the oldest leaders, among the least educated leaders, and among those with low occupational ratings. Generally, the relationship was strengthened among those who were younger, those with more education, and those with higher occupational status.

Additionally, it is interesting to note from tables not presented here,

[35] These data used in the construction of the Index of Knowledge of the Jamaican leaders were collected in 132 interviews with a 25 per cent random sample of households in a selected squatter-housing area in West Kingston. These interviews were completed in the months immediately preceding independence. Additional findings from this survey will be available in James A. Mau, "Political Mobilization and Belief in Progress in Jamaican Slums," revised version of a paper read at the meetings of the American Sociological Association, Chicago, Ill., September, 1965, forthcoming.

Table 8. PERCENTAGE OF JAMAICAN LEADERS WHO BELIEVE IN PROGRESS
BY THE INDEX OF KNOWLEDGE

Index of Knowledge	Percentage Who Believe In Progress	No. of Cases on Which the Per Cent is Based
High knowledge	62	(34)
Low knowledge	45	(20)

that all of the Catholics who were knowledgeable believed in progress; all of the clergy who were knowledgeable regardless of denomination believed in progress; and among the Members of Parliament, 83 per cent of those who were knowledgeable believed in progress.

From these data we may generally conclude that belief in progress is not an uninformed idealism that should be relegated simply to the realm of utopian fantasy. For the most part it is based on a realistic awareness of the demands of the urban lower classes.

We have seen that each of three variables, attitudes toward the reduction of social inequality in Jamaica, the leaders' relative power in public affairs concerning West Kingston, and the leaders' knowledge of the problems of the West Kingston people, was associated with variation in belief in progress. We now simultaneously examine the effect of all three variables. Unfortunately, the number of cases on which the analysis is based prohibits the presentation of the four-variable tabulation which logically follows. Therefore, a composite index of the three variables was constructed which would allow the simultaneous elaboration of the relationship between these three variables and the belief in progress.[36] Scores of zero or one were given to the leaders on each of the three variables. Zeros were assigned to the leaders with inegalitarian attitudes, little power, and less knowledge. The categories given a one-point value were, conversely, egalitarian attitudes, and relatively high power and knowledge. The sum of these three assigned values is the total score on the composite index. These scores range from zero to three.

Having constructed this index, we may now look at the cumulative effect of this composite variable upon the Jamaican leaders' beliefs in progress. The percentage of leaders who expressed belief in progress is presented in Table 9 by the composite index of egalitarianism, relative power, and knowledge. Eighty-two per cent of the leaders who were egalitarian, powerful, and knowledgeable (score 3) believed in progress, compared with one-third of those who were assigned low

[36] See Herbert Hyman's discussion of the creation of a composite or configurational index, which, though synthetic, allows more complex and refined analysis; *Survey Design and Analysis*, Glencoe, Ill.: The Free Press, 1955, pp. 271–272.

scores (0 or 1) in the composite index.[37] In the intermediate position, 57 per cent of those leaders who were assigned score two believed in progress.

Table 9. PERCENTAGE OF JAMAICAN LEADERS WHO BELIEVE IN PROGRESS BY THE COMPOSITE INDEX OF EGALITARIANISM, POWER, AND KNOWLEDGE

Composite Index Scores	*Percentage Who Believe In Progress*	*No. of Cases on Which the Per Cent is Based*
3 (Highest)	82	(11)
2	57	(23)
0–1 (Lowest)	33	(18)

In tables not shown here, it is apparent that each of the three variables in the composite index makes an additional contribution to the prediction of belief in progress. Seventy per cent of those who were both knowledgeable and egalitarian, and 72 per cent of those who were both knowledgeable and relatively powerful were leaders who indicated a belief in Jamaica's future progress. Similarly, 73 per cent of those who were both egalitarian and powerful believed in progress. The percentage of leaders who believed in progress is raised to 82 per cent by the simultaneous consideration of all three of the predicting variables. In sum, those leaders who were egalitarian, powerful, and knowledgeable were more likely to believe in progress than those who did not favor the extension of equality, who were relatively powerless, and who were relatively ignorant of the specific interests and needs of the people for whom and to whom they were responsible.

SUMMARY

The research reported in this chapter is a study of images of the future held by public leaders. Jamaican leaders' attitudes toward the progressive development of their nation's potential, specifically, their beliefs in progress, were analyzed in relation to their commitments to the ideal of equality, their relative power in public affairs, and their knowledge of the discontents and complaints of the urban lower-class people whose welfare was their responsibility.

[37] The zero and one scores were combined in Table 9, again because of the small number of cases in the low scored cells of the table. It should be noted, however, that the leaders who scored "zero" on the composite index were somewhat more likely to believe in progress than those leaders who scored "one." It is possible that this reversal is not spurious, but the size and consistency of differences in this and preceding tables warrant general confidence in the conclusions to be drawn from Table 9 as it is presented.

The close link between the ideals of equality and progress that emerged from the democratic revolution of the eighteenth century was evident among Jamaican leaders. Those leaders who favored the extension of equality of opportunity to all persons, and opposed the maintenance of ascriptive barriers to full participation in Jamaican society, were likely to believe in progress. The leaders not clearly favoring the reduction of such barriers to participation in the society, economy, and polity were less likely to believe in the progressive character of Jamaica's developing potential. Thus, for these leaders, the belief in progress was associated with desired changes in Jamaica's social structure, particularly the incorporation of the less privileged social, economic, and racial segments of the population into equal and meaningful participation in the nation's future. On the whole, the Enlightenment tradition of thought and its influence throughout Western civilization may be seen among the leaders studied here as well as among those studied by Bell, Moskos, and Oxaal. Of the majority who affirmed the value of equality, most were believers in progress.

The command of some measure of control in the movement toward the future, the possession of access to the means of decisions which affect the future of the nation, also contributed to the frequency of belief in progress. In expressing their images of the future, those leaders who were relatively powerful most often indicated their faith in the favorability of Jamaica's coming history. The less powerful leaders were most likely to negate the possibility of Jamaica's potential for progress.

It was suggested that knowledge, in addition to power and egalitarianism, is a critically important component in the process of making the decisions that shape the future. Further, it was contended that it is through knowledge that we can hope to control society and fulfill the positive images of the future. In this context, the association between knowledge and belief in future progress was examined. Knowledge was found to play an important role in the leaders' belief in progress. Those leaders who were most knowledgeable about the urban-lower classes were likely to hold favorable views of Jamaica's potential. The less knowledgeable leaders did not as frequently express faith in the progressive future for their island-nation. This finding suggests that belief in progress was not to be lightly dismissed as the expression of an unrealistic and unknowing idealism. The more pessimistic view of the future, which some might prefer to call "realism," was founded on ignorance.

Each of these three major variables, egalitarianism, power in public affairs, and knowledge, was found to predict a different and additional portion of the variance in attitudes toward progress. In sum, those leaders who were egalitarian, powerful, and knowledgeable were more likely to believe in progress than those who did not favor equality, were less powerful, and less knowledgeable about the discontents of the lower-class people whose welfare was their responsibility.

The findings reported here would appear to suggest a favorable view of Jamaica's new history. Slightly more than half of the leaders studied expressed belief in Jamaica's future potential for progressive change. The believers in progress tended to be persons who were in positions to exert some control in the councils of decision which will shape the nation's future. They tended to be knowledgeable people who will be guided in their history-making decisions by commitments to the ideal of equality. If the assumptions made here are well founded, we shall see the past and present trends of progressive change continue, and even accelerated by the support of more and more members of Jamaican society. But, we must note that even belief in the idea of progress can be a damning kind of fatalism, if it becomes a faith that fosters inaction and a negation of the normative implications of the idea of progress. Or, if the leaders who are capable of influencing the trends of change abdicate their responsibility and shed their ideology for reasons of self-interest or despair, then those progressive trends may falter.

Epilogue

WENDELL BELL

The studies reported in this book focus on the investigation of a challenge and a struggle that transcend the boundaries of any one nation and that are today global in scale. Although correlated with race, what these studies reveal is not primarily a racial problem — despite the rhetoric of both the extreme racialists and anti-racialists alike. It is rather an interrelated set of political, economic, social and cultural problems, and it stems from the world-wide discrepancy, both within and between countries, between the ideals of democracy and equality and the actualities of too frequent repression and inequality, between progress and despair, between knowledge and ignorance.

This discrepancy is a problem of Western civilization in that these ideals have been most consistently codified and explicitly stated in Western culture, but it is faced by men everywhere as the vision of the democratic revolution spreads around the world. This we have tried to illustrate by giving some of the details of the modern political and social history of the emergent nations of the West Indies.

There is the common complaint of the new states that most of the histories available to them are not *their* histories, but histories provided for them by others. The national histories of the emergent nations of the Caribbean, like those of new nations everywhere, still have to be written, and in an important sense still have to be made. West Indian scholars are at work, of course, but the effort required to amend the record and to overcome the centuries of distortion is Herculean. New images of the past consistent with the emerging future, new images of the future that will mold both past and future, the making of history in the present through valid action that expresses a continuity with the new images of both the past and future — all are needed. A new cycle of social change is called for. We have tried in our studies to look at the realities of West Indian political, economic, and social life at a crucial time in West Indian history through the eyes and with the hopes of the West Indian leaders and people as they faced the decisions of nationhood. Whether we have succeeded or not remains for others to judge, but it is our hope that the results of our labors will help in some small way to fill the historical gap left by the degrading aspects of colonialism.

Some West Indians may resent that we seven Americans have intruded into *their* history. For many reasons we cannot blame them if they do; they may rightly think us rash or impudent, or they may view us as agents of exploitation as they view the United States as now replacing the European powers in the Caribbean in a neocolonial version of the "mother country." We doubt very much if they want any "help" from us.

We can only say to them that we are not only Americans, we are also part of that universal enterprise that is social science, dwellers in universities, and intellectuals whose thinking cannot end at the boundaries of that particular nation-state to which we by chance happen to belong. We are also part of another universal: a concern for human dignity and common decency transcends national boundaries and is the responsibility of all men.

But perhaps the most important fact of all is that the democratic revolution is unfinished business not just in the West Indies, not just in the new states, but everywhere. The Atlantic community in the eighteenth century may have been the seedbed from which the drive toward equality sprang, but today it is world-wide. It arrived dramatically on the world stage with the birth of the new states in the last two decades, but it smoulders, and occasionally bursts forth, in the old nations as well. While the new nations demanded political independence in the name of their right to equality, we witnessed in the old nations demands for change in the name of the same value. In the United States, for example, it is no accident that the civil rights movement and the war on poverty are motivated by and justified on grounds similar to those used by the new nationalist leaders to explain their desire for political independence. Each is a manifestation of the democratic revolution and each is part of an effort to alter the facts of social life to conform more closely to an egalitarian ethic. Of course, gains have been made. But the challenge remains: Much more must be accomplished in new and old nations alike if the full promise of the democratic revolution is to be achieved. No society can honestly boast a present state of affairs that is not in some important respects negated by the image of a future egalitarian society. As long as that is true and images of a better future outdistance the realities of the present, one can rely on the fact that some men everywhere will continue the struggle.

Name Index

Subject Index